Mobile Learning
Transforming the Delivery of Education and Training

Edited by

Mohamed Ally

1

Mobile Learning
Transforming the Delivery of Education and Training

Edited by

Mohamed Ally

AU PRESS

Issues in Distance Education series

© 2009 Mohamed Ally
Second printing 2010

Published by AU Press, Athabasca University
1200, 10011 – 109 Street
Edmonton, AB T5J 3S8

Library and Archives Canada Cataloguing in Publication

Mobile learning: transforming the delivery
of education and training / edited by Mohamed Ally.

(Issues in distance education)
Includes index.
Also available in electronic format (ISBN 978-1-897425-44-2).
ISBN 978-1-897425-43-5

1. Mobile communication systems in education. 2. Distance education.
I. Ally, Mohamed II. Series: Issues in distance education series (Print)

LB1044.84.M62 2009   371.33   C2009-900642-1

ISSN 1919-4382 Issues in Distance Education Series (Print)
ISSN 1919-4390 Issues in Distance Education Series (Online)

Book design by Infoscan Collette, Québec
Cover design by W2 Community Media Arts Lab | Vancouver

Printed and bound in Canada by Marquis Book Printing

Contents

Mohamed Ally
Athabasca University, Canada

PART ONE: Advances in Mobile Learning

Chapter 1
John Traxler
University of Wolverhampton, United Kingdom

Chapter 2
Marguerite L. Koole
Athabasca University, Canada

PART TWO: Research on Mobile Learning

Chapter 3
Torstein Rekkedal and Aleksander Dye
Norwegian School of Information Technology & NKI Distance Education,
Norway

Foreword

Normally I'm an enthusiast and early adopter of new educational technologies, but for years after I first heard people talk about mobile learning, I didn't get it. Instead, I focused on the challenges of working with learning management systems on tiny screens, the cost to purchase and operate mobile devices, their large battery requirements, and the limited coverage footprints. Two things have changed my mind.

First was the purchase of an iPhone 3G. With easily available software add-ons, my "phone" can become a piano, a guitar, a drum machine, a level, a ruler, a bookshelf, a camera, a fake zippo lighter, a database, a web browser, an email client, a game machine, a "TV" (for watching YouTube), a voice recorder, a weather forecaster, and a GPS. As a Canadian, I need to know the location of the nearest Tim Horton's! Every day, the app store offers me yet more ways (including 75 applications categorized under "education") that this phone can morph itself into a universal and ubiquitous information, education, and entertainment portal.

The second came about after attending two e-learning conferences and reading books by innovative educators such as those in this volume. Editor Mohamed Ally has drawn together an eclectic selection of authors who show us that the power of context and the capacity to provide information where and when it can be used can overcome the challenges of small screens and limited (but ever-increasing) battery capacity.

This second book in AU Press's Issues in Distance Education Series offers both theoretical and very practical insights into the diverse uses of mobile devices for formal and informal learning. I am confident that every reader will find ideas and inspiration in the writings of these innovators and early adopters, who demonstrate and evaluate the emerging affordances and current practicability of mobile learning technologies and applications. More than any previous generation of technology, such applications demonstrate achievement of the often elusive goal of every distance educator – to support quality learning, anywhere/anytime.

Terry Anderson
Edmonton, Canada
February 3, 2009

Contributing Authors

Tom Boyle is director of the Learning Technology Research Institute (LTRI) at London Metropolitan University. He has a long history of developing and evaluating innovative multimedia learning technology. Tom led a major project in the development, use and evaluation of learning objects that won an EASA (European Academic Software Award) in 2004. He is the director of the Centre for Excellence in Teaching and Learning (CETL) in Reusable Learning Objects. The CETL involves collaboration between three universities – London Metropolitan University, the University of Cambridge and the University of Nottingham – to develop and evaluate high quality learning objects across a range of subject areas.

Claire Bradley is a research fellow at the Learning Technology Research Institute at London Metropolitan University. She has a master's degree in interactive multimedia from the Royal College of Art. For the past eleven years she has worked on a number of UK and European research projects involved in e-learning, online communities, multimedia, and in the general application and evaluation of digital technologies in teaching and learning. Her recent work focuses on mobile learning. She has co-authored a number of journal articles and papers in these areas.

Pamela A. Burton is an instructor with the Collaboration for Academic Education in the Nursing Program (Bachelor of Science in Nursing) at North Island College in Courtenay, British Columbia, Canada. Her research interests include the use of mobile technologies in nursing education and prevention of medication errors.

Gill Clough is a full time PhD student with the Institute of Educational Technology at The Open University (OU). Her doctoral work investigates how mobile devices are used to support informal learning, in particular the role of GPS-enabled devices in engaging people with both physical and social contexts and triggering sustained collaborative learning. She is currently researching the activities of geocachers, looking at the informal learning that occurs through setting and finding geocaches, and at how geocachers collaborate through their geocache descriptions, logs and web forum posts. This interest in the social networks of geocachers is echoed in consultancy work for the Schome Project (not school, not home, Schome). When Schome began to investigate the educational potential of virtual 3D worlds, Gill migrated an avatar to the OU's educational island on the teen grid, Schome Park. Here she worked with the teenagers on the project, participating in group work and running world workshops for the students.

John Cook has over fourteen years previous experience as a full-time lecturer at various HEIs and six years of project management experience; the latter includes AHRB, BECTA and HEFCE work. Furthermore, Cook has been principal investigator or co-investigator on research and development projects that have attracted $3.4 million in competitive external funding; he has also helped to obtain $500,000 of internal funds. He has published over one hundred refereed articles in the area of e-learning and conducts review work for the ESRC, EPSRC, EU, and Science Foundation of Ireland. Cook was chair/president of the Association for Learning Technology (2004-06), and his current mobile learning interest centres on user generated contexts.

Davide Diamantini is professor at the University of Milano-Bicocca in the Department of Education and vice director of the Nomadis Lab. He coordinates projects related to distance learning, specifically mobile learning. His research areas, as well as distance learning, are the analysis of methodological, cognitive and social aspects of the processes of scientific and technological transfer. He is the author of many national and international publications in his field.

Aleksander Dye has worked with NKI Distance Education since 2001 in the Research and Development Department as a system developer. He has for many years been a member of the team developing SESAM (Scalable Educational System for Administration and Management), the learning management system developed internally in NKI for online distance education. He has specifically worked with different solutions of system adaptation for different purposes, such as mobile learning. The last years he has worked with both system developments and research in four EU Commission projects on mobile learning. Presently, he works as researcher in the field of distance education with emphasis on mobile learning and is also project manager for the development of SESAM.

Merryl Ford is the manager of the ICT in Education Research Group of the Meraka Institute of the Council for Scientific and Industrial Research (CSIR), South Africa. The ICT in Education Research Group works in partnership with local and international tertiary and research institutions to accelerate the application of ICTs in the education sector to help ensure social and economic development in South Africa and Africa more generally. Merryl has fifteen years of expertise in the ICT domain and was responsible for setting up and managing the largest ISP in South Africa as an incubation project within the CSIR. Merryl has also worked for IBM, where she was a member of a team that provided e-business consulting services to industry. After returning to the CSIR to pursue her passion for innovation, she now focuses on seeking ways to harness the digital knowledge economy to benefit all sectors of the community.

Jon Gregson is currently Director of Global Networks and Communities, University of London External System and he formerly directed for several years the Wye Distance Learning Programme (DLP) of Imperial College London until the DLP was transferred to SOAS in August 2007. He is responsible for the Learning Technology and Production Team and oversees the development of electronic courseware and learning environments. He also looks after the development of educational and student support systems used for the distance learning programme. He manages a range of international collaborations on behalf of the programme, including support for a large number of Commonwealth Scholarship students in Southern Africa in cooperation with University of Pretoria, and involvement in the Global Open Food and Agricultural University (GOFAU) initiative, which is lead by the International Food Policy Research Institute (IFPRI), and is developing a range of courses based on open educational resources. Jon holds a master's degree from the University of London in managing rural change, and another from the University of Lancaster in distributed interactive systems. He is one of the founding fellows of the University of London Centre for Distance Education (www.cde.london.ac.uk) and is the grant holder for a two year mobile learning project focussed on the needs of postgraduate distance learning students in the Southern African Development Community. Over the last five years he has been involved in authoring and online tutoring of courses in ICT for development and NGO management.

Richard Haynes is a multimedia developer at London Metropolitan University with over ten years of experience developing learning and support materials. Trained originally at Artec in Islington he has worked on many art gallery and educational projects. For the last few years he has worked on learning object design for PCs and mobiles, and was a member of the award winning EASA Learning Object Team in 2004. He has developed learning objects for mobile phones in the areas of marketing and study skills, developing such mobile learning resources as "How to reference books" and "What is your learning style?"

Ann C. Jones is senior lecturer in the Institute of Educational Technology at The Open University and co-director of the Computers and Learning Research Group in the Centre for Research in Education and Educational Technology. One of her interests in mobile learning concerns the affective aspects of using handheld devices which echoes one of her key research interests in educational technology more generally. In recent work she has focused on adults' use of handheld devices in different contexts and particularly on the motivating features of using mobile devices for informal learning. She is currently an investigator on the ESRC/EPSRC funded Personal Inquiry Project in which researchers at The Open University and the University of Nottingham are researching how children can best take advantage of hand-held devices – both inside and outside the classroom – to personalize the way they learn about science-related topics.

Dolf Jordaan is an e-learning project manager within the Department for Education Innovation at the University of Pretoria. He is a manager of an e-education division (including instructional designers and other support staff) within the department, and this division supports academic staff at the university with e-learning projects. He is also involved as a project manager in Web and multimedia projects, and he has lectured in multimedia design and development and in project management at the university. A consultant for national and international e-learning projects, Dolf is a qualified educator and holds a master's degree in computer assisted education. During the last few years he has been involved in international collaboration projects, and he has participated in the management of the e-campus at the university since 2003. He is responsible for the coordination of e-learning and learning management system-related applications, and he currently serves as project manager for the implementation of Blackboard Vista Enterprise Edition on campus.

Richard F. Kenny is an associate professor with the Centre for Distance Education at Athabasca University, where he teaches instructional design and learning theory. His research interests include instructional design and change agency, emerging technologies to foster higher-order thinking, and mobile learning applications and strategies.

Marguerite Koole is the program administrator for the Doctor of Education Program and instructional media analyst for the Centre for Distance Education at Athabasca University. Marguerite has a bachelor's degree in modern languages, a college diploma in multimedia production, and a master's degree in distance education. For her thesis, she developed a theory of mobile learning, the FRAME model, and conducted an analysis of mobile devices. Marguerite also has experience in teaching instructional design and multimedia programming. She has designed interactive, online learning activities for various learning purposes and platforms – including print, Web, and mobile devices. Marguerite has taught at the University of Lethbridge, Athabasca University, and private schools in Canada and overseas.

Agnes Kukulska-Hulme is a senior lecturer in educational technology in The Open University's Institute of Educational Technology, where she led the TeleLearning Research Group and chaired the production of the postgraduate course "Innovations in eLearning." Agnes has been working in mobile learning since 2001 and is the co-editor of *Mobile Learning: A Handbook for Educators and Trainers*. She has led two JISC funded projects: case studies of wireless and mobile learning in the post-16 sector, and the landscape study on the use of mobile and wireless technologies for learning and teaching. She also led the literature review for a project on the use of Tablet PCs in schools. Agnes' background is in foreign language learning and from this perspective she has a long standing research interest in user interface design for effective communication.

Teemu Leinonen leads the Learning Environments Research Group of the Media Lab, University of Art and Design, Helsinki, Finland. The group is involved in the research, design, and development of New Media tools, as well as their use and application, in the field of learning. Teemu has more than a decade of experience in the field of research and development in web-based learning, computer-supported collaborative learning (CSCL), online cooperation, educational planning, and educational politics. Teemu conducts research and publishes in different forums. He has delivered a number of papers at national and international conferences, has given in-service courses for teachers, and has carried out consulting and concept design for ICT and media companies. He is currently undertaking doctoral dissertation research on learning and design with collaborative computer tools in unconventional learning communities.

Patrick McAndrew is senior lecturer at The Open University's Institute of Educational Technology. He has led a range of research projects addressing how materials and environments can support learning through the use of learning design and the provision of tools for learners. He was responsible for the final evaluation stages within the European MOBILearn Project that reviewed models for mobile learning and developed and demonstrated a flexible task based environment. Patrick has a degree in mathematics from the University of Oxford and a PhD in computer science from Heriot-Watt University in Edinburgh. He is currently the research and evaluation director of OpenLearn, a major initiative to provide open content for free education supported by the William and Flora Hewlett Foundation.

Jan Meiers is an instructor with the Collaboration for Academic Education in Nursing Program, Bachelor of Science in Nursing (BSN), at North Island College in Courtenay, British Columbia, Canada. Her research interests include the use of mobile technologies in nursing education and student attrition in BSN education programs.

Laura Naismith is a research assistant and PhD candidate in the Department of Educational and Counselling Psychology at McGill University in Canada. Her current research interests include the development of cognitive tools to support learning and assessment in medicine. In her previous position with the Centre for Learning, Innovation and Collaboration (CLIC) at the University of Birmingham in the United Kingdom, she worked with subject specialists to develop a needs-driven research program in educational technology with funding from Microsoft UK Ltd. Her recent publications include an activity-based literature review of mobile technologies and learning, commissioned by Futurelab UK. Laura holds a BASc in systems design engineering from the University of Waterloo in Canada, and an MPhil in medicine from the University of Birmingham.

Caroline Park is an associate professor with the Centre for Nursing and Health Studies at Athabasca University, where she teaches in the Master's of Health Studies and the Master's of Nursing programs. Besides an interest in handheld devices for learning, she is participating in research relating to inter-disciplinary research teams.

Kristine Peters is director of KPPM Organisational Strategists where her work includes research into emerging learning trends. Notable publications include *Learning on the Move: Mobile Technologies in Business and Education* (republished as "M-learning: Positioning Educators for a Mobile, Connected Future" in the *International Review of Research in Open and Distance Learning*), *E-learning for Youth* for the Australian Flexible Learning Framework, and *Differentiating Needs: Customer Demand for Online Learning*. Kristine's consulting work provides strategic planning, social research, and organizational development for government, non-profit and private sectors. Her previous experience includes management of a pilot for vocational education in schools, and management roles in training, consumer finance and retail, and she started her career as a teacher. Kristine has a teaching diploma, a master's in business administration, and is currently undertaking a PhD at Flinders University, exploring the influence of knowledge within social capital networks.

John Pettit is a lecturer at The Open University's Institute of Educational Technology. He has chaired the postgraduate course *Implementing Online, Open and Distance Learning*, and has written on innovation and on audiographics for *Innovations in eLearning* – another module within The Open University's MA programme for online and distance education. He is currently researching the emergent uses of mobile devices among the alumni of that programme, and has a particular interest in what these reveal about Web 2.0 practices. He is a member of IET's Centre for Educational Development and a core member of the TeleLearning Research Group. John has also led a blended-delivery programme supporting The Open University's learning and teaching strategy, and he continues to develop university teaching in the area of synchronous and asynchronous conferencing.

Michelle Pieri is specialized in analysis and management of public and company communication and in methodology and theory of teaching at the secondary school level. Since 2005 she has been in a post-doctoral position with the University of Milano-Bicocca' NOMADIS Lab. Her research interests are concentrated mainly on the psychological and social aspects of communication through the computer and virtual communities, in particular the distance learning field, and specifically in mobile learning. She has published articles on distance learning and computer mediated communication at the national and international level.

Torstein Rekkedal is professor of distance education and director of research and development at NKI Distance Education, Norway. He has worked in distance education research since 1970, producing a stream of research publications in the field of distance education and online learning. He has chaired the research committees of the European Association for Distance Learning (EADL) and the International Council for Open and Distance Education (ICDE). In 2003 he was conferred honorary doctor of the British Open University for his research work in the field. He has for many years chaired the Standing Committee for Quality of the Norwegian Association for Distance and Flexible Education. Presently, he is member of the board of the Norwegian state organization for distance education in higher education, Norway Opening Universities. During the last ten years he has participated in over ten EU Commission projects on distance, online and mobile learning. In 2005-2007 he was project manager of the Leonardo da Vinci Project, megatrends in e-learning provision.

Eileen Scanlon is professor of educational technology and co-director of the Centre for Education and Educational Technology at The Open University, and visiting professor at Moray House School of Education at the University of Edinburgh. Eileen has a long history of research and teaching in the area of educational technology. Recent projects related to mobile learning include Mobile Learning in Informal Science Settings (MELISSA), a project that explored the consequences of mobile technologies for learning science. In particular it investigated what this means in the area of informal learning in science; where, for example, learners might use portable devices to support their field work as naturalists, geologists or in weather forecasting. She is currently principal investigator on the ESRC/EPSRC funded Personal Inquiry Project in which researchers at The Open University and the University of Nottingham are researching how children can best take advantage of handheld devices – both inside and outside the classroom – to personalize the way they learn about science related topics.

Carl Smith (PGDip, MA) has concentrated on exploiting the various ways that computer based modeling can be used in the design, construction and generation of Reusable Learning Objects (RLOs) and Mobile Learning Objects (MLOs). His primary research involves the investigation of learning objects from the point of view of their units of construction – to see across the whole range of constituent parts, schemas and key narratives involved in their successful development and application. He uses rich media visualization techniques to produce highly interactive and engaging learning resources for both the Web and mobile devices. His other research interests include visualization as interface, augmented reality, intermediality, mediascapes, 3Dweb art, open source learning, Web 2.0, and the emerging practice within the arts and sciences that merges digital virtual experiences and technologies with physical spatial experiences. His previous projects were based at the Humanities Computing departments at Glasgow and Sheffield universities.

Paul Smith is the director of the Lapworth Museum of Geology at the University of Birmingham in the United Kingdom. He is also a professor of palaeobiology and head of the School of Geography, Environmental and Earth Sciences. Paul trained as a geologist and micropaleontologist at the universities of Leicester and Nottingham, and developed an interest in museums whilst working at the Sedgwick Museum in Cambridge and the Geological Museum in Copenhagen.

John Traxler is reader in mobile technology for e-learning and director of the Learning Lab at the University of Wolverhampton. John has co-written a guide to mobile learning in developing countries and is co-editor of a book on mobile learning. He publishes and presents regularly on conceptualising, evaluating and embedding mobile learning, and is interested in the profound social consequences of using universal mobile devices. He is jointly responsible for national workshops on mobile learning for UK universities and has delivered similar workshops to university staff in Africa, Canada and India. He advises UK universities on mobile learning projects, for example in large-scale-messaging, podcasting and broadcasting with Bluetooth, and was recently invited to the Microsoft Mobile Learning Summit in Seattle. He was the evaluator for the EU FP6 M-learning Project, and is advising a Swiss project for Kenya farmers that uses blended web-based and phone-based technology. He is continuing to work with the Kenyan government implementing national support for Kenyan teachers' in-service training using mobile phones and video, and has links with South Africa's Meraka Institute.

Jocelyne M. C. Van Neste-Kenny is the Dean of health, human services and applied business technology at North Island College in Courtenay, British Columbia, Canada. Her research interests include practice education models, emerging technologies in practice education, and interprofessional education.

Jocelyn Wishart is currently a lecturer in science education at the University of Bristol specialising in teacher training. She first entered initial teacher education at Loughborough University in 1996 where she taught both PGCE science (physics) and PGCE ICT. Prior to that she taught science, psychology and ICT in secondary schools. She has been involved in research into the use of information and communication technologies for learning since investigating children's learning through computer games and educational software for her PhD in the 1980s. Her current research focuses on the use of mobile technologies to support teachers in training. Other recent research projects include developing online resources for education in ethical issues within science and evaluating the use of online role play to teach safety on the Internet.

Introduction

Mobile learning through the use of wireless mobile technology allows anyone to access information and learning materials from anywhere and at anytime. As a result, learners have control of when they want to learn and from which location they want to learn. Also, all humans have the right to access learning materials and information to improve their quality of life regardless of where they live, their status, and their culture. Mobile learning, through the use of mobile technology, will allow citizens of the world to access learning materials and information from anywhere and at anytime. Learners will not have to wait for a certain time to learn or go to a certain place to learn. With mobile learning, learners will be empowered since they can learn whenever and wherever they want. Also, learners do not have to learn what is prescribed to them. They can use the wireless mobile technology for formal and informal learning where they can access additional and personalized learning materials from the Internet or from the host organization. Workers on the job can use the mobile technology to access training materials and information when they need it for just-in-time training. Just-in-time learning encourages high level learning since learners access and apply the information right away rather than learn the information and then apply the information at a later time. Educators and trainers are empowered since they can use the mobile technology to communicate with learners from anywhere and at anytime. At the same time, educators and trainers can access learning resources from anytime and anywhere to plan and deliver their lessons.

This book is timely since there is significant growth in the use of mobile technology by people around the world, especially in developing countries. As the citizens of the world use mobile technology to complete everyday tasks and to socialize with friends and colleagues, they will demand access to learning materials using mobile technology. Also, other sectors of society such as business, are allowing citizens around the world to use mobile technology to complete everyday transactions. Hence, education and training have no other choice but to deliver learning materials on mobile devices. The research studies and projects in this book show how mobile learning can transform the delivery of education and training.

Rather than acquiring another technology to receive learning materials, people throughout the world will want to access learning materials on their existing mobile devices. As a result, educators and trainers must design learning materials for delivery on different types of mobile devices. The design of learning materials for mobile devices must follow good learning theories and proper instructional design for the learning to be effective. The twenty-first century learner and worker will benefit from well designed learning materials so that they can learn from anywhere and at anytime using mobile technology. The nomadic learner and worker who travel frequently from place to place will similarly use mobile technology to access information and learning materials from anywhere and at anytime.

A major benefit of using wireless mobile technology is to reach people who live in remote locations where there are no schools, teachers, or libraries. Mobile technology can be used to deliver instruction and information to these remote regions without having people leave their geographic areas. This will benefit communities in such places since students and workers will not have to leave their families and jobs to go to a different location to learn or to access information. At the same time, business owners, agriculture workers, and other working sectors can access information to increase productivity and improve the quality of their products. People living in remote communities will be able to access health information to improve their health hence, enhancing quality of life. Finally, because remote access using wireless mobile technology reduces the need for travel, its use can reduce humanity's carbon footprint on earth to help maintain a cleaner environment.

The first book on the use of mobile technology in education and training was published four years ago. In the last four years, mobile devices have become more sophisticated and easy to use. At the same time, there have been many applications of mobile technology in education and training. This book contains current research initiatives and applications in mobile learning. Recently, there have been many conceptual papers on mobile learning and initiatives to use mobile technology for learning and training. Also, there were many conferences on mobile learning for educators and researchers to present their projects and research findings. For example, the First International Conference on M-libraries was held recently to explore the use of mobile technology in libraries to disseminate information and learning materials to anyone, anywhere, and at anytime. This conference was attended by delegates from twenty-six different countries. Also, the Sixth International Mobile Learning Conference was held recently with people from twenty-one countries attending. Papers on the use of mobile technology in teaching and learning were presented at this conference.

Intended audience for this book

This book can be used by anyone who is interested in mobile learning in education and training. Faculty can use this book as a textbook in a course on "mobile learning" or "emerging technology in learning." Faculty, researchers, teachers, instructors, and trainers can use this book to learn about mobile learning and how to design learning materials for delivery on mobile technology. They can also use this book to become informed on current research and initiatives on mobile learning to learn best practices on mobile learning from other educators, trainers, and researchers. At the same time, business and government can use this book to gain knowledge on how-to design information and learning materials for delivery on mobile devices.

Book organization

This book consists of three parts. Part One deals with advances in mobile learning and sets the stage for the other parts of the book. This first part presents the current status of mobile learning, explores what mobile learning is, and presents a model that can be used to guide the development and implementation of mobile learning. The first part also provides theoretical information on mobile learning, discusses the definition of mobile learning, and outlines some of the challenges faced when designing and implementing mobile learning. Part Two includes chapters that present the latest research on mobile learning so that readers can learn from current findings to guide the development of mobile learning materials and better implement future mobile learning initiatives. Part Three covers various examples of how mobile learning is used in different subjects and places around the world. As a result, readers will discover how to successfully design and implement mobile learning regardless of where they live. The chapters in the last part of the book also identify lessons learned which will be helpful for future implementation of mobile learning in educational and training settings.

Part One: Advances in mobile learning

The first part of the book consists of two chapters. That by John Traxler provides information on the current state of mobile learning and where it is going. It also identifies challenges organizations face when implementing mobile learning and what must be done to make mobile learning successful. For those who are new to mobile learning, it is important to know about the challenges of implementing it so that they can plan for success. It is important to know the development of the field, its current state, and potential challenges for the future. This chapter provides good background information for the chapters that follow.

The chapter by Marguerite Koole presents a theoretical model for developing and implementing mobile learning: the Framework for the Rational Analysis of Mobile Education (FRAME). It is a comprehensive model that covers different aspects of mobile learning including the learner and device usability. The model explains the pedagogical issues of information overload, knowledge navigation, and collaborative learning in mobile learning. Koole makes a significant contribution by introducing the convergence of mobile technologies, human learning capacities, and social interaction in mobile learning. FRAME will help educators and trainers to develop mobile learning materials and to use effective teaching and learning strategies for mobile education. It will also help guide the development of mobile devices for mobile learning.

Part Two: Research in mobile learning

The second part of the book consists of four chapters. Torstein Rekkedal and Aleksander Dye's chapter presents experiences from three European Union (EU)-supported Leonardo da Vinci projects on mobile learning. In the studies reported, researchers tested the use of many features on the mobile device including video, chat, and synthetic speech. This chapter makes an important contribution as it discusses research conducted on the use of multimedia for mobile learning.

The chapter by Richard F. Kenny, Caroline Park, Jocelyne M. C. Van Neste-Kenny, Pamela A. Burton, and Jan Meiers reports on research studies concerning the use of mobile technology in nursing. Use of mobile technology in the health care field is growing at a fast rate because of the nature of the work health care workers perform. They are on the move most of the time and need to access information for just-in-time application. Hence, the use of mobile technology to work from anywhere and access information at any time is important for this group. The research reported in this chapter will be helpful to anyone planning to develop mobile learning for workers on the move.

The chapter by Gill Clough, Ann Jones, Patrick McAndrew, and Eileen Scanlon discusses the use of mobile devices in informal learning and reports on research that was conducted on the use of mobile devices to deliver informal learning. Allowing people to use mobile technology for informal learning will empower them to access information anytime and from anywhere to improve their quality of life. Most of what people learn in their lives is learned informally. As the Internet continues to grow, there will be more informal learning. This chapter will benefit those who are interested in using mobile technology for informal learning.

The chapter by Kristine Peters looks at the use of mobile learning in business and how the use of mobile technology results in flexible learning. Since most employees in businesses have mobile technology that they use for work related tasks, they can use the same technology to access learning materials for application on the job. In this study, information on use of mobile devices was collected through interviews with manufacturers of mobile devices and education providers. As more businesses start using mobile technology for learning, they will need to know about the best practices when implementing mobile learning, and this chapter provides valuable information in this regard.

Part Three: Applications of mobile learning

The third part of the book presents different applications of mobile learning and consists of seven chapters. The chapter by Agnes Kukulska-Hulme and John Pettit examines learners' use of mobile devices and reports on learners' experience using four different types of mobile devices. The practices reported in this chapter provide valuable information to those who are interested in designing mobile learning materials. One of the challenges in mobile learning is how to design good instruction for delivery on mobile devices. This chapter addresses the design of learning materials based on learners' experience using mobile devices.

The chapter by Claire Bradley, Richard Haynes, John Cook, Tom Boyle, and Carl Smith describes how to design learning objects for use on mobile devices. The use of learning objects in mobile learning is essential since the learning objects can be stored in repositories for access at anytime and from anywhere. Also, learning objects can be re-used many times. Developers of learning materials should seriously think about developing learning materials in the form of learning objects for storage in electronic repositories for flexibility in delivery. This chapter provides valuable information on how to design learning materials using learning objects for delivery on mobile devices.

The chapter by Michelle Pieri and Davide Diamantini presents a project where mobile learning is used in a blended delivery format for training in the workplace. In some cases, training is delivered using mobile learning along with other delivery methods in a blended format. Pieri and Diamantini report on the blended approach and describes a mobile learning application to train managers to improve their knowledge and skills. The authors also compared the effectiveness of mobile learning and e-learning to train managers. As workplace training moves towards using different delivery methods, trainers will need to know which delivery methods to use. This chapter addresses how a blended approach that includes mobile learning can be used in workplace training.

The chapter by Merryl Ford and Teemu Leinonen examines the use of mobile learning in both formal and informal learning. The authors describe implementations that are being carried out around the world and provide suggestions for implementing mobile learning in different parts of the globe. This is a good case study on how mobile learning can be implemented internationally.

The chapter by Jon Gregson and Dolf Jordaan describes the experience of implementing mobile learning in developing countries and the challenges one could face during the implementation. The authors also cover how to design learning materials for delivery on mobile devices for distribution to such countries. Those who will receive the most benefits from mobile learning are individuals who live in developing countries and in remote locations since they can access learning materials from anywhere and at anytime. This chapter will help those involved in international education and training to implement mobile learning in a variety of contexts.

The chapter by Laura Naismith and M. Paul Smith describes how to design for learner-centred experience when touring museums. They also reported on learners' feedback when touring museums with the help of mobile technology. This chapter illustrates how mobile technology can be used in contexts outside the classroom for learning.

The chapter by Jocelyn Wishart describes the use of mobile technology for teacher training to get teachers involved in the use of technology in education. The chapter describes the activities teachers prefer to complete with the mobile devices and why the technology was not fully utilized. This case study will be important to those who would like to involve teachers in mobile learning.

In conclusion, this timely book will benefit learners, educators, and trainers by encouraging flexibility in the learning process, and thereby improve learning. The information presented in this book will help citizens of the world to use mobile technology to access information and learning materials while also improving their ability to communicate with each other.

Mohamed Ally, Ph.D.

PART ONE

• • •

Advances in Mobile Learning

Current State of Mobile Learning[1]

JOHN TRAXLER
UNIVERSITY OF WOLVERHAMPTON
UNITED KINGDOM

Abstract

Since the start of the current millennium, experience and expertise in the development and delivery of mobile learning have blossomed and a community of practice has evolved that is distinct from the established communities of "tethered" e-learning. This community is currently visible mainly through dedicated international conference series, of which MLEARN is the most prestigious, rather than through any dedicated journals. So far, these forms of development and delivery have focused on short-term small-scale pilots and trials in the developed countries of Europe, North America, and the Pacific Rim, and there is a taxonomy emerging from these pilots and trials that suggests tacit and pragmatic conceptualisations of mobile learning. What has, however,

---

1. Originally published in the *International Review on Research in Open and Distance Learning* (*IRRODL*) 8, no. 2. This article is subject to Creative Commons License 2.5 (c) 2007. The original article is published at: www.irrodl.org/index.php/irrodl/article/view/346/875. Reproduced with permission of AU Press, Athabasca University.

developed less confidently within this community is any theoretical conceptualisation of mobile learning and with it any evaluation methodologies specifically
aligned to the unique attributes of mobile learning. Some advocates of mobile
learning attempt to define and conceptualize it in terms of devices and technologies; other advocates do so in terms of the mobility of learners and the
mobility of learning, and in terms of the learners' experience of learning with
mobile devices.

Introduction

The role of theory is, perhaps, a contested topic in a community that encompasses philosophical affiliations from empiricists to post-structuralists, each
with different expectations about the scope and legitimacy of theory in their
work. The mobile learning community may nevertheless need the authority
and credibility of some conceptual base. Such a base would provide the
starting point for evaluation methodologies grounded in the unique attributes
of mobile learning. Attempts to develop the conceptualizations and evaluation of mobile learning, however, must recognize that mobile learning is
essentially personal, contextual, and situated; this means it is "noisy," which
is problematic both for definition and for evaluation.

   Furthermore, defining mobile learning can emphasize those unique
attributes that position it within informal learning, rather than formal.
These attributes place much mobile learning at odds with formal learning
(with its cohorts, courses, semesters, assessments, and campuses) and with
its monitoring and evaluation regimes. The difference also raises concerns
for the nature of any large-scale and sustained deployment and the extent to
which the unique attributes of mobile learning may be lost or compromised.
Looking at mobile learning in a wider context, we have to recognize that
mobile, personal, and wireless devices are now radically transforming societal
notions of discourse and knowledge, and are responsible for new forms of
art, employment, language, commerce, deprivation, and crime, as well as
learning. With increased popular access to information and knowledge anywhere, anytime, the role of education, perhaps especially formal education,
is challenged and the relationships between education, society, and technology are now more dynamic than ever. This chapter explores and articulates
these issues and the connections between them specifically in the context of
the wider and sustained development of mobile learning.

   The use of wireless, mobile, portable, and handheld devices are gradually
increasing and diversifying across every sector of education, and across both
the developed and developing worlds. It is gradually moving from small-scale,

short-term trials to larger more sustained and blended deployment. Recent publications, projects, and trials are drawn upon to explore the possible future and nature of mobile education. This chapter concludes with an examination of the relationship between the challenges of rigorous and appropriate evaluation of mobile education and the challenges of embedding and mainstreaming mobile education within formal institutional education.

Mobile learning has growing visibility and significance in higher education, as evidenced by the following phenomena. First, there is the growing size and frequency of dedicated conferences, seminars, and workshops, both in the United Kingdom and internationally. The first of the series, MLEARN 2002 in Birmingham, was followed by MLEARN 2003 in London (with more than two hundred delegates from thirteen countries), MLEARN 2004 in Rome in July 2004, MLEARN 2005 in Cape Town in October 2005, MLEARN 2006 in Banff, Alberta in November 2006, and MLEARN 2007 in Melbourne, Australia. Another dedicated event, the International Workshop on Mobile and Wireless Technologies in Education (WMTE 2002), sponsored by IEEE, took place in Sweden in August 2002 (http://lttf.ieee.org/wmte2002/). The second WMTE (http://lttf.ieee.org/wmte2003/) was held at National Central University in Taiwan in March 2004, the third in Japan in 2005, and a fourth in Athens in 2006. Both these series report buoyant attendance. There are also a growing number of national and international workshops. The June 2002 national workshop in Telford on mobile learning in the computing discipline attracted sixty delegates from UK higher education (http://www.ics.ltsn.ac.uk/events). The National Workshop and Tutorial on Handheld Computers in Universities and Colleges at Telford (http://www. e-innovationcentre.co.uk/eic_event.htm) on June 11, 2004, and subsequent events on January 12, 2005 and November 4, 2005 (http://www.aidtech. wlv.ac.uk) all attracted over ninety delegates. The International Association for Development of the Information Society (IADIS) (www.IADIS.org) now runs a conference series, the first taking place in Malta in 2005, the second in Dublin in 2006, and the third in Lisbon in 2007. Secondly, there have also been a rising number of references to mobile learning at generalist academic conferences; for example, the Association for Learning Technology conference (ALT-C) every September in the UK (http://www.alt.ac.uk).

The mobile learning currently exploits both handheld computers and mobile telephones and other devices that draw on the same set of functionalities. Mobile learning using handheld computers is obviously relatively immature in terms of both its technologies and its pedagogies, but is developing rapidly. It draws on the theory and practice of pedagogies used in technology enhanced learning and others used in the classroom and the community, and takes place as mobile devices are transforming notions of space, community, and discourse (Katz and Aakhus 2002; Brown and Green 2001) along with investigative ethics and tools (Hewson, Yule, Laurent, and Vogel 2003). The term covers the personalized, connected, and interactive use of handheld computers in classrooms (Perry 2003; O'Malley and Stanton 2002), in collaborative learning (Pinkwart, Hoppe, Milrad, and Perez 2003), in fieldwork (Chen, Kao, and Sheu 2003), and in counselling and guidance (Vuorinen and Sampson 2003). Mobile devices are supporting corporate training for mobile workers (Gayeski 2002; Pasanen 2003; Lundin and Magnusson 2003) and are enhancing medical education (Smordal and Gregory 2003), teacher training (Seppala and Alamaki 2003), music composition (Polishook 2005), nurse training (Kneebone 2005), and numerous other disciplines. They are becoming a viable and imaginative component of institutional support and provision (Griswold, Boyer, Brown, et al. 2002; Sariola 2003; Hackemer and Peterson 2005). In October 2005, the first comprehensive handbook of mobile learning was published (Kukulska-Hulme and Traxler 2005), but accounts of mobile distance learning are still infrequent.

There are now a large number of case studies documenting trials and pilots in the public domain (Kukulska-Hulme and Traxler 2005; JISC 2005; Attewell and Savill-Smith 2004). In looking at these, we can see some categories of mobile learning emerging (Kukulska-Hulme and Traxler forthcoming):

- **Technology-driven mobile learning** – Some specific technological innovation is deployed in an academic setting to demonstrate technical feasibility and pedagogic possibility
- **Miniature but portable e-learning** – Mobile, wireless, and handheld technologies are used to re-enact approaches and solutions already used in conventional e-learning, perhaps porting some e-learning technology such as a Virtual Learning Environment (VLE) to these technologies or perhaps merely using mobile technologies as flexible replacements for static desktop technologies
- **Connected classroom learning** – The same technologies are used in classroom settings to support collaborative learning, perhaps connected to other classroom technologies such as interactive whiteboards
- **Informal, personalized, situated mobile learning** – The same technologies are enhanced with additional functionality, for example location-awareness or video-capture, and deployed to deliver educational experiences that would otherwise be difficult or impossible
- **Mobile training/ performance support** – The technologies are used to improve the productivity and efficiency of mobile workers by delivering

information and support just-in-time and in context for their immediate priorities (for an early account, see Gayeski 2002)

- **Remote/rural/development mobile learning** – The technologies are used to address environmental and infrastructural challenges to delivering and supporting education where conventional e-learning technologies would fail, often troubling accepted developmental or evolutionary paradigms

Mobile distance learning could fall into any of these categories (with the exception of the connected classroom learning); how it develops will depend in part on the affordances of any given situation. These affordances might include:

- Infrastructure, meaning power supply, postal services, Internet connectivity, etc.
- Sparsity, giving rise to infrequent face-to-face contact, lack of technical support, etc.
- The wider policy agenda including lifelong learning, inclusion (of rural areas for example), assistivity, participation, and access
- Mobile distance learning within a framework of blended distance learning and the affordances of other delivery and support mechanisms

Defining Mobile Education

In spite of the activity cited above, the concept of mobile education or mobile learning is still emerging and still unclear. How it is eventually conceptualized will determine perceptions and expectations, and will determine its evolution and future. There are different stakeholders and factors at work in this process of conceptualising mobile education and the outcome is uncertain.

There are obviously definitions and conceptualisations of mobile education that define it purely in terms of its technologies and its hardware, namely that it is learning delivered or supported solely or mainly by handheld and mobile technologies such as personal digital assistants (PDAs), smartphones or wireless laptop PCs. These definitions, however, are constraining, technocentric, and tied to current technological instantiations. We, therefore, should seek to explore other definitions that perhaps look at the underlying learner experience and ask how mobile learning differs from other forms of education, especially other forms of e-learning.

If we take as our starting point the characterisations of mobile learning found in the literature (the conference proceedings from MLEARN and WMTE for example), we find words such as "personal, spontaneous, opportunistic, informal, pervasive, situated, private, context-aware, bite-sized, portable." This is contrasted with words from the literature of conventional "tethered" e-learning such as "structured, media-rich, broadband, interactive, intelligent, usable." We can use these two lists to make a blurred distinction between mobile learning and e-learning. This distinction, however, is not only blurred – but in part it is also only temporary. Among the virtues of e-learning is the power of its technology (and the investment in it), and soon this virtue will also be accessible to mobile devices as market forces drive improvements in interface design, processor speed, battery life, and connectivity bandwidth. Nevertheless, this approach underpins a conceptualisation of mobile learning in terms of the learners' experiences and an emphasis on ownership, informality, mobility, and context that will always be inaccessible to conventional tethered e-learning.

Tackling the problem of definition from another direction, we see that mobile devices and technologies are pervasive and ubiquitous in many modern societies, and are increasingly changing the nature of knowledge and discourse in these societies (whilst being themselves the products of various social and economic forces). This, in turn, alters both the nature of learning (both formal and informal) and alters the ways that learning can be delivered. Learning that used to be delivered "just-in-case," can now be delivered "just-in-time, just enough, and just-for-me." Finding information rather than possessing it or knowing it becomes the defining characteristic of learning generally and of mobile learning especially, and this may take learning back into the community.

Mobile technologies also alter the nature of work (the driving force behind much education and most training), especially of knowledge work. Mobile technologies alter the balance between training and performance support, especially for many knowledge workers. This means that "mobile" is not merely a new adjective qualifying the timeless concept of "learning"; rather, "mobile learning" is emerging as an entirely new and distinct concept alongside the mobile workforce and the connected society.

Mobile devices create not only new forms of knowledge and new ways of accessing it, but also create new forms of art and performance, and new ways of accessing them (such as music videos designed and sold for iPods). Mobile devices are creating new forms of commerce and economic activity as well. So mobile learning is not about "mobile" as previously understood, or about "learning" as previously understood, but part of a new mobile conception of society. (This may contrast with technology enhanced learning or technology supported, both of which give the impression that technology does something to learning.)

In a different sense, ongoing developments on implementing e-learning, for example in developing the ontologies of learning objects, makes us examine and question how knowledge is organized and interrelated. Here too our notions of knowledge and learning are evolving. It could be argued that the need to organize and navigate through bite-sized pieces of mobile learning content (whether or not as learning objects) will also impact on these notions of knowledge and learning and perhaps individual learners will create their own ontologies on-the-fly as they navigate through a personalized learning journey.

One can also focus on the nature of mobility in order to explore the nature of mobile learning. For each learner, the nature of mobility has a variety of connotations and these will colour conceptualisations of mobile education. It may mean learning whilst traveling, driving, sitting, or walking; it may be hands-free learning or eyes-free learning. These interpretations impact on the implementation and hence the definition of mobile learning.

Having earlier discounted technology as a defining characteristic of mobile learning, it may in fact transpire that different hardware and software platforms support rather different interpretations of mobile learning. At the risk of over-simplification, the philosophy behind the Palm™ based brand of handheld computers (or rather, organizers) initially led to a zero-latency task-oriented interface with only as much functionality as would fit inside the prescribed size of box, and this would coax maximum performance out of the processor, the memory, and the battery. *Microsoft*-based mobile devices by comparison inherited a PC-based interface with considerable latency, making much higher demands on memory, battery, and processor. This dichotomy may be less sharp than it once was, but it could be viewed as underpinning two different interpretations of mobile learning; the former a bite-sized, just-in-time version near to the one described above, the latter more like a portable but puny version of tethered e-learning described above. Similarly, if we were to address whether learning delivered or supported on the current generation of laptop and *Tablet* PCs should be termed "mobile learning," then the answer must be no. Learners, and indeed people in general, will carry and use their phones, their *iPods*, or their PDAs habitually and unthinkingly; however, they will seldom carry a laptop or *Tablet* PC without a premeditated purpose and a minimum timeframe.

Another technical factor, however, may hinder direct comparison with e-learning. That is the geometry of mobile devices. For several years, proponents of mobile learning have looked for the eventual convergence of mobile phone technologies and handheld computer technologies, creating a basic generic mobile learning platform to which extra (learning) functionality could be added as desired. This might include camera and other data capture, media player capacity, and location awareness using, for example, global positioning systems (GPS). This now looks unlikely to happen and currently the hardware manufacturers and vendors treat their markets as highly segmented and differentiated. This may be due to the nature of the hardware itself. Unlike desktop PCs, where functionality and connectivity can be easily added or subtracted by adding or subtracting internal chips and cards, mobile technologies are fairly monolithic. In the case of laptops, external slots and ports can provide extra connectivity or memory. Anything smaller, such as a handheld or palmtop computer, has one or at best, two slots. This means that most handheld devices have only the functionality with which it was made. Manufacturers cannot position and reposition variations on a basic chassis to suit changing markets. Therefore, it is unlikely that we will be able to build a conceptualization of mobile learning upon the idea of a generic and expandable mobile hardware platform in the way that tethered e-learning has implicitly been built upon the PC or personal computer platform.

In any case, hardware devices and technical systems are all without exception designed, manufactured, and marketed for corporate, retail, or recreational users. Any educational uses of the devices and the systems are necessarily parasitic and secondary. Therefore, conceptualisations of mobile learning are also constrained by the distorting nature of the technologies and the devices.

The community of practice cohering around mobile learning nevertheless may feel the need for a theory of mobile learning (although in a postmodern era, the role of theory as an informing construct is under threat). Such a theory may be problematic since mobile learning is inherently a "noisy" phenomenon where context is everything. E-learning has certainly gained credibility from the work of many outstanding authors. Finding similar beacons for mobile learning may be more challenging and proponents of mobile learning are still struggling to find a literature and rhetoric distinct from conventional tethered e-learning.

The discussion so far has implicitly focused on conceptions of mobile learning based on the culture and affordances of developed countries. If we look at the emerging practice of mobile learning based around phones and PDAs in developing countries, especially the poorest, a different picture emerges based on wholly different affordances. The radically different physical infrastructure and cultural environment – including landline telephony, Internet connectivity, electricity, the rarity of PCs, and the relative inability of societies to support jobs, merchandising, and other initiatives based around these prerequisites – has meant that prescriptions for mobile learning are more cautious than in the developed world (Traxler and Kukulska-Hulme 2005). It has also meant that mobile phones are now being recognized as the pre-eminent vehicle not only for mobile learning, but also for wider social change (Traxler and Dearden 2005). It is entirely possible that the emergence of mobile learning in developing countries will take the evolution of e-learning along a trajectory that is very different from that in developed countries, where it has been predicated on massive, static, and stable resources. Distance learning will form a significant component of this because of its existing status within the development communities.

The Case for Mobile Education

It is possible to make a strong case for mobile education on "purist" or theoretical pedagogic grounds. This purist case for mobile learning includes the idea that mobile learning will support a wide variety of conceptions of teaching, and the idea that mobile learning is uniquely placed to support learning that is personalized, authentic, and situated.

Different teachers and disciplines will have different conceptions of teaching (Kember 1997) that they will attempt to bring to education. These conceptions of teaching may vary from ones primarily concerned with the delivery of content to those focused on supporting student learning (i.e., by discussion and collaboration). Mobile learning technologies clearly support the transmission and delivery of rich multimedia content. They also support discussion and discourse, real-time, synchronous and asynchronous, using voice, text and multimedia. Different disciplines, say for example sociology or literature as opposed to engineering, may also require broadly different conceptions of teaching. Distance learning versus site-based/face-to-face education forms another alternative axis to the subject axis; distance educators will have their own conceptions of teaching, often influenced by Illich (1971), Freire (1972), and Gramsci (1985).

What are called "styles of learning" will also exert an influence on how mobile learning is conceptualized. This is currently a contested area (Coffield, Moseley, Hall, and Ecclestone 2005), but similar arguments could be advanced about the capacity of mobile learning to fit with the various preferred approaches to learning adopted by different (distance) students at different times.

By personalized learning, we mean learning that recognises diversity, difference, and individuality in the ways that learning is developed, delivered, and supported. Personalized learning defined in this way includes learning that recognizes different learning styles and approaches (though perhaps this phrase should not be related too literally to the established literature of learning styles; see for example Coffield et al. 2005), and recognizes social, cognitive, and physical difference and diversity (in the design and delivery of interfaces, devices, and content). We would argue that mobile learning offers a perspective that differs dramatically from personalized conventional e-learning in that it supports learning that recognizes the context and history of each individual learner and delivers learning to the learner when and where they want it.

By situated learning, we mean learning that takes place in the course of activity, in appropriate and meaningful contexts (Lave and Wenger 1991). The idea evolved by looking at people learning in communities as apprentices by a process of increased participation. It can be, however, extended to learning in the field (in the case of botany students for example), in the hospital ward (in the case of trainee nurses), in the classroom (in the case of trainee teachers), and in the workshop (in the case of engineering students), rather than in remote lecture theatres. Mobile learning is uniquely suited to support context-specific and immediate learning, and this is a major opportunity for distance learning since mobile technologies can situate learners and connect learners.

By authentic learning, we mean learning that involves real-world problems and projects that are relevant and interesting to the learner. Authentic learning implies that learning should be based around authentic tasks, that students should be engaged in exploration and inquiry, that students should have opportunities for social discourse, and that ample resources should be available to students as they pursue meaningful problems. Mobile learning enables these conditions to be met, allowing learning tasks built around data capture, location-awareness, and collaborative working, even for distance learning students physically remote from each other.

Mobile learning uniquely supports spontaneous reflection and self-evaluation and the current e-Portfolio technologies (see for example, www.pebblepad.co.uk/) are expected to migrate to mobile devices in the near future.

It is equally possible, however, to make a strong case for mobile education on practical or "impurist" grounds. This impurist case recognises that learning takes place in a wider social and economic context, and that students must be recognized to be under a range of pressures, most obviously those of time, resources, and conflicting/competing roles. This is true of distance learning and part-time students. Mobile learning allows these students to exploit small amounts of time and space for learning, to work with other students on projects and discussions, and to maximize contact and support from tutors.

Evaluating Mobile Education

This section makes the case that the increasing diversity of mobile education and the increasing power, sophistication, and complexity of mobile technologies call into question the adequacy of the conventional repertoire of evaluation techniques based largely around formal, sedentary, and traditional learning. This has always been the case with informal and distance learning anyway. There is a need for a more comprehensive, eclectic, and structured approach to evaluation based on sound and transparent principles. The section briefly elucidates these principles and shows how they can be used to underpin evaluation methodologies appropriate to mobile education.

There are a variety of problems associated with evaluating mobile learning. Perhaps the most fundamental is the problem of defining the characteristics of a "good" or acceptable evaluation though, of course, the issue of evaluating mobile learning will also take us back to the issue of defining and conceptualizing mobile learning. A definition or conceptualization of mobile learning in terms of learner experience will take evaluation in a different direction from a conceptualisation of mobile learning in terms of hardware platforms. Of course, the categorization of mobile learning (above) will also influence the practicalities and the priorities of evaluation.

What is not always accepted is that there are no *a priori* attributes of a good evaluation of learning (to say that there are would be to take an implicitly realist or essentialist position that not every stakeholder would agree with, and would also confront a widely held view that in fact evaluation is a contingent activity). In an earlier work (Traxler 2002), we tried to outline some tentative candidate attributes of a good evaluation, but we also identified the reasons why evaluation of mobile learning is unusually challenging. Briefly some of these attributes of a good evaluation could be:

- Rigorous, meaning roughly that conclusions must be trustworthy and transferable
- Efficient, in terms of cost, effort, time, or some other resource
- Ethical, specifically in relation to the nuances of evolving forms of provision, in terms of standards from legal to normative
- Proportionate, that is, not more ponderous, onerous, or time-consuming than the learning experience or the delivery and implementation of the learning itself (bearing in mind earlier remarks about the learners' experiences of mobile learning)
- Appropriate to the specific learning technologies, to the learners, and to the ethos of the learning – ideally built in, not bolted on

- Consistent with the teaching and learning philosophy and conceptions of teaching and learning of all the participants
- Authentic, in accessing what learners (and perhaps teachers and other stakeholders) really mean, really feel, and sensitive to the learners' personalities within those media
- Aligned to the chosen medium and technology of learning

Consistent across:
 - different groups or cohorts of learners in order to provide generality
 - time, that is, the evaluation is reliably repeatable
 - whatever varied devices and technologies are used

The last of these attributes is challenging in mobile learning, since the technologies are changing at an exceptional pace and consequently reaching any understanding of underlying issues is difficult. Nevertheless, some issues around ethics have been explored elsewhere recently (Traxler and Bridges 2004), and mobile learning continues to evolve.

A recent review of practice in the evaluation of mobile learning (Traxler and Kukulska-Hulme 2005) suggests that not many accounts articulated an explicit position on pedagogy or epistemology (none of the evaluations concerned distance learning anyway). They seldom cited any works from the literature of evaluation or any works from the literature of the ethics of evaluation. They seldom, if ever, mentioned any ethical issues in relation to their evaluation. Most accounts cited focus groups, interviews, and questionnaires as their elicitation instruments. Some used observation and some used system logs. A few accounts mentioned several techniques and were triangulated, but most accounts used only one or, at most, two techniques. None of these elicitation techniques were particularly consistent with mobile learning technologies, and all accounts of such evaluations assumed that the evaluators were told the truth by subjects (that is, learners and teachers). Hopefully those engaged in mobile distance learning evaluation will learn from this critique.

Clearly, there are problems with the epistemology and ethics of evaluating mobile learning; there are also challenges in developing suitable techniques to gather, analyse, and present evaluation. Nevertheless, the credibility of mobile (including distance) learning as a sustainable and reliable form of educational provision rests on the rigour and effectiveness of its evaluation.

Mobile Education in Universities and Colleges

Mobile education, however innovative, technically feasible, and pedagogically sound, may have no chance of sustained, wide-scale institutional deployment in higher education in the foreseeable future, at a distance or on site. This is because of the strategic factors at work within educational institutions and providers. These strategic factors are different from those of technology and pedagogy. They are the context and the environment for the technical and the pedagogic aspects. They include resources (that is, finance and money but also human resources, physical estates, institutional reputation, intellectual property, and expertise) and culture (that is, institutions as social organizations, their practices, values and procedures, but also the expectations and standards of their staff, students, and their wider communities, including employers and professional bodies).

Implementing wireless and mobile education within higher education must address these social, cultural, and organizational factors. They can be formal and explicit, or informal and tacit, and can vary enormously across and within institutions. Within institutions, different disciplines have their own specific cultures and concerns, often strongly influenced by professional practice in the "outside world" – especially in the case of part-time provision and distance learning. Because most work in mobile learning is still in the pilot or trial phase, any explorations of wider institutional issues are still tentative (Traxler 2005; JISC 2005) but it points to considerable hurdles with infrastructure and support.

Conclusion

This has been a very wide-ranging exploration of mobile learning's nature and possibilities. It draws together much existing work, but this is still a relatively immature field. This chapter has sought to define questions for discussion rather than provide answers for what might in fact be premature or inappropriate questions. It is too early to describe or analyse the specifics of mobile learning for distance learning since the field, as a whole, is new and accounts are relatively sparse. The synergy between mobile learning and distance learning, however, holds enormous potential.

References

Attewell, J., and C. Savill-Smith, eds. 2003. Learning with mobile devices: Research and development. In *mLearn 2003 book of papers*. London: Learning and Skills Development Agency.

Brown, B., and N. Green. 2001. *Wireless world: Social and interactional aspects of the mobile age*. New York: Springer-Verlag.

CHEN, Y., T. KAO, and J. SHEU. 2003. A mobile learning system for scaffolding bird watching learning. *Journal of Computer Assisted Learning* 19 (3):347-59.

COFFIELD, F., D. MOSELEY, E. HALL, and K. ECCLESTONE. 2004. *Should we be using learning styles? What research has to say to practice.* London: Learning and Skills Research Centre.

FREIRE, P. 1972. *Pedagogy of the oppressed.* London: Penguin.

GAYESKI, D. 2002. *Learning unplugged: Using mobile technologies for organisational and performance improvement.* New York: AMACON – American Management Association.

GRAMSCI, A. 1985. *Selections from cultural writings.* London: Lawrence & Wishart.

GRISWOLD, W., R. BOYER, S. BROWN, T. TRUONG, E. BHASKER, G. JAY, and B. SHAPIRO. 2002. *Using mobile technology to create opportunistic interactions on a university campus.* San Diego: Computer Science and Engineering, University of California, San Diego.

HACKEMER, K., and D. PETERSON. 2005. Campus-wide handhelds. In Kukulska-Hulme and Traxler 2005.

HEWSON, C., P. YULE, D. LAURENT, and C. VOGEL, eds. 2003. *Internet research methods: A practical guide for the social and behavioural sciences.* London: Sage, New Technologies for Social Research Series.

ILLICH, T. 1971. *Deschooling society.* London: Marion Boyars.

Joint Information Services Committee (JISC). 2005. *Innovative practice with e-learning.* Bristol, UK: JISC.

KATZ, J., and M. AAKHUS, eds. 2002. *Perpetual contact: Mobile communications, private talk, public performance.* Cambridge, UK: Cambridge University Press.

KYNÄSLAHTI, H. and P. SEPPÄLÄ, eds. 2003. Mobile learning. Helsinki, Finland: IT Press.

KEMBER, D. 1997. Reconceptualisation of research into university academics' conceptions. *Learning and Instruction* 7 (3):255-75.

KNEEBONE, R. 2005. PDAs for PSPs. In Kukulska-Hulme and Traxler 2005, 106-15.

KUKULSKA-HULME, A., and J. TRAXLER. 2005. *Mobile learning: A handbook for educators and trainers.* London: Routledge.

———. Forthcoming. Learning design with mobile and wireless technologies. In *Rethinking pedagogy for the digital age*, ed. H. Beetham and R. Sharpe. London: Routledge.

LAVE, J., and E. WENGER. 1990. *Situated learning: Legitimate peripheral participation.* Cambridge, UK: Cambridge University Press.

LUNDIN, J., and M. MAGNUSSON. 2003. Collaborative learning in mobile work. *Journal of Computer Assisted Learning 19* (3):273-83.

O'MALLEY, C., and D. STANTON. 2002. Tangible technologies for collaborative storytelling. In proceedings, *mLearn 2002, European workshop on mobile and contextual learning,* June 20-21, University of Birmingham, Birmingham, UK.

PASANEN, J. 2003. Corporate mobile learning. In Kynäslahti and Seppälä 2003, 115-23.

PERRY, D. 2003. *Handheld computers (PDAs) in schools.* Coventry, UK: BECTA.

PINKWART, N., H. HOPPE, M. MILRAD, and J. PEREZ. 2003. Educational scenarios for cooperative use of Personal Digital Assistants. *Journal of Computer Assisted Learning 19* (3):383-91.

POLISHOOK, M. 2005. Music on PDAs. In Kukulska-Hulme and Traxler 2005.

SARIOLA, J. 2003. The boundaries of university teaching: Mobile learning as a strategic choice for the virtual university. In Kynäslahti and Seppälä 2003, 71-78.

SEPPÄLÄ, P., and H. ALAMAKI. 2003. Mobile learning in teacher training. *Journal of Computer Assisted Learning 19* (3):330-35.

SMORDAL, O., and J. GREGORY. 2003. Personal Digital Assistants in medical education and practice. *Journal of Computer Assisted Learning 19* (3):320-29.

TRAXLER, J. 2002. Evaluating m-learning. In proceedings, *mLearn 2002, European workshop on mobile and contextual learning,* June 20-21, University of Birmingham, Birmingham, UK.

———. 2005. Institutional issues: Embedding and supporting. In Kukulska-Hulme and Traxler 2005, 173-88.

TRAXLER, J., and N. BRIDGES. 2004. Mobile learning: The ethical and legal challenges. In proceedings, *mLearn 2004,* June, Bracciano, Italy.

TRAXLER, J., and P. DEARDEN. 2005. The potential for using SMS to support learning and organisation in sub-Saharan Africa. In proceedings, *Development Studies Association conference*, September, Milton Keynes, UK.

TRAXLER, J., and A. KUKULSKA-HULME. 2005a. Mobile learning in developing countries. In *A report commissioned by the Commonwealth of Learning*, ed. G. Chin. Vancouver, BC: Commonwealth of Learning.

——. 2005b. Evaluating mobile learning: Reflections on current practice. In proceedings, *mLearn 2005*, October 25-28, Cape Town, South Africa.

VUORINEN, R., and J. SAMPSON. 2003. Using mobile information technology to enhance counselling and guidance. In Kynäslahti and Seppälä 2003, 63-70.

A Model for Framing Mobile Learning

MARGUERITE L. KOOLE
ATHABASCA UNIVERSITY
CANADA

Abstract

The Framework for the Rational Analysis of Mobile Education (FRAME) model describes mobile learning as a process resulting from the convergence of mobile technologies, human learning capacities, and social interaction. It addresses contemporary pedagogical issues of information overload, knowledge navigation, and collaboration in learning. This model is useful for guiding the development of future mobile devices, the development of learning materials, and the design of teaching and learning strategies for mobile education.

Introduction

Research in the field of mobile learning is on the rise. Visionaries believe mobile learning offers learners greater access to relevant information, reduced cognitive load, and increased access to other people and systems. It may be argued that wireless, networked mobile devices can help shape culturally sensitive learning experiences and the means to cope with the growing amount of information in the world. Consider, for a moment, an individual who is learning English. There is a myriad of available resources on grammar, vocabulary, and idioms; some resources are accurate and useful; others less so. Equipped with a mobile device, the learner can choose to consult a web page, access audio or video tutorials, send a query via text message to a friend, or phone an expert for practice or guidance. She may use one or several of these techniques. But, how can such a learner take full advantage of the mobile experience? How can practitioners design materials and activities appropriate for mobile access? How can mobile learning be effectively implemented in both formal and informal learning? The Framework for the Rational Analysis of Mobile Education (FRAME) model offers some insights into these issues.

The FRAME model takes into consideration the technical characteristics of mobile devices as well as social and personal aspects of learning (Koole 2006). This model refers to concepts similar to those as found in psychological theories such as Activity Theory (Kaptelinin and Nardi 2006) – especially pertaining to Vygotsky's (1978) work on *mediation* and the *zone of proximal development*. However, the FRAME model highlights the role of technology beyond simply an artefact of "cultural-historic" development. In this model, the mobile device is an active component *in equal footing* to learning and social processes. This model also places more emphasis on constructivism: the word *rational* refers to the "belief that reason is the primary source of knowledge and that reality is constructed rather than discovered" (Smith and Ragan 1999, 15). The FRAME model describes a mode of learning in which learners may move within different physical *and* virtual locations and thereby participate and interact with other people, information, or systems – anywhere, anytime.

The FRAME Model

In the FRAME model, mobile learning experiences are viewed as existing within a context of information. Collectively and individually, learners consume and create information. The interaction with information is mediated through technology. It is through the complexities of this kind of interaction that information becomes meaningful and useful. Within this context of information, the FRAME model is represented by a Venn diagram in which three aspects intersect (Figure 1). [2]

---

2. The nomenclature used in the Venn diagram has been altered from previous publications. Previously the *device aspect* was called the *device usability aspect*, the *device usability intersection* was called the *learner context intersection*, and the *social technology intersection* was called the *social computing intersection*.

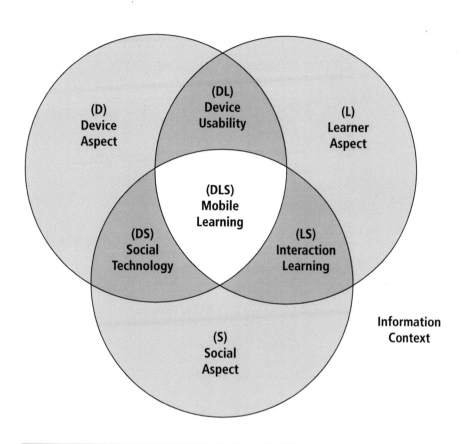

FIGURE 1 The FRAME Model

The three circles represent the device (D), learner (L), and social (S) aspects. The intersections where two circles overlap contain attributes that belong to both aspects. The attributes of the device usability (DL) and social technology (DS) intersections describe the *affordances* of mobile technology (Norman 1999). The intersection labelled interaction learning (LS) contains instructional and learning theories with an emphasis on social constructivism. All three aspects overlap at the primary intersection (DLS) in the centre of the Venn diagram. Hypothetically, the primary intersection, a convergence of all three aspects, defines an ideal mobile learning situation. By assessing the degree to which all the areas of the FRAME model are utilized within a mobile learning situation, practitioners may use the model to design more effective mobile learning experiences.

Aspects

Device Aspect (D)

The device aspect (D) refers to the physical, technical, and functional characteristics of a mobile device (Table 1). The physical characteristics include input and output capabilities as well as processes internal to the machine such as storage capabilities, power, processor speed, compatibility, and expandability. These characteristics result from the hardware and software design of the devices and have a significant impact on the physical and psychological comfort levels of the users. It is important to assess these characteristics because mobile learning devices provide the interface between the mobile *learner* and the *learning task*(s) as described later in the device usability intersection (DL).

TABLE 1 The Device Aspect

Criteria	Examples & Concepts	Comments
Physical Characteristics	Size, weight, composition, placement of buttons and keys, right/left handed requirements, one or two-hand operability[1].	Affects how the user can manipulate the device and move around while using the device.
Input Capabilities	Keyboard, mouse, light pen, pen/stylus, touch screen, trackball, joystick, touchpad, hand/foot control, voice recognition[1].	Allows selection and positioning of objects or data on the device[1]. Mobile devices are often criticized for inadequate input mechanisms.
Output Capabilities	Monitors, speakers or any other visual, auditory, and tactile output mechanisms.	Allows the human body to sense changes in the device; allows the user to interact with the device. Mobile devices are often criticized for limitations in output mechanisms such as small screen-size.

File Storage and Retrieval	Storage on the device (RAM or ROM) or detachable, portable mechanisms such as USB drives, CDs, DVDs, and SD cards.	Consistency and standardization of storage and retrieval systems greatly affect usability.
Processor Speed	Response rates; speed with which the device reacts to human input.	Determined by the amount of RAM, file storage speed, user-interface speed, and system configuration. Unusually long or short response rates may affect error rates as the user may forget initial goals and/or task sequences[1].
Error Rates	Malfunctions resulting from flaws in hardware, software, and/or interface design.	Users may not be able to perform desired tasks and may lose confidence in the device.

1. Shneiderman and Plaisant (2005).

As the bridge between the human being and the technology, devices must be constructed so as to maintain high physical and psychological comfort levels. In other words, the device characteristics have a significant impact upon usability. In order for a device to be portable, for example, the size, weight, structure, and composition must match the physical and psychological capacities of the individual users. In particular, input and output capabilities must be suited to human perception and motor functions. Similarly, the capacity and speed of the device memory, processor, file storage, and file exchange require error-free response rates appropriately timed to the human user's needs and expectations. Learners equipped with well-designed mobile devices should be able to focus on cognitive tasks such as those described in the learner aspect (L) rather than on the devices themselves.

Learner Aspect (L)

The learner aspect (L) takes into account an individual's cognitive abilities, memory, prior knowledge, emotions, and possible motivations (Table 2). This aspect describes how learners use what they already know and how they encode, store, and transfer information. This aspect also draws upon learning theories regarding knowledge transfer and learning by discovery.

TABLE 2 The Learner Aspect

Criteria	Examples & Concepts	Comments
Prior knowledge	Cognitive structures already in memory, anchoring ideas[1], schema theory, Gagne's conditions for learning[2].	Affects how easily a learner can comprehend new concepts. Potential problems include "assimilation bias" (a reluctance to adopt new procedures)[3].
Memory	Techniques for successful encoding with the use of contextual cues: categorization, mnemonics, self-questioning, semantic & episodic memory[5], tactile, auditory, olfactory, visual imagery[4], kinaesthetic imagery, dual coding[6], and encoding specificity[4].	Inclusion of multimedia by providing a variety of stimuli may help learners understand and retain concepts more easily.
Context and Transfer	Inert vs. active knowledge.	Actively using information aids for learners to remember, understand, and transfer concepts to varied contexts.
Discovery Learning	Application of procedures and concepts to new situation; solutions for novel problems.	May stimulate learner to develop skills to "filter, choose, and recognize" relevant information in different situations[7].
Emotions and Motivations	Feelings of the learner towards a task; reasons or accomplishing a task.	A learner's willingness or ability to adopt new information may be affected by his/her emotional state or desire to accomplish a task. Activity Theory may provide additional avenues of investigation into motivation.

1. Ausubel (1968), 2 Gagne (1977), 3. Caroll and Rosson (2005), 4. Driscoll (2005), 5. Tulving and Donaldson (1972), 6. Paivio (1979), 7. Tirri (2003, p. 26).

While it is recognized that prior knowledge (Ausubel 1968) and past experience will influence learning, so too will a learner's environment, task authenticity, and presentation of content in multiple formats. Tulving and Donaldson (1972) proposed that *semantic* memory is composed of general, non-contextually based concepts. Mobile learning, however, can help learners utilize *episodic* memory. This type of memory is grounded in actual, authentic experiences such as traveling to foreign countries, visiting museums, visiting historic sites, and case studies in professional settings. Using concepts makes them *active*, and the ability of a learner to remember a concept is largely dependent upon the learner remembering its use (Driscoll 1994). Remembering the use of a concept or tool may also aid the learner in transferral of the concept into other contexts. Finally, some theorists recommend that materials be presented in different formats – as proposed in Dual Coding Theory – allowing the brain to actively process content through various channels (Paivio 1979).

The learner aspect (L) is grounded in the belief that the learner's prior knowledge, intellectual capacity, motivation, and emotional state have a significant impact upon encoding, retaining, and transferring information. Actively selecting or designing learning activities rooted in authentic situations as well as encouraging learners to discover laws within physical and cultural environments are powerful pedagogical techniques. Mobile learning may help to enhance encoding, recall, and transfer of information by allowing learners to access content in multiple formats and highlighting the contexts and uses of the information.

Social Aspect (S)

The social aspect takes into account the processes of social interaction and cooperation (Table 3). Individuals must follow the rules of cooperation to communicate – thereby enabling them to exchange information, acquire knowledge, and sustain cultural practices. Rules of cooperation are determined by a learner's culture or the culture in which an interaction take place. In mobile learning, this culture may be physical or virtual.

TABLE 3 The Social Aspect

Criteria	Examples & Concepts	Comments
Conversation and Cooperation	Social constraints; 4 maxims (rules): quantity, quality, relation, and manner[1].	Affects quality and quantity of communication; miscommunications may occur when any of the 4 maxims are not met[1].
Social Interaction	Conversation as a cooperative activity, sharing of signs and symbols.	Agreement on the meaning of signs and symbols may affect reinforcement of social and cultural beliefs and behaviours[2].

1. Wardhaugh (1968), 2. Kearsly (1995).

It is important to realize that there may be constraints upon participants in a conversation. Such constraints provide guidelines and predictability for behaviour that enable effective communication. When a person joins a new community, he must share his own "sign systems" and learn those of the new community (Driscoll 2005, 173). Cooperative communication requires that contributions are as informative as necessary, accurate, relevant, and sufficiently clear. When a participant neglects to follow one or more of the rules, miscommunication may occur (Wardhaugh 1986). Participants may also purposely break rules about procedures and etiquette in order to achieve certain effects (Preece, Rogers, and Sharp 2002). It is important that participants pay attention to each other during conversations in order to detect breakdowns and interpret them appropriately (Preece, Rogers, and Sharp 2002). It is through interaction that people receive feedback which, in turn, reinforces social and cultural beliefs and behaviours (Kearsley 1995).

Intersections

Device Usability Intersection (DL)
The device usability intersection contains elements that belong to both the device (D) and learner (L) aspects (Table 4). This section relates characteristics of mobile devices to cognitive tasks related to the manipulation and storage of information. These processes, in turn, can affect the user's sense of psychological comfort and satisfaction by affecting

cognitive load, the ability to access information, and the ability to physically move to different physical and virtual locations.

TABLE 4 The Device Usability Intersection

Criteria	Examples & Concepts	Comments
Portability	Portability and durability (dependent on physical characteristics, number of components, and materials used to construct the device).	Affects the user's ability to move the device to different environments and climates.
Information Availability	Anytime, anywhere access to information stored on a device. (This is a distinct from information transfer, a characteristic of social technology (DS).)	Enables just-in-time learning; information accompanies the user; the user can retrieve stored information when and where it is needed.
Psychological Comfort	Learnability[1], comprehensibility, transparency, intuitiveness, memorability[1], and metaphors.	Psychological comfort affects cognitive load and the speed with which users can perform tasks. Metaphors, chunking information, mnemonics, simplification of displays, and reduction of required actions may reduce cognitive load.
Satisfaction	Aesthetics of the interface, physical appearance of the device, functionality, preferred cognitive style.	Because satisfaction and enjoyment is highly personal and culturally determined, it is very difficult to predict.

1. Nielsen, 1993.

Portability and access to information are significant concepts in mobile usability. Device portability is dependent upon the physical attributes of the device such as size and weight, the number of peripherals, and the materials used in the construction of the device. Highly portable devices must resist humidity, dust, and shock. Information access complements portability, and it enables information to travel with the user rather than the user moving to the information. In the past, learners were required to learn information just in case they needed it in the future. Now, learners can access stored information anytime or anywhere, making just-in-time learning possible.

Psychological comfort refers to how intuitive the device is or how quickly a learner can understand and begin using the device. Users should be able to learn the main functions quickly so they can accomplish desired tasks as soon as possible (Nielsen 1993). A high degree of transparency suggests that the device is easy to use and that the user can concentrate on cognitive tasks rather than the manipulation of the device itself. Some ways to increase transparency and reduce cognitive load include lowering the number of actions necessary to complete a task, using mnemonic devices, providing sufficient training, and using simple displays (Shneiderman and Plaisant 2005). Interfaces based on carefully considered metaphors that draw on learners' prior experiences or social-cultural knowledge are, hypothetically, more learnable and memorable. Flexibility permitting the user to select themes and functionality may help to increase satisfaction and comfort.

Designers should strive to minimize memory load on the user (Shneiderman and Plaisant 2005; Bransford, Brown, and Cocking 2000). A commonly cited rule is the seven-plus-or-minus-two rule. Miller (1956) proposed that most people are capable of retaining approximately seven chunks of information give or take two. More information can be stored depending up the person's familiarity with the chunk patterns and with the information (Shneiderman and Plaisant 2005; Bransford, Brown, and Cocking 2000).

The device usability intersection (DL) bridges needs and activities of learners to the hardware and software characteristics of their mobile devices. Highly portable, intuitive, and transparent devices can help to reduce cognitive load and increase task completion rates because the learner can concentrate on the tasks rather than the tools.

Social Technology Intersection (DS)
While the device usability intersection (DL) in the FRAME model describes the relationship between *one* learner and a device, the social technology intersection (DS) describes how mobile devices enable communication and collaboration amongst *multiple* individuals and systems (Table 5). Device hardware and software provide various means of connectivity. Many mobile devices come equipped with various technical capabilities, such as short messaging service (SMS), telephony, and access to the Internet through wireless networks. What is of greater importance here, however, are the means of information exchange and collaboration between people with various goals and purposes.

TABLE 5. The Social Technology Intersection

Criteria	Examples & Concepts	Comments
Device Networking	Personal area networks (PANs), wide area networks (WANs), wireless local area networks (WLAN), synchronization software, wireless fidelity (WiFi), cellular connectivity.	The various connectivity standards allow users to connect to other users, systems, and information. Networking in mobile systems is often hindered by low bandwidth on wireless networks.
System Connectivity	Internet access and document transfer protocols.	Users must be able to exchange documents and information within and across systems. This affects the organization of individuals and systems that are attempting to interact.
Collaboration Tools	Shared tools such as calendars, authoring tools and project management tools.	Collaboration tools allow co-authoring documents; coordinating tasks; attending or providing lectures and demonstrations; holding meetings synchronously or asynchronously, voting, decision-making, performing commercial transactions; and accessing laboratory or other rare equipment[1].

1. Shneiderman & Plaisant (2005).

Devices should include mechanisms for connecting to a variety of systems through multiple means. Networks often require various types of wired (such as telephone lines and/or Ethernet cables) or wireless frequencies. Common wireless technology standards that are important for mobile learning include WiFi, infrared, Bluetooth, GSM, and CDMA. The Internet and the World Wide Web have become a central gateway to scientific, procedural, and cultural information. Speed and quality of data transfer can suffer without adequate standards. The rules and constraints of data exchange may affect workflow in that it can force certain types of organization upon the individuals who are interacting. Coordination of activity can be accomplished through various electronic technologies such as "shared calendars, electronic schedulers, project management tools, and workflow tools" (Preece, Rogers, and Sharp 2002, 122). Using such tools, users can engage in a number of different types of collaboration.

Wireless networking is, perhaps, the most significant feature of mobile tools within the social technology intersection (DS). When people are able to exchange relevant information at appropriate times, they can participate in a variety of community and collaborative situations that normally could not take place by distance. Therefore, the socio-cultural setting becomes an integral part of interaction. Mobile learning practitioners must consider providing mobile "media spaces" or computer mediated communications environments that will assist learners to communicate even though they are physically and temporally separated (Preece, Rogers, and Sharp 2002).

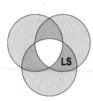

Interaction Learning Intersection (LS)

The interaction learning intersection (LS) represents a synthesis of learning and instructional theories, but relies very heavily upon the philosophy of social constructivism. In this view, "[learning] is collaborative with meaning negotiated from multiple aspects" (Smith and Ragan 1999, 15). Adherents to social constructivist philosophy vary in the degree to which they place emphasis on social interaction. Some support the idea that learners indirectly negotiate the meaning of materials by comparing their interpretation with that of the author's. Others contend that learners interact and negotiate meaning with other individuals directly (Smith and Ragan 1999). It seems clear that individuals do both, depending on the circumstances. The interaction learning intersection (LS) presented here is balanced between these viewpoints (Table 6). This intersection takes into account the needs of distance learners as individuals who are situated within unique cultures and environments. Such settings impact a learner's ability to understand, negotiate, integrate, interpret, and use new ideas as needed in formal instruction or informal learning.

TABLE 6 The Interaction Learning Intersection

Criteria	Examples & Concepts	Comments
Interaction	Learner-learner, learner-instructor, learner-content[1]; computer-based learning (CBL); intelligent tutoring systems, zone of proximal development[2].	Different kinds of interaction can all stimulate learning to varying levels of effectiveness depending on the situation, learner, and task.
Situated Cognition	Authenticity of context and audience.	A real purpose and audience for a learning task may serve to increase learner motivation.
Learning Communities	Cognitive apprenticeships, dialogue, problem solving, communities of practice.	Learners work with others in an effort to achieve mutual goals. Learners have varying degrees of control over the learning process.

1. Moore (1989), 2. Vygotsky (1978).

Moore (1989) proposed three types of interaction in distance education: learner-content, learner-instructor, and learner-learner. Learner-content interaction refers to the cognitive changes that occur as a result of a learner actively engaging with course materials. While a learner can access a variety of information through textbooks, audio tapes, and video tapes, the learner cannot have a dialogue directly with these media. Neither CBL nor intelligent tutoring systems can adequately stimulate metacognitive skills necessary for decision making, information selection, and self regulation (Kommers 1996; Sharples 2000). The significance of context and social negotiation of meaning is highlighted by Vygotsky's (1978) *zone of proximal development*. The zone of proximal development is the gap between what a learner is currently able to do and what she could potentially do with assistance from more advanced peers. Hence, interaction with other people provides a potentially more powerful form of learning.

The main precept of situated cognition is that learning tasks should be situated within authentic contexts (Smith and Ragan 1999). Authenticity does not necessarily imply that the learners must interact directly with other learners, but that the products of learning activities are intended for members of a real and larger community. In such situations, then, the learner is not passive, but "action-oriented" (Farmer, Buckmaster, and LeGrand 1992, 47).

Learning communities and cognitive apprenticeships are two examples of highly social methods of learning offering varying degrees of learner control. Learning communities may be thought of as collections of learners who work together toward mutual goals (Reigeluth and Squire 1998). Through technology, they can enter into dialogues and problem solving activities with other learners in different locations. In a cognitive apprenticeship situation, a learner has the opportunity to observe a human model operating within a real and relevant situation. The learner then has opportunities to try the techniques in a similar situation. Part of the process requires the learner to plan, reflect upon, and articulate her actions during the process. The learner receives gradually less support from the mentor as she gains competence and confidence until, finally, the learner is able to work independently (Farmer, Buckmaster, and LeGrand 1992).

While social constructivism can be taken to extremes, few can deny the impact of interaction on human learning. Encouraging learners to participate in communities and cognitive apprenticeships permits them to utilize a greater variety of situations in which to negotiate meaning. Combining these socially grounded learning practices with the affordances of wireless, mobile devices completes the FRAME model in the centre of the Venn diagram.

Mobile Learning Process (DLS)

Effective mobile learning, the primary intersection of the FRAME model, results from the integration of the device (D), learner (L), and social (S) aspects. Mobile learning provides enhanced collaboration among learners, access to information, and a deeper contextualization of learning. Hypothetically, effective mobile learning can empower learners by enabling them to better assess and select relevant information, redefine their goals, and reconsider their understanding of concepts within a shifting and growing frame of reference (the information context). Effective mobile learning provides an enhanced cognitive environment in which distance learners can interact with their instructors, their course materials, their physical and virtual environments, and each other (Table 7).

TABLE 7 The Mobile Learning Process

Criteria	Examples & Concepts	Comments
Mediation	Task artefact cycle[1], mediation[2].	The nature of the interaction itself changes as learners interact with each other, their environments, tools, and information.
Information Access and Selection	Information noise, identification of patterns and relationships, relevancy, and accuracy.	As the amount of information available increases, learners must increase their efforts to recognize and evaluate the appropriateness and accuracy of information.
Knowledge Navigation	Knowledge production vs. knowledge navigation[3].	In knowledge production, teachers determine what and how information should be learned. In knowledge navigation, learners acquire skills to appropriately select, manipulate, and apply information to their own unique situations and needs.

1. Caroll, Kellogg, and Rosson (1991), 2. Vygotsky (1978), 3. Brown (2005).

The concept of mediation is crucial for understanding the integration of the three aspects of the FRAME model. According to Vygotsky (1978), the nature of the interaction itself changes as learners interact with each other, their contexts, tools, and information. In keeping with the concept of mediation, the *task-artefact cycle* posits that the artefacts themselves introduce possibilities and constraints that, in effect, redefine the uses for which the artefact was originally intended (Carrol and Rosson 2005). The process of mobile learning is itself defined and continuously reshaped by the interaction between the device (D), learner (L), and social (S) aspects.

As the amount of information available on the Internet grows, it is increasingly important for learners to be able to identify relevant and accurate information. They must be able to identify patterns and relationships between facts amongst a growing variety of resources. "When knowledge is subject to paucity, the process of assessing worthiness is assumed to be intrinsic to learning. When knowledge is abundant, the rapid evaluation of knowledge is important" (Siemens 2005, 3). In addition, both the relevance and the accuracy of the information may shift as other information becomes available. Educators need to respond with more flexible methods of knowledge management in order to prepare learners to navigate within an information rich world. Because the mobile learning process is defined by social, cognitive, environmental, and technological factors, mobile learning can help learners gain immediate and ongoing access to information, peers, and experts (not necessarily teachers) who can help them determine the relevance and importance of information found on both the Internet and in their real-world environments. This kind of access to other learners and experts can help to mitigate the negative effects of information noise and assimilation bias (Marra 1996) in which learners may be overwhelmed by the volume of information or may be reluctant to learn new procedures.

Kommers (1996, 38) posits that while student control is beneficial for motivation and empowerment, "both simulation and explorative information retrieval need some navigational assistance to prevent the student from being lost or trapped in misconceptions." Brown (2005) documents the transition from a knowledge production paradigm to a knowledge navigation paradigm. In knowledge production, teachers determine what should be learned and how information should be learned. In knowledge navigation, teachers or experts help learners understand how to navigate through knowledge in order to select, manipulate, and apply already existing information for unique situations. In this paradigm, formal and informal learning techniques may blend and teachers' roles shift that of coaches and mentors.

Towards More Effective Mobile Learning Environments

While learners may not actually share the same physical environment, they can use mobile devices to share aspects of their personal and cultural lives. To solve problems unique to their situations, learners can readily choose from a seemingly unlimited quantity of data. The Internet has ushered in an era in which information has become easy to access and easy to publish. Now, learners must acquire the skills and tools to navigate through this growing body of information. Mobile learning enables learners to interact using additional tools such as text messaging, mobile Internet access, and voice communications – all through wireless networks. Although this medium may be hindered by low bandwidth and limited input and output capabilities, there are some distinct advantages:

- Wireles s, networked mobile devices can enable learners to access relevant information when and where it is needed. Mobile learners can travel to unique locations, physically *with* or virtually *through* their mobile devices.
- The ability to access a variety of materials from anywhere at anytime can provide multiple cues for comprehension and retention.
- Learning within specific contexts can provide authentic cultural and environmental cues for understanding the *uses* of information which may enhance encoding and recall.
- Well-implemented mobile education can assist in the reduction of cognitive load for learners. While it is difficult to determine how to chunk information, differing patterns of presentation and amounts of information can potentially help learners to retain, retrieve, and transfer information when needed.

The FRAME model can help practitioners and researchers to leverage these benefits and to better comprehend the complex nature of mobile learning. For example, in attempting to repair a carburetor on a car, can the learner retrieve appropriate instructions at the exact time it is needed? If she can, indeed, access information when it is needed, is she able to choose the best resources? Is the information easy to hear or view on the device? Is the underlying networking infrastructure adequate? Is the learner fully utilizing the affordances of the device? If this learning task is taking place in a formal educational system, are the learning tasks designed in a way that encourages meaningful interaction with peers or experts? The checklist in Appendix A can help answer such questions and guide the development and assessment of mobile learning environments. While reading through the remaining chapters in this book, one can refer to the FRAME model and this checklist to assess the extent to which learners are engaged in balanced and effective mobile learning experiences.

References

AUSUBEL, D. 1968. *Educational psychology: A cognitive view.* Toronto: Holt, Rinehart and Winston.

BRANSFORD, J., A. BROWN, and R. COCKING. 2000. *How people learn: Brain, mind, experience, and school.* Expanded ed. Washington: National Academy of Sciences.

BROWN, T. 2005. *Beyond constructivism: Exploring future learning paradigms.* http://www.dreamland.co.nz/educationtoday/Tom_Brown_Beyond_Constructivism.pdf.

BRUNER, J. 1960. *The process of education: A searching discussion of school education opening new paths to learning and teaching.* New York: Vintage Books.

CAROLL, J., W. KELLOGG, and M. ROSSON. 1991. Chapter 6: The task-artifact cycle. In *Designing interaction: Psychology at the human-computer interface*, ed. J. Caroll. New York: Cambridge University Press.

CAROLL, J., and M. ROSSON. 1985. *Paradox of the active user.* Online reprint with permission, 2005. http://www.winterspeak.com/columns/paradox.html.

———. 2005. Getting around the task-artifact cycle: How to make claims and design by scenario. *ACM Transactions on Information Systems* 10 (2): 181-212. http://sin01.informatik.uni-bremen.de/sin/lehre/02w/03-860-globallife/download/p181-carroll.pdf.

DRISCOLL, M. 1994. *Psychology of learning for instruction.* 1st ed. Toronto: Allyn and Bacon.

———. 2005. *Psychology of learning for instruction.* 3rd ed. Toronto: Pearson Education Inc.

ERSTAD, O. 2002. Norwegian students using digital artifacts in project-based learning. *Journal of Computer Assisted Learning* 18 (4):427-37.

FARMER, J., A. BUCKMASTER, and B. LEGRAND. 1992. Cognitive apprenticeship: Implications for continuing professional education. *New Directions for Adult and Continuing Education* 55:41-49.

GAGNÉ, R. 1977. *The conditions of learning.* 3rd ed. Toronto: Holt, Reinhart, and Winston.

KAPTELININ, V., and B. NARDI. 2006. *Acting with technology: Activity theory and interaction design.* Cambridge, MA: MIT Press.

KEARSLEY, G. 1995. The nature and value of interaction in distance education. In *Distance Education Symposium 3: Instruction.* State College: Pennsylvania State University.

KOMMERS, P. 1996a. Chapter 1: Definitions. In Kommers, Grabinger, and Dunlap 1996.

———. 1996b. Chapter 2: Multimedia environments. In Kommers, Grabinger, and Dunlap 1996.

———. 1996c. Chapter 3: Research on the use of hypermedia. In Kommers, Grabinger, and Dunlap 1996.

KOMMERS, P., S. GRABINGER, and J. DUNLAP, eds. 1996. *Hypermedia learning environments*. Mahwah, NJ: Lawrence Erlbaum Associates.

KOOLE, M. 2006. Framework for the rational analysis of mobile education (FRAME): A model for evaluating mobile learning devices. Thesis, Centre for Distance Education, Athabasca University.

MARRA, R. 1996. Chapter 6: Human-computer interface design. In Kommers, Grabinger, and Dunlap 1996.

MILLER, G. 1956. The magical number seven, plus or minus two: Some limits on our capacity for processing information. *The Psychological Review* 63 (2):1-14.

MOORE, M. 1989. Editorial: Three types of interaction. *The American Journal of Distance Education* 3 (2):1-6.

NIELSEN, J. 1993. *Usability engineering*. San Francisco: Morgan Kaufmann.

NORMAN, D. 1999. Affordance, conventions and design. *Interactions* 6 (3):38-43.

PAIVIO, A. 1979. *Imagery and verbal process*. Hillsdale, NJ: Lawrence Erlbaum Associates.

PIAGET, J. 1970. *Science of education and the psychology of the child*. New York: Orion Press.

PREECE, J., Y. ROGERS, and H. SHARP. 2002. *Interaction design: Beyond human-computer interaction*. New York: John Wiley & Sons.

REIGELUTH, C., and K. SQUIRE. 1998. Emerging work on the new paradigm of instructional theories. *Educational Technology* (July/August): 41-47.

SHARPLES, M. 2000. The design of personal mobile technologies for lifelong learning. *Computers & Education* 34:177-93.

SHNEIDERMAN, B., and C. PLAISANT. 2005. *Designing the user interface: Strategies for effective human-computer interaction*. 4th ed. Toronto: Pearson Education.

SIEMENS, G. 2005. Connectivism: A learning theory for the digital age. *International Journal of Instructional Technology and Distance Learning* 1. http://www.itdl.org/Journal/Jan_05/article01.htm.

SMITH, P., and T. RAGAN. 1999. *Instructional design*. 2nd ed. Toronto: John Wiley & Sons.

TIRRI, H. 2003. Chapter 2: Promises and challenges of mobile learning. In *Mobile Learning*, ed. by H. Kynäslahti and P. Seppälä. Helsinki, Finland: Edita Publishing.

TULVING, E., and W. DONALDSON. 1972. *Organization of memory*. New York: Academic Press.

VYGOTSKY, L. 1978. *Mind in society: The development of higher psychological processes*. Ed. M. Cole, V. John-Steiner, S. Scribner, and E. Souberman. Cambridge: Harvard University Press.

WARDHAUGH, R. 1986. *An introduction to sociolinguistics*. Oxford: Basil Blackwell.

Appendix A

CHECKLIST Planning and Analysis of Mobile Learning Environments

Device Aspect	In the selection and use of mobile devices, have you considered
D	❑ selecting a device with comfortable physical characteristics?
	❑ allowing users to adjust input and output settings (i.e., font sizes, addition of peripherals)?
	❑ selecting devices with processing speeds and input and output capabilities that will best complement user tasks?
	❑ providing instructions for storing and retrieving files?
	❑ taking measures to identify and limit perceived and real error rates of the mobile hardware and software?
Learner Aspect	In designing mobile learning activities, have you considered
L	❑ assessing the learners' current level of knowledge (if possible)?
	❑ using schemas, anchoring ideas, advance organizers, or other instructional techniques?
	❑ using contextual cues and multimedia to provide a variety of stimuli to assist comprehension and memory?
	❑ structuring learning activities around authentic contexts and audiences?
	❑ designing learning situations to stimulate *active* transfer of concepts and procedures to different contexts?
	❑ allowing learners to explore, discover, select information relevant to their own unique problems?

Social Aspect 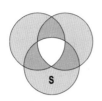	**In terms of culture and society, have you considered** ❏ clarifying definitions, cultural behaviours (etiquette), or symbols that participants might require while interacting? ❏ providing methods or guidance for ensuring sufficient, accurate, and relevant communications among participants in the mobile media space?
Device Usability Intersection 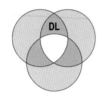	**While using mobile devices in learning activities, have you considered** ❏ the locations and climates in which the learner may wish to carry a device? ❏ if the learner's device will permit access to information whenever and wherever needed (just-in-time learning)? ❏ reducing cognitive load by chunking content, reducing the number of required actions to complete tasks, using mnemonic devices, and simplifying displays? ❏ making the device aesthetically pleasing and functional for learners by allowing them to choose themes and adjust preferences?
Social Technology Intersection 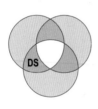	**In accessing or providing networks for interaction, have you considered** ❏ selecting appropriate wireless standards in light of the amount of data, speed, and security with which the data must be transferred? ❏ selecting appropriate collaboration software to meet the needs of the learning or social tasks?

Interaction Learning Intersection 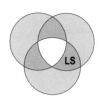	**With regard to interaction, have you considered** ❑ the learner's relationships with other learners, experts, and systems? ❑ the learner's preferences for social interaction and for learning information and/or skills? ❑ providing mobile media spaces for the development of communities of practice, apprenticeships, and mentorship between learners and experts?
Mobile Learning 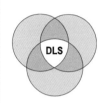	**In a mobile learning system, have you considered** ❑ how use of mobile devices might change the process of interaction between learners, communities, and systems? ❑ how learners may most effectively use mobile access to other learners, systems, and devices to recognize and evaluate information and processes to achieve their goals? ❑ how learners can become more independent in navigating through and filtering information? ❑ how the roles of teachers and learners will change and how to prepare them for that change?

PART TWO

● ● ●

Research on Mobile Learning

Mobile Distance Learning with PDAs: Development and Testing of Pedagogical and System Solutions Supporting Mobile Distance Learners

TORSTEIN REKKEDAL
AND ALEKSANDER DYE
NORWEGIAN SCHOOL OF INFORMATION
TECHNOLOGY & NKI DISTANCE EDUCATION
NORWAY

Abstract

The article discusses basic teaching-learning philosophies and experiences from the development and testing of mobile learning integrated with the online distance education system at NKI (Norwegian Knowledge Institute) Distance Education. The chapter builds on experiences from three European Union (EU) supported Leonardo da Vinci projects on mobile learning: From e-learning to m-learning (2000-2003), Mobile learning – the next generation of learning (2003-2005), and the ongoing project, Incorporating mobile learning into mainstream education (2005-2007).

Introduction

This chapter discusses NKI[3] basic philosophies of distance learning and their consequences for development of a learning environment supporting mobile distance learners. Most NKI courses are not designed to function as online interactive e-learning programmes, although some parts of the courses may imply such interaction with multimedia materials, tests, and assignments. NKI courses normally involve intensive study, mainly of text-based materials and include problem solving, writing essays, submitting assignments, and communicating with fellow students by email or in the web-based conferences. This means that most of the time the students will be offline when studying. From experience, we know that students often download content for reading offline and print content for reading on paper.

When developing system solutions for mobile learning, it is assumed that the NKI students will have access to a desktop or laptop computer with an Internet connection. This means that when students are mobile and wishing to study, the equipment and technologies they use will be in addition to the equipment use at home or at work. It should also be noted that the solutions developed were based on the absolute assumption that mobile learners would study within the same group of students who do not have access to mobile technology. Thus, the design of the learning environment must efficiently cater to both situations and both types of students.

During the first project, NKI developed solutions for mobile learning applying mobile phones and Personal Digital Assistants (PDAs) with portable keyboard. Learning materials were developed mainly for downloading to the PDA and offline study, while online access to forum discussions, responding to forum messages, reading in forums, communication with fellow students and tutors, and submitting assignments, were handled online via mobile equipment when students were on the move.

During the second project, NKI developed and tested solutions for an "always-online multimedia environment" for distance learners based on the use of PDAs with access to wireless networks. During this project, NKI first developed one specific course for mobile access with PDAs. Cost and efficiency considerations, however, required server-side solutions that made access independent of devices on the user-side. Thus, during the second year of the second mobile learning project, NKI installed software and solutions

---

3. Originally published in the *International Review on Research in Open and Distance Learning* (IRRODL), 8, no. 2. This article is subject to Creative Commons License 2.5 (c) 2007. The original article is published at: http://www.irrodl.org/index.php/irrodl/article/view/349/871. Reproduced with permission of Athabasca University – Canada's Open University.

which, in principle, made all online courses accessible independent of devices on the receiving side – for example, most types of pocket PCs, PDAs, and mobile phones.

One of the main challenges concerning the use of mobile devices was to find acceptable solutions adapted to the small screen. There is simply not enough space on a small screen for all the information found on a traditional web page. Another problem encountered was the limited data transfer rate and processing power found in mobile devices. When people use a mobile device with Internet connectivity, the connection speed is traditionally lower than, for instance, that of a traditional mobile phone. Thus, the project tried out solutions designed for a future, as we believe it might be, with online high speed access wherever the student is located.

The aim of the third and present project is to develop mobile learning course content and services that will enter into the mainstream and take mobile learning from a project-based structure and into mainstream education and training. This chapter presents and discusses the student experiences from the first two trials of mobile learning and their consequences for further developments within an online distance learning system.

Although it is difficult to foresee what will be the technical solutions for mobile devices in the years to come, there is no doubt that the research on mobile technology in online distance learning at NKI has inspired developments that also increase the quality of our online distance learning in general, helping make us better prepared to serve mobile students now and in the future, independent of which technology students prefer to use when on the move.

Context

NKI Distance Education is the largest distance teaching institution in Norway, recruiting 7,000 to 10,000 students every year. NKI Distance Education is one unit in the NKI group, a non-governmental educational institution offering full-time and part-time training on the secondary and tertiary levels.

NKI Distance Education was one of the first institutions worldwide to offer online distance education when, in 1987, we started the first trials on our in-house developed Learning Management System (LMS), EKKO (Norwegian acronym for "electronic combined education"). Since then, online education has continuously been offered to increasing numbers of students. At time of writing, NKI has approximately 9,000 active online students, studying one of more than 80 study programmes or over 400 courses offered on the Internet/Web. Since 1987 NKI online distance education has had 60,000 course enrolments. In 2001 we launched what we consider to be the fourth generation online distance education system at NKI: the internally developed LMS called Scalable Educational System for Administration and Management (SESAM), a solution that totally integrates NKI's web-based LMS with its overall Student Administration System (SAS) and a number of other applications designed for the efficient operation and administration of the logistics and student support measures in online distance education (see Figure 1). We consider the total integration of distance education information technology systems as one major prerequisite for operating an efficient and effective large-scale distance education system. A description of SESAM and its functionalities has been given by Paulsen, Fagerberg, and Rekkedal (2003).

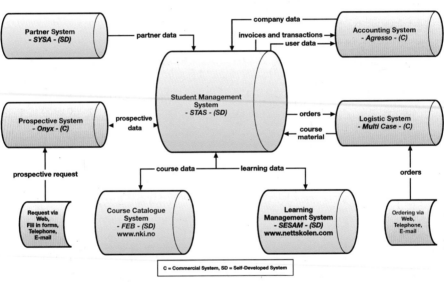

Systems Integration of NKI's Online Student Support Services

FIGURE 1 NKI's integrated systems for online administration and student support.

When engaging in the EU Leonardo da Vinci m-learning projects, the NKI research and development group was very clear that our aim would be to develop solutions that increase access and flexibility, and refine the total distance learning environment to meet the needs of the mobile distance learner.

NKI's Basic Philosophies Concerning Distance Learning

Increasing the flexibility of distance education

A number of evaluation studies among distance and online learners at NKI have demonstrated that students emphasize flexibility (Rekkedal 1990; 1998; 1999; Rekkedal and Paulsen, 1997).

We have argued that distance education generally seems to develop in two quite different directions. The solution at one end of the flexibility continuum can be described as an individual, flexible solution that allows students the freedom to start at any time and follow their own progression according to their personal needs for combining studies with work, family, and social life: This solution is called the "individual flexible teaching model." This model represents a development of the generic model of distance teaching institutions and normally applies media and technologies independent of time (and place), such as asynchronous computer communication, and pre-produced video, audio, and printed materials. On the opposite end of the flexibility continuum is the "extended classroom model," which assumes that students should be organized into groups that meet regularly at local study centres, and favours the application of technologies such as video conferencing, satellite distribution, radio, and television (Gamlin 1995).

In this connection, we have chosen the philosophy for the development of Internet-based education at NKI: "Flexible and individual distance teaching with the student group as social and academic support for learning." Each year, NKI recruits nearly 10,000 students to more than 400 courses and over 130 study programmes by correspondence-based and Internet-based distance teaching. In 2006-07, approximately 70 per cent of NKI students choose online study. Students can enrol in any course or programme or combination of courses anytime and progress at their own pace. This flexibility does not exclude group-based solutions in cooperation with one single employer, trade organization, or local organizer, nor individual students on their own initiative, or by the initiative of their tutor. According to the NKI philosophy on online learning as expressed in the strategic document (NKI 2005): "NKI Distance Education facilitates individual freedom within a learning community in which online students serve as mutual resources without being dependent on each other" (translated from Norwegian, p. 6).

Faced with the challenge of supporting distance students within a flexible distance learning context wherein they must identify and invite fellow students to become their learning partner, NKI has developed different kinds of social software solutions within the LMS-system. As such, all students are urged to present themselves in ways that invites social interaction for learning purposes. This information may be open to all – for example, members of the learning society of NKI Distance Education, to fellow students studying the same programme, or to tutors and administration only. Student lists contain information about where individual students live and which module they are studying at any given time. Software solutions for inviting and accepting learning partners and for establishing connections have been developed in parallel to the research on mobile learning (Paulsen, 2004). There is no doubt that mobile technology may increase possibilities for efficient interaction between distance students, making them more independent of time and space. The potential of social software for developing solutions that allow students within "maximum freedom and flexibility" modes of distance learning to engage in cooperative learning activities has been presented by Anderson (2005).

Views on knowledge and learning

When we started our first discussions on m-learning and planning for the first m-learning solution development, it was very clear that the learning aims, content, and teaching/ learning methods in the NKI online courses and programmes were, for the most part, very different from most e-learning courses, which are typically designed with self-instructional programmed learning materials (Dichanz 2001).

To us, learning results in a change in students' perception of reality related to the problem areas under study. Learning also results in students' increased competence in problem-solving, ability to differentiate between focal and more peripheral questions, and increased analytical skills and competence in using various tools within a field, in appropriate ways. This means that learning results in qualitative changes taking place in students' understanding, academic, social, and technical competence. Learning is a result of students' active processing of learning material and solving problems individually and/or in groups. This view is different from what often we find in many so-called e-learning programmes, wherein "knowledge" often is seen as providing students a large amount of information and testing their ability to recall and reproduce facts. In addition to cost considerations, this is why NKI has generally placed little emphasis on developing interactive programmed learning courses or modules based on a tradition more related to behaviouristic pedagogy and knowledge transmission (for more on students' conceptions of learning, deep level, and surface level approaches to learning see Marton, Dahlgren, Svensson, and Säljö 1987; Marton, Hounsell, and Entwistle 1997; and Morgan 1993). We also hold the view that learning is an individual process that can be supported by adequate interaction and/

or collaboration in groups (Askeland, 2000), a viewpoint that is stated in the NKI strategic plan (2005).

From the discussion of NKI philosophy of learning, views on knowledge, and aims and objectives in formal studies, we came to the conclusion that we should experiment with mobile learning based on more advanced technology than what was available on mobile phones in 2001, the WAP and Smart phones. Thus, we found that the Compaq iPAQ PDA in combination with mobile phone communication was suitable for our purposes. Our experiences, combined with the experiences of other project partners (Fritsch, 2002) during the first project, resulted in continuing the developments of mobile learning with PDAs in further m-learning projects.

Our main objective in the first m-learning project was to extend the distribution of learning materials and communication to lighter equipment, specifically PDAs and mobile phone. During the first project, we understood that for NKI, our long-term challenge would be to develop a system and server-side solution that presented learning materials in ways suitable for PDA and other mobile technologies. We also had to determine acceptable solutions for access to, and interaction with, NKI learning materials and for teacher-to-student, student-to-teacher, and student-to-student communication. We should also add at this juncture, that parallel to the m-learning projects, NKI was also engaged in projects aimed at developing universal accessibility of distance learning (Mortensen, 2003), which, it should be noted, has similar consequences concerning server-side solutions for making content available to anyone independent of physical handicaps or technology on the receiver-side.

Our aim in designing the environment for the mobile learner was to extend, enhance, or arguably even restore, flexibility that should be inherent in distance education. Indeed, to a great extent, the flexibility aspects of distance education took a step backwards when we converted from paper-based to online learning, making a situation wherein students were oftentimes required to study at a place (and at a time) where a computer with access to the Internet was available. This aim was still in focus during the second and third m-learning projects.

By trying out the didactic and system solutions with different types of students in different settings, we studied the results and effects of the developments of mobile learning solutions in the two first projects. Students' opinions and experiences concerning mobile learning were assessed through our use of structured interviews. As well, because of our need to make comparisons with project partner experiences, formal questionnaires containing the same questions to students studying in different mobile learning environments in other European countries were applied.

Designing and Testing the Environment for Mobile Learners in the project, "From e-learning to m-learning"

Studying online and offline

In line with the above discussions on learning and studying, most NKI courses are not designed to function as online interactive e-learning programmes, although some parts of the courses may imply such interaction with multimedia materials, tests, and assignments. NKI courses normally involve intensive study mainly of text-based materials that requires students to solve problems, write essays, submit assignments, and communicate with fellow students via email or during web-based conferences. This means that most of the time NKI students will be offline when studying. From experience, we also know that students often download content for reading offline and print-out content for reading on paper.

Technical solution

It should be emphasized that we assume that NKI distance education students will have access to a desktop or laptop computer with an Internet connection. This means that the equipment and technologies students use when mobile are, in fact, "additions" to the equipment they normally use when studying at home or at work. It should also be noted that our developments were based on the absolute assumption that NKI's mobile learners would be studying with students who do not have access to mobile technology. Thus, the design of the learning environment had to cater efficiently to both learning contexts.

When planning for the m-learning environment of the first project, the NKI project team engaged in long discussions on whether to develop the learning materials for online or offline study. Given the above experiences, coupled with cost considerations concerning mobile access to online learning materials, we concluded that the learning environment for the first course should include the following aspects (Fagerberg, Rekkedal and Russell 2002; Rekkedal 2002a):

Technology
- Pocket PC/ PDA
- Mobile phone
- Portable keyboard

Learning Content and Communication

Learning content to be downloaded to the mobile device could be studied offline, if the student so desires. Downloaded content included all course materials, such as:

- Contents page
- Preface
- Introduction
- All study units
- Resources (articles on the Web, references to other resource materials)
- Online access to the discussion forum, with capacity that allows students quick access to readings in the forum, and writing and responding to contributions made in the forum
- Email with capacity that allows students to communicate with tutors and fellow students, and for submitting assignments either as text-based emails or as Word or Text attachments

Students' and tutor's use of technology when mobile

When mobile – and using mobile technologies – we found that it was generally satisfactory for students (and tutors) to have the course content available to study on the PocketPC. In addition, when mobile, students must be able to:

- Access the course forum to read archived messages (if necessary). Messages on the forum were also emailed to participants
- Access their course forum to submit their contributions to the course discussions
- Send email to fellow students, their teacher, and to administration (i.e., study advisor)
- Receive email from fellow students, their tutor, or from administration
- Submit their assignments by email, including attachments
- Receive assignments back from their tutor, corrected and commented on, as attachments

To access email and discussion forums, mobile phones with infrared connection to the PDA were used.

Trial of two Project 1 courses

In the first project, two courses were tested and evaluated with students using mobile phones and PDAs. The two courses were "The Tutor in Distance Education" (Norwegian version of the introductory course for tutors); "Online Teaching and Learning" (Master's level course 5 ECTS credits).

The first course, comprising nine ($n = 9$) students, was a simulated distance teaching setting. The second course, comprising three ($n = 3$) students studying with other students not using mobile technology, was trial of a "real setting" – a context expected to be the normal situation for mobile learning in NKI's distance education setting. In both cases, technological evaluations were carried out using qualitative methods employed in field research models. The first course was a trial designed to evaluate the use, functionality, and acceptance of the technology. The researcher functioned as tutor and used the course to test and evaluate its mobile learning aspects. Rather than asking subject related questions in connection with assignments and forum discussions however, the researcher instead asked students questions related to the technology itself. The educational background of the nine students taking the first course ranged from two associates degrees to PhD; the age of participants ranged from 24 to 56. All participants were competent in the use of information technologies.

The second course was administered in a normal study setting, and the researcher had access to the course forum and carried out the evaluation by asking participants questions on the use of the technology, while another tutor was teaching of the course. This test course had five ($n = 5$) registered students: four in Norway and one in Canada. Three of the Norwegian students used mobile devices (mobile telephone and PDA with a foldable keyboard). The three "mobile learners" included one male (age 32, with a BSc in computer science) and two females (the first, age 55, with a PhD in Chemistry and working as webmaster, and the second age 35, with a BEd and director of studies at a technical research centre). Both questions and answers on mobile learning were distributed as contributions to the course forum.

In addition to the open qualitative questions given during the study, students in both trials answered a questionnaire consisting mainly of statements to be answered on a 5-point Likert scale. The questionnaire was used as part of the common evaluations in the international project. For our purpose, the qualitative evaluation was found to produce the most relevant and valid data.

Main Conclusions: Project 1 trials

We learned that downloading and synchronizing learning materials to the students' PDAs caused few (if any) problems. The learning content was delivered in two versions: HTML and Microsoft Reader e-book format. As students' preference for the e-book format was evident from the results of first trial course, the second course applied e-book materials only. During the first, we found that figures and illustrations were hard to read on the

PDA. Taking notes was also a problem. Therefore, for the second trial, we equipped students with keyboards, which resolved these problems and enabled students to write longer texts with assignments. Using mobile phones to submit assignments and respond to the course forums was found to be fairly easy, with few problems encountered. Costs were also acceptable, but only on the condition that students produced their lengthy texts offline before sending them.

Our main aim in designing solutions for mobile learners was to support and maximize students' freedom to study with increased flexibility. This supports findings in previous trials, which shows that the main advantage of m-learning (as designed in these trials) is that it increases flexibility for students studying at a distance (Rekkedal, 2002b; 2002c).

In Figure 2, the picture on the left shows a tutor writing and sending emails to his students from Düsseldorf Himmelturm. The picture on the right is of a student on holiday communicating from the garden of his hotel in Rome.

FIGURE 2 Tutor and student communicating with a mobile device

Designing and Testing an Always-Online Environment for Mobile Learners in the project "Mobile Learning: The next generation of learning"

Based on the results and our experiences gained from the first project, NKI continued its research on m-learning, this time based on the PDA solutions that were available in 2003-2005. After examining the different brands available, we decided to develop solutions for the HP iPAQ Pocket PC 5500 series with a built-in wireless network card. Again, all developments were undertaken with the main objective of developing generic solutions.

For NKI, a large-scale provider of flexible online distance learning, it is extremely important to deliver cost-effective solutions. For instance, we needed to find system solutions that suited the needs of mobile learners in addition to students who wish to study using more standard technologies, such as desktop PCs. Any solution must be designed in ways to allow both groups to participate in the same course. In other words, we had to find optimal solutions for communication and for distributing course content, independent on whether students and tutors choose to use mobile technologies or standard desktop PCs.

When planning the first m-learning project, we determined online access to course content to be the best solution to meet NKI's needs. However, when we started researching the first m-learning project, it was neither technologically nor economically feasible to provide continuous online access. By 2004, however, technological advancements where such that they allowed us to start developing and experimenting with solutions based on the notion that students had access to an "always-online mobile learning environment." Today, the always-online mobile learning environment is almost a reality and will likely be the norm in the near future.

Provisional Developments during Year 1 of the Project

The NKI project team committed itself to develop one standard NKI course, "Sales and Services," to an always-online mobile learning environment during the first year, and a second course, "Administration Systems and Support Services for Online Education," during the second year.

The first course, *Sales and Services*, was developed with an additional version with specific materials for mobile learners. This version was produced on the server in a format *adapted* to the PDA screens and multimedia materials specifically developed to be accessed by the PDA. These developments have been described by Dye, Faderberg, and Midtsveen (2004).

We found that the text used was perfectly adapted to the PDA screen. For ease of navigation, the menu link was fixed at the bottom of the screen. Multimedia elements were also developed using Macromedia Flash. We designed and tried different solutions to ensure that the multimedia elements were readable on the PDA, but we really did not arrive at any good solutions. Our conclusion, both during development and beta testing with students, was that most multimedia elements included details, which were very difficult to read on the PDA. We also found that it was more useful to focus our efforts on the readability of text versus the background colour combinations. We found that the choice of font was also important.

It was clear during internal testing that the solutions functioned according to expectations; they allowed all students in the course, irrespective if they were mobile or tied to a desktop computer, to participate and communicate in the same course. However, because additional materials had to be developed specifically for the mobile learners, we found that these solutions could never be applied cost-effectively on a large scale.

Second Year Functionalities of the Always-Online Environment developed by NKI in the project "mLearning: The next generation of learning"

When planning for this second project, the project team sought to develop m-learning solutions wherein students and tutors using wireless PDA/PocketPC could benefit an always-online environment. In the first project, although the downloaded course contents could be accessed any time, some significant disadvantages were found, mainly that:

- Participants in the course often lacked incentive to log into the Internet College to take advantage of the larger learning community
- Participants had no access to interactive materials
- Participants encountered low – or no – access to other Internet resources
- Participants were restricted in their communication, likely due to costs but also because of having to connect to mobile networks for email, submitting assignments, and contribute to the forum.

During the planning process, we described the following aspects of an always-online solution, which we determined would be necessary to increase the quality of service for those teaching and learning in a mobile environment:

- Access to high bandwidth networks, which enable faster uploading and downloading of course content and use of streaming audio, video, and advanced graphics
- Mobile technologies that are not tied to and operate independent of students' and tutors' desktop PCs
- Access to the Internet, 24/ 7
- Access to email, 24/ 7
- Access to online assessments, assignments, course activities
- Options that enables group collaboration
- Options that support synchronous communication such as chat and IP telephony
- ADSL or free access to WLAN, needed to make mobile learning affordable

During the first phase of this project, an "ideal" description of require-ments for a mobile learning management system (mLMS) for the NKI context was developed by Dye and Fagerberg (2004). These requirements were based on the assumption that the NKI Learning Management System, SESAM, would be further developed to accommodate the needs of mobile learners using PocketPCs. The specifications proposed by Dye and Fagerberg (2004) are presented below and divided into the following categories:

1. Overall framework needs

The mLMS must be a part of an LMS so that it supports both the mobile client as well as traditional clients. It should also automatically provide different types of content on different devices. It must also create a comfortable learning environment for mobile learners.

2. Course content

The mLMS must be able to archive course content, provide easy navigation, and provide a zoom function for display of illustrations and pictures.

3. Access to courseware

The mLMS should provide access to online resources such as libraries, refer-ences, glossaries, exams, databases, and to course planning tools and calen-dars. Students must be allowed to submit assignments, and tutors must be allowed to comment on, and return, students' assignments using mobile devices. Students must have access to a class list with tutor and student information. They should be allowed to answer questions using multiple choices, drag-and-drop test/exercises, etc. Text-to-speech options (that are available on PCs for all NKI courses) would similarly be very desirable. Further, the mLMS must support graphics, audio and video, moving images, pro-vide access to search engines, and provide capacity for immediate response and feedback.

4. Communication

The system must provide access to online synchronous communication tools such as chat, and to asynchronous communication tools such as email, and Short Messages Service (SMS) to allow for broadly distributed information such as notices on grades and assignments. Multimedia Messaging Service (MMS) should be also supported. Students and tutors must have access to message boards, course forums, and online lists that contain tutor and student information.

5. Other

The mLMS should allow for students to enrol in a course online, and provide export features that allow students to access their course materials offline. Personal settings should be adjustable (i.e., changing passwords or email addresses). The system should provide access to technical support services, frequently asked questions, contact information, general study information such as exam dates, course syllabi and handbooks, regulations, and so forth. A site map should also be provided for easy navigation. Ideally, users should be able to print from their mobile devices and access an area where they can upload and store personal files.

Conclusions from Testing

During year two of the project, NKI developed SESAM into a functioning mLMS and then beta tested mLMS system.

The test students were 18 NKI employees registered as regular students in the course, Sales and Services (Dye & Rekkedal, 2005), seven ($n = 7$) males, and eleven ($n = 11$) females. All had no previous connection to the m-learning project. Ages of the participants ranged from 30 to 60 (10 were between the age of 51 and 60). All had higher education.

The trial was carried out in a sort of laboratory situation, after which the students had the opportunity to study the course for three weeks. The test was administered by two researchers in the project; one researcher functioned as a tutor and the other as an observer. The evaluation was carried out using the same questionnaire with Likert attitude scales, plus some open ended questions used in Project 1. In addition, the researchers observed the participants, made note of students' viewpoints, and asked students questions concerning their use of the technology in connection with their assignments, forum contributions, and use of email with other students and tutors.

User friendliness

User-friendliness of mobile learning in the context examined. Nearly all the students reported that they found the equipment easy to use. Some indicated that the "experience was fun." When asked whether or not they would like to take another m-learning course or recommend an m-learning course to others, some students were more reserved, however. We speculate that students' experiences of the trial situation may have influenced their answers, as they did not provide decisive answers.

Didactic efficiency

In terms of didactic efficiency, taken the assumed context of m-learning as a supplement to NKI's established distance online learning environment, students in this trial project agreed that "m-learning increases quality," that "objectives can be met by m-learning," that "accessing course content and communication with the tutor was easy," and that "m-learning is convenient for communication with other students."

A majority agreed that "evaluation and questioning" was effective. Again, however, some students in this trial were uncertain and in some cases negative. The negative attitudes of some students may be related to the fact that during the trial phase, some of the test and questioning materials were distributed with graphical materials, which was far from perfectly presented on their PDAs. The students were also exposed to graphical materials specifically developed for the PDA (part of Year 1 developments) and to the standard graphical course materials presented on the PDA. Both types had definitely significant weaknesses. The size of the illustrations specifically developed for the PDA had to be reduced to make the number of details readable on the small screen. Moreover, illustrations were generally too detailed to be easy to read on the small screen.

Technical feasibility

Most students found navigation easy. They did not agree, however, whether the graphics and illustrations were necessary. More than half of the students in the trial course were uncertain – or disagreed – with the statement that "graphics and illustrations are necessary for m-learning to be effective." We speculate, however, that this finding may partly be based on students' learning context at NKI, which assumes that students would also be accessing their learning materials on standard desktop PCs equipment and that their course work would consist primarily of text-based learning materials.

Cost efficiency

Most participants agreed that m-learning increases access to learning. Access to technology, however, is still lacking. Mobile phones with more PocketPC-like functionalities may resolve this problem in the near future, however. Previously, we have shown that communication costs, even when communicating by mobile phone, are low. As such, in these trial situations, we assumed that the learning could take place in an "always-online" environment with free access. For most users today, however, sending emails is still easier to send via their mobile phone than taking the time needed to configure their PDA for sending emails through different network providers.

Students tried synchronous communication both via chat and IP telephony. Based on their experiences in the m-learning test, it generally seemed that they assumed that the chat function would be similar to chatting on an ordinary PC. When questioned, the majority of participants indicated that they believed that the chat function could be useful in m-learning.

Functionalities and quality

Video on the PDA (Figure 3) using small video clips worked very well using the *Windows Media Player*. No problems were reported in viewing the picture and audio files, and most participants reported them to be high quality. We did, however, encounter problems when we tried to stream video directly from the web browser. Unlike Internet Explorer (IE) for a PC, the pocket version of IE is not capable of streaming video directly from the browser; nor can it start the *Windows Media Player*. This means that users must copy the URL into the *Media Player* to access and watch the video. While this tactic seemed to work okay, it is clearly a cumbersome way to watch a video. The students' opinions concerning the functionality of the video also differed. It was clear to us, however, that their "uncertain" and "negative" responses were related to the difficulties they encountered in playing the video than to the quality of the video itself. In fact, the students in this trial course found the quality of the streamed video to be quite good.

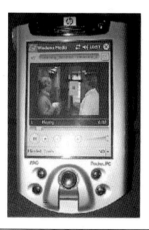

FIGURE 3 Video on the PDA

As a result of previous projects working with universal accessibility (Mortensen, 2003), we also tested the use of synthetic speech. We implemented a technology that makes it possible to save the text on a web page as an MP3 file and have it "read" afterwards using the PDA. The students reported that they were generally positive concerning the quality of both human and synthetic sound on the PDA – all responding on the positive side of the scale. The quality of both digital human voice and synthetic speech was found to be sufficient.

Generally, participants also indicated that they were generally impressed by the quality of IP telephony on the PDAs. Most agreed with the statement that "IP telephony could be useful in mobile learning." The one participant, however, disagreed with this statement, likely because s/he held the position that synchronous communication generally is not useful in distance learning, which, in principle, is fully inline with the NKI philosophy and strategy premised on asynchronous communication.

According to students functions such as sending and receiving emails, making posts to their course forum, submitting assignments as Word attachments, and receiving tutor feedback on projects, functioned well. There were a few negative responses, however.

Students were generally very positive towards reading text on the PDAs, with the majority holding positive opinions to most of the questions asked concerning the m-learning environment. Despite these positive opinions, however, many indicated to us that they did not find the solutions of sufficient quality for mobile access only. This finding falls in line with our assumptions that m-learning in the NKI online system, should only be seen as an addition to increase access and enhance flexibility.

The students agreed that the always-online mobile solutions increase the flexibility of distance learning. To a large extent, they also agreed that the m-learning solutions increase the quality of course arrangements. More than half of the students, however, reported that they were uncertain as to whether the solutions used in the course trial could actually increase the quality of learning outcomes. This, of course, is a very difficult question to answer based on the experiences from this trial situation.

It was clear that students with a technical background and working in IT-positions were less enthusiastic about mobile learning than students with limited technical backgrounds. According to their statements, this group of students were less tolerant of functions that were more complicated or took longer than similar functions found on standard PC equipment. This could be seen as an indication that the technology still needs to be developed further before it will be attractive enough for online learners in general. The research undertaken to date, however, has demonstrated that developing solutions that make courses available in sufficient quality, and independent of devices on the user-side, seems to be a sound strategy.

Incorporating Mobile Learning into the Mainstream of Education and Training

Introduction

The project "Incorporation of Mobile Learning into Mainstream Education and Training" was completed over two years. The scope of this project is based on what we learned during the two earlier projects reported in this chapter. We now feel it is time to take mobile learning from its project trial status and incorporate more formalized m-learning solutions into mainstream education and training in Europe. It is also time to disseminate the results of our research to interested parties in Europe and around the world.

For NKI, this final project builds on the situation that all online distance courses will be available on PDAs (and also on smart phones with web browser capacities) without any need for adaptation for individual courses. As such, during this final project we are seeking to develop services using primarily Short Message Service (SMS) technology to support online distance education within the context of a cost-efficient, large-scale distance education institution. Infrastructure for new and additional services must be developed to be applied in all courses, irrespective if they are tied to ordinary PCs or available on mobile devices.

Specification for the project

The term "mobile," as used in the project, includes all types of devices that are connected to the mobile phone system. These devices will include capacity for voice communication, and in many cases, SMS and Multimedia Message Service (MMS) messages. Advanced versions of these devices will include Wireless Application Protocol (WAP), a secure specification that allows users to access online information instantly (i.e., send and receive email and surf the Web) via handheld wireless devices such as mobile phones and smart phones. Mobile technologies can be divided into two basic categories.

Push: MMS and SMS are the two leading push technologies for mobile devices. Push technologies send the information directly to the user. SMS functionality is available on nearly all mobile phones in use today, thus making it the most robust platform for push technologies for communications where guaranteed delivery is needed. MMS is catching up with SMS, as it is very, very close to becoming a universal standard as well.

Pull: Key technologies used for pull communication will include WAP, HTML, and email. Pull communication occurs when the user sign on to the system to access information. For optimal use, an analysis of the market penetration of these technologies will be required. As well, a market penetration of

JAVA/*Flashlite* and other relevant technologies will also be ascertained. The more valuable – or critical – a given service is to students, the more important it will be for students to own and make use of the service. Important and valuable services will be delivered using SMS because of its ubiquitous availability and proven track record of reliability.

Hardware

To set up a basic infrastructure, a SMS/ MMS gateway is needed, which should include the ability to send and receive SMS/ MMS messages. Received SMS/MMS messages should be made available to a computer, so that they can be processed either by NKI staff responsible for handling students requests, errors, and so forth. An in-house SMS service which consist of one or more GSM modem terminals, along with software (housed on a server) that enables different devices to "talk" to the GSM modem terminals, will be needed as well.

Service requirements

The mobile service development process will start with the smallest and easiest service that will deliver a business function to NKI, which means increasing to the quality of NKI's distance education offerings. The next phase will then deal with more complex and advanced services. All services should handle error messages and log them, record costs, and so forth.

As mentioned, NKI will focus its efforts on services that support mobile phones for all online courses and programmes. The first service that will be evaluated is an SMS message, which will include practical information such as how to log on to the NKI Internet College, how to get a username and password, etc. This SMS message will be sent to new NKI students whom we, for whatever reason, have not been able to reach via email. This SMS message will also include a link to "Learning to Learn," an introductory course applicable to all online programmes, in that it offers students tips on how to study and what to expect as an NKI student. This will be a lightweight WAP version of the original Learning to Learn course.

We will also use the system to get in touch with students who have registered using invalid email addresses. Our plan is to develop a solution that automatically sends an SMS message to the student if an invalid email address is detected by the system.

Possible services

There are numerous possibilities for the use of SMS/MMS services suitable for supporting online distance learners. NKI practices flexible pacing and free start-up times, and has developed advanced support systems to follow-up with students and teachers alike.

The following services might be developed and implemented for mobile technologies during the present project (Russell, 2005):

- Password retrieval for students who have forgotten their password
- Welcome message to students, which includes their user name and password and could include tips on how to log on to course web pages. Messages should be stored on mobile phones, and provide links to other services available from mobile devices. The message may also include a question for permission to communicate to the student via mobile phone
- The introductory course, Learning to Learn, will be designed specifically for delivery to mobile devices, preparing news students on what to expect as an NKI student. We hope to include an introduction on study techniques available for mobile via WAP
- Reminders to students who fall behind their studies
- Reminders to students to register and enroll for exams via mobile phones
- Delivery of interactive quizzes
- Delivery of notification to teachers, indicating that a student has submitted an assignment, and possibly automated follow-ups if the teacher is late in responding
- Delivery of notifications related to assignments and grade posted
- Development of a web interface that allows teachers and administrators to send SMS messages to students, and allows students to send messages to other students
- Allow students to upload pictures and text to their presentation
- Allow students to upload pictures and text to their blog
- As much of the NKI teaching/learning site as feasible to be made available to mobile web browsers

Because this third project is in its first stage at the time of writing, it is difficult to describe in detail exactly what services will be developed and tested. It is also premature to determine any costs involved to students or NKI, along with this usefulness and general level of acceptance by users.

Conclusion

NKI's research and development on mobile learning in connection with the three EU Leonardo da Vinci projects have led to better, more flexible mobile solutions needed to serve distance learners studying online. Through trial and error, we have learned that cost-efficiency considerations did not permit us to develop parallel versions of courses. Instead, we found that courses must be developed, presented, and distributed in a manner that allow both mobile and non-mobile distance learners to participate in the same course, using the same course materials that can be accessed from standard and mobile technologies. Moreover, we found that course content available on mobile devices must be of minimum acceptable quality. Interaction with course content and multimedia materials, as well as communication with tutors and fellow students, must function adequately using both standard and mobile technologies.

The question remains on what the 'ideal' device and solution for mobile learning will look like. In all probability, however, the answer will very likely rest with students' individual preferences. That is why NKI has found it extremely important to experiment with different solutions which, in turn, have inspired further developments in finding the right mix of course design and system solutions that serve the needs of all learners, independent of whether they are using a desktop PC or whether they are using mobile devices.

References

ANDERSON, T. 2005. Distance learning: Social software's killer ap. Paper presentation, *Open and Distance Learning Association of Australia conference, breaking down boundaries*, Adelaide, November 9-11. http:// www.unisa.edu.au/odlaaconference/PPDF2s/13%20odlaa%20-%20 Anderson.pdf (accessed June 26, 2005).

ASKELAND, K. 2000. Fjernundervisning i spenningsfeltet mellom pedagogen og teknogen. In G. Grepperud and J. Toska, *2000 Mål, myter, marked – Kritiske perspektiv på livslang læring og høgre utdanning. SOFF-rapport 1/2000*. Tromsø: SOFF.

DICHANZ, H. 2001. E-learning: A linguistic, psychological and pedagogical analysis of a misleading term. Paper presentation, *20th ICDE world conference*, April, Düsseldorf, Germany.

DYE, A., T. FAGERBERG, and B. MIDTSVEEN. 2004a. Technical working paper 2004, NKI Distance Education: Exploring online services in a mobile environment. http://learning.ericsson.net/mlearning2/files/workpackage2/ NKI_technical_workingpaper_2004.pdf (accessed June 26, 2006).

———. 2004b. *Mobile learning management system specification*. http://learning.ericsson.net/mlearning2/files/workpackage1/nki.pdf (accessed June 27, 2006).

DYE, A., and T. REKKEDAL. 2005. Testing of an "always-online mobile environment." Evaluation paper for mLearning project: *The next generation of learning.* http://learning.ericsson.net/mlearning2/files/workpackage6/testing.doc (accessed June 26, 2006).

FAGERBERG, T., T. REKKEDAL, and J. RUSSELL. 2002. Designing and trying out a learning environment for mobile learners and teachers. Sub-project of the EU Leonardo Project, "From e-learning to m-learning." http://www.nettskolen.com/forskning/55/NKI2001m-learning2.html (accessed June 27, 2006).

FRITSCH, H. 2002. mLearning for Smartphones. Conference presentation, *mLearning: The Cutting Edge*, November 11, Dublin, Ireland. http://learning.ericsson.net/mlearning2/project_one/presentation/helmut1911.ppt (accessed June 7, 2006).

GAMLIN, M. 1995. Distance learning in transition: The impact of technology: A New Zealand perspective. Keynote address, *1995 EDEN conference: The open classroom, distance learning, and new technologies in school level education and training*, September 18-20, Oslo, Norway.

Leonardo Da Vinci Project. n.d. European Commission Leonardo Da Vinci Project website. http://ec.europa.eu/education/programmes/leonardo/leonardo_en.html (accessed April 17, 2007).

MARTON, F., L. DAHLGREN, L. SVENSSON, and R. SÄLJÖ. 1987. *Inlärning och omvärldsuppfatning* [in Swedish]. Stockholm: Almquist & Wiksell. 6. opplag.

MARTON, F., D. HOUNSELL, and N. ENTWISTLE. 1997. *The experience of learning: Implications for teaching and studying in higher education.* Edinburgh: Scottish Academic Press.

MORGAN, A. 1993. *Improving your students' learning: Reflections on the experience of study.* London: KoganPage.

MORTENSEN, I. 2003. *Universell tilrettelegging av nettbasert studium i 'Ledelse og organisasjon'* [in Norwegian]. Bekkestua: NKI. http://www.nettskolen.com/forskning/soffrapport_universell.pdf (accessed June 27, 2006).

NKI. 2005. *Strategisk plan for NKI Fjernundervisning 2005-2007* [in Norwegian]. Internal document. Bekkestua: NKI.

PAULSEN, M. 2006. COGs, CLIPs and other instruments to support cooperative learning in virtual environments. Paper presentation, *4th EDEN research workshop, research into online distance education and e-learning*, October 25-28, Barcelona, Spain.

Paulsen, M., T. Fagerberg, and T. Rekkedal. 2003. Student support systems for online education available in NKI's integrated systems for Internet based e-learning. Oslo: NKI. http://learning.ericsson.net/socrates/doc/norwayp3.doc (accessed June 27, 2006).

Rekkedal, T. 1990. Recruitment and study barriers in the electronic college. In *The electronic college: Selected articles from the EKKO project*, ed. M. F. Paulsen and T. Rekkedal. Bekkestua: NKI/SEFU.

——. 1998. Courses on the WWW: Student experiences and attitudes towards WWW courses. Evaluation report, *MMWWWK*, Leonardo On-line Training Project. http://www.nki.no/eeileo/research/eei/Rekkeval.htm (accessed June 27, 2006).

——. 1999. Courses on the WWW: Student experiences and attitudes towards WWW courses, II. Evaluation report, *MMWWWK*, Leonardo On-line Training Project. http://www.nki.no/eeileo/research/Rekkedalcorrected.html (accessed June 27, 2006).

——. 2002a. Enhancing the flexibility of distance education: Experiences with a learning environment for mobile distance learners. Paper presentation, mLearning conference, *The Cutting Edge*, November 22, Dublin, Ireland. http://learning.ericsson.net/mlearning2/project_one/presentation/torstein1911.ppt (accessed June 26, 2006).

——. 2002b. Trying out a learning environment for mobile learners. Evaluation of the course, "The Tutor in Distance Education," Phase 1 of the NKI sub-project of the EU Leonardo Project, "From e-learning to m-learning." http://learning.ericsson.net/mlearning2/project_one/NKI2001m-learningevaluationFinal.doc (accessed June 26, 2006).

——. 2002c. Trying out a learning environment for mobile learners. Evaluation of the course, "Online Teaching and Learning," Phase 2 of the NKI sub-project of the EU Leonardo Project, "From e-learning to m-learning." http://learning.ericsson.net/mlearning2/project_one/student_use_year_2_nki.doc (accessed June 26, 2006).

Rekkedal, T., and M. Paulsen. 1997. The third generation NKI electronic college: A survey of student experiences and attitudes. Evaluation report, *MMWWWK*, Leonardo On-line Training Project. http://www.nki.no/eeileo/research/nki/evaluati.htm (accessed June 27, 2006).

Russell, J. 2005. SMS: *The in house development experience* (unpublished technical working paper). Oslo: NKI Distance Education.

Using Mobile Learning to Enhance the Quality of Nursing Practice Education

RICHARD F. KENNY
CAROLINE PARK
ATHABASCA UNIVERSITY
CANADA
JOCELYNE M. C. VAN NESTE-KENNY
PAMELA A. BURTON
JAN MEIERS
NORTH ISLAND COLLEGE
CANADA

Abstract

This chapter reviews the research literature pertaining to the use of mobile devices in nursing education and assess the potential of mobile learning (m-learning) for nursing practice education experiences in rural higher education settings. While there are a number of definitions of m-learning, we adopted Koole's (2005) FRAME model, which describes it as a process resulting from the convergence of mobile technologies, human learning capacities, and social interaction, and use it as a framework to assess this literature. Second, we report on the results of one-on-one trials conducted during the first stage of a two stage, exploratory evaluation study of a project to integrate mobile learning into the Bachelor of Science Nursing curriculum in a western Canadian college program. Fourth year nursing students and instructors used Hewlett Packard iPAQ PDAs for a two week period around campus and the local community. The iPAQs provided both WiFi and GPRS wireless capability and were loaded with selected software, including MS Office Mobile along with nursing decision-making and drug reference programs. Our participants reported on a variety of benefits and barriers to the use of these devices in nursing practice education.

Introduction

Wagner (2005) has claimed that evidence of the widespread adoption in North American society of mobile wireless technology such as cell phones, Personal Digital Assistants (PDAs), laptop computers, and MP3 players, is irrefutable. Current mobile technologies (especially wireless) – frequently referred to as third generation (3G) – provide an unprecedented opportunity for inexpensive and beneficial computing power for learners (Hill and Roldan 2005; Wagner 2005).

Wagner (2005) then asks why, with the continuing expansion of wireless networks and improved capacity portable electronic devices, this mobility should not apply to learning. Keegan (2002, 2005) agrees that it should, declaring that the future of distance education is wireless and noting that there has never been a technology that has penetrated the world with the depth and rapidity of mobile telephony. He claims that the challenge for distance educators is to accept this fact and to now develop pedagogical environments for mobile devices.

What then do we mean by m-learning and what does it allow educators to do differently than other forms of teaching and learning? Keegan (2005) defined the term simply as the provision of education and training on PDAs[4]/palmtops/handhelds, smart phones and mobile phones. Trifonova and Ronchetti (2003) agreed, noting that m-learning is often defined as e-learning carried out by means of mobile computational devices and point out that this refers mainly to PDAs and digital cell phones. M-learning could "employ any device that is small, autonomous and unobtrusive enough to accompany us in every moment of our everyday life" (p. 32). Kukulska-Hulme and

---

4. "PDA" refers to a Personal Data Assistant. The term originated in reference to devices providing features such as electronic calendars, organizers, and task lists. PDAs typically now include mobile phones, digital cameras and, in higher end devices, mobile computing capability.

Traxler (2005) view the most significant attributes of mobile technologies as their ability to support learning that is more situated, experiential, and contextualized within specific domains and to support the creation and use of more up-to-date and authentic content.

The FRAME Model

In our study of m-learning in nursing education, we used the Framework for the Rational Analysis of Mobile Education (FRAME) model (Koole 2005; Koole and Ally 2006) to guide our understanding of m-learning, as well as to provide framework for our review of the literature on m-learning in health care, and more specifically, in nursing practice education.

In her model, Koole (2005; Koole and Ally 2006) describes m-learning as a process resulting from the convergence of mobile technologies, human learning capacities, and social interaction. The FRAME model is represented as an intersecting set of three circles representing device usability, learner, and social aspects of learning (see Figure 1).

Device Useability Aspect

This describes the physical, technical, and functional components of mobile devices, the medium through which mobile learners and mobile community members interact. This interface is both enabled and constrained by the hardware and software design of the devices and can have a significant impact on the physical and psychological comfort levels of the users.

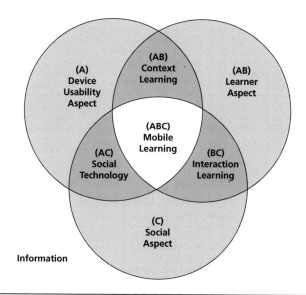

FIGURE 1 Koole's FRAME Model (reproduced with permission)

LEARNER ASPECT

This refers to the individual learner's cognitive abilities, memory, and prior knowledge and those situations and tasks in which a learner needs to succeed. It encompasses the wide range of theories of how learners learn (Driscoll 2005; Mayes and de Freitas, 2004) and explains how mobile learning offers an extended environment where learners can interact within their physical and social environments.

SOCIAL ASPECT

This aspect refers to the processes of social interaction and cooperation and conveys an underlying thread of social constructivist philosophy. The way in which individuals exchange information affects how groups of people develop knowledge and sustain cultural practices.

CONTEXT LEARNING (AB)

This secondary intersection relates the characteristics of mobile devices to cognitive tasks and to the effective manipulation and storage of information. Highly portable devices permit learners to move with their mobile tools to more relevant or more comfortable locations and can affect the user's sense of psychological comfort and satisfaction by reducing cognitive load and increasing access to information.

SOCIAL COMPUTING INTERSECTION (AC)

This secondary intersection describes how mobile devices enable users to communicate with each other and to gain access to other networked systems and information. When people are able to exchange relevant information at appropriate times, they can participate in collaborative situations that are normally difficult at a distance.

INTERACTION LEARNING (BC)

This secondary intersection (BC) focuses on social interaction. Participation in learning communities and cognitive apprenticeships can provide socially based learning environments in which learners can acquire information and negotiate meaning.

MOBILE LEARNING PROCESS (ABC).

All three aspects overlap at the primary intersection (ABC), which represents a convergence of all three aspects and defines the m-learning process. As such, m-learning can afford learners access to a variety of human, system, and data resources, as well as to assist them to assess and select relevant information and redefine their goals (Koole 2005). M-learning is, however, also constrained by the mobile device hardware and software configurations and dependent upon adjustments in teaching and learning strategies.

The Use of Mobile Learning in Health Care and Nursing: Review of the Literature

Mobile Learning in Health Care Education

The education of health care professionals in the context of a rapidly changing health care system is a prime example of how the mobility of learners within a variety of real life learning environments has posed increasing challenges and where mobile technologies have the potential to support and enhance teaching and learning. The high acuity and pace of practice in institutional environments, combined with an explosion of knowledge and technology, increasingly requires practitioners to access and process clinical data efficiently by drawing on current resources to support safe care and evidence-informed practice at the point-of-care.

Moreover, the shift of client care to the community requires that the education of health care professionals take place increasingly in this more autonomous and diverse practice environment where resources are not readily accessible, where client acuity is increasing, and where more traditional methods of directly observing and working with students are not as feasible. These shifts in practice, along with more limited education and practice resources to support students' practice, raise concern for the quality of their education and the safety of their practice. This is particularly significant for rural practice education where resources are limited and geography poses additional challenges. Addressing these "new age" challenges requires "new age" approaches and tools to support the teaching and learning of health care professionals.

Experiences with Mobile Learning in Nursing

Rosenthal (2003) outlines a number of useful functions identified by nurses using PDAs: address book, "to do" lists, date book, memo pad, expense tracking, "find" functions, diagnostic tools, clinical guidelines, medical dictionaries, lab values, and patient, student, and staff management programs. She categorizes these as tools that enhance productivity, promote risk management/error reduction, and through their rapid access to critical information lead to stress reduction.

Cahoon (2002) groups the functions into five categories: clinical services, calculators, data collection, medical record system, and content tools. Newbold (2003) notes that if the PDA is also a wireless device, the uses increase in both number and complexity. She lists potential applications such as: interdisciplinary consultations, electronic ordering and test results, patient histories, progress notes and assessments, references, protocols, and prescription information. Increased PDA wireless capacity to include phone and camera capabilities permits rapid chart access, improved workflow, increased time for patients, cost savings, enhanced productivity and, therefore, boosts professional satisfaction.

The utilization of PDAs in nursing practice has not been confined to acute care settings. George and Davidson (2005) note that nurses are utilizing the new technology to enhance their practices in both long term care and community-based sites. Community based nurses are using PDAs to provide patient teaching information and to track patient progress.

Several authors have outlined benefits and barriers to PDA use. Davenport (2004) identified 38 barriers and 68 benefits to PDA use and, based on a survey completed by nurses, she produced six themes in each category, ranked in priority order. The benefits were: a) quick access to current drug database and nursing reference books (highest ranking), b) the ability to manage patients and procedure information, bedside data entry, and data collection for research and teaching (tied for the 2nd, 3rd, and 4th rankings) c) patient health management (ranked 5th), and d) improved team communication (ranked 6th).

Davenport also found the following barriers, ranked by priority: a) the risks of storing confidential patient information, b) the cost of PDAs and ease of loss or damage, c) not enough research on PDA use in nursing, d) difficult to read, e) slow data entry, and f) difficult to understand. These barriers were rated as modest to moderate.

Experiences with Mobile Learning in Nursing Education

Lehman (2003) identified challenges faced by nursing instructors in the practice setting. She reported using PDAs to keep records of student assignments, checklists for completing physical assessments, and as a source of point-of-care reference (drug software). This eliminates the need for carrying hardcopy drug references. Lehman also used the PDA on-the-spot to document student progress. It was reported that previous studies found electronic data to be more accurate than paper documentation.

Miller et al. (2005) conducted a pre-post and comparative study to identify nursing "students information seeking behaviours and the effectiveness and cost of innovation strategies associated with incorporation of PDAs into students' clinical practice" (p.19). Due to limitations of the study, authors note that differences among the two groups in seeking information cannot be attributed to PDA use. It was however determined that students utilizing PDAs had increasing numbers of questions when in the practice setting, as well as a greater recognition of the need to use current resources.

Goldsworthy, Lawrence, and Goodman (2006) examined the relationships between the use of Personal Digital Assistants, self-efficacy, and the preparation for medication administration. Thirty six second-year baccalaureate nursing students were randomly assigned to either a PDA or control group. The authors reported that the PDA group showed a significant increase in self-efficacy.

Stroud, Erkel, and Smith (2005) reported on the patterns of use and demographics of users within nurse practitioner (NP) programs. A 20 item questionnaire was sent to students and faculty in 150 organizations across the United States. The 227 returned questionnaires represented 27 per cent of the sample. A high percentage, 67 per cent of those returning the questionnaire, used PDAs, generally to "support clinical decision-making" (p.67). The list of uses and frequency cited is reported in Table 1.

In June 2006, Western Canadian University's Centre for Nursing and Health Studies polled their nurse practitioner students on PDA use. Students were asked to respond to one of two anonymous surveys: "I use a PDA" and "I don't use a PDA." One hundred and fifty students responded: 64 (42.6 per cent) in the "use" category and 86 (57.3 per cent) in the "do not use" category (Park 2006). The respondents had a wide range of perceptions of reasons to recommend PDAs to other nurse practitioners, as well as of the barriers to use (Table 1).

TABLE 1 Nurse Practitioner Insights – Park (2006)

Reasons to recommend	Barriers to use
1. Valuable with right software	1. Cost
2. Lighter to carry than textbooks	2. Lack of knowledge about technology
3. Decrease in medication errors,	and software
safer than memory	3. Difficult to set up
4. Convenient, useful tool	4. No time to learn
5. Information available is immense	5. Confidentiality issues
and valuable	6. Technology failures (batteries die)
6. Back-up quick reference, security blanket	7. Loss of personal touch
7. Concise and easy to transport	
8. The way of the future	
9. Looks professional	

Reasons to recommend	Barriers to use
10. Can edit & highlight the most important information & add personal notes	8. They aren't necessary
11. You can use it to explore options with client	9. They don't teach you to be a Nurse Practitioner
12. Organizational benefits	
13. Up-to-date information	
14. Aids mobility	

The Relationship between FRAME Model and Research on Mobile Learning in Nursing

Effective mobile learning is defined by the convergence of the device usability, learner, and social aspects to extend their impact beyond their natural boundaries. Mobile learning affords enhanced collaboration among learners, ready access to information, and a deeper contextualization of learning. Mobile learning can help learners gain immediate and ongoing access to information, peers, and experts who can help them determine the value of information found on both the Internet and in their real-world environments (Koole and Ally 2006). The relationship between the FRAME Model and the themes reported in the research literature are shown in Table 2.

A number of research articles relating to health care professionals use as PDAs focus on the aspect of device usability (for example, Cahoon 2002; Newbolt 2003; Rosenthal 2003). Health care professionals have traditionally carried small booklets and index cards in their pockets, so they are natural early adopters for PDAs as content providers. Students are always in the market for the latest and best, so new innovation permeates the field.

The learner aspect of Koole's FRAME model is demonstrated by the health care professional/students' experience and interaction within the clinical setting, which includes the clients/patients, the facility or home and multiple caregivers. Besides reference content, many existing tasks such as sending pharmacy and laboratory requisitions have translated to PDAs easily. The ongoing recording of patient information is also facilitated. These activities are documented in the research (Cacace, Cinque, Crudele, Iannello and Venditti 2004; Thomas, Coppola, and Feldman, 2001).

TABLE 2 The correspondence between PDA uses and Koole's FRAME model.

Cahoon (2002)	Stroud et al. (2005)	Park (2006)	FRAME Model
Clinical services	To do list; Memo pad	Pharmacy; lab uses	Device Usability
Calculators	Calculator: Expense tracker	Calculator	Device Usability
Data collection		Keeping up-to-date	Learner Aspect Context learning
Medical record tools	Calendar/date book	Calendar	Device Usability
Content tools	Patient management tools; Clinical reference materials; Address/phone book	Referring to texts & guidelines; Studying	Learner Aspect
Communication tools	Information exchange via beaming (Bluetooth)		Social Computing
Interaction tools	Games; Recreational reading		Context learning
Communication tools	E-mail; Internet access E-mail		Social Computing

Less, however, is reported on the psychological comfort of the user when carrying out this research using mobile devices. The Western Canadian University Nurse Practitioner students used the term "security blanket" and "safer than memory" in their list of reasons to recommend the use of PDAs (Park 2006). The use of PDAs in medication error research also exemplifies this comfort (Rothschild, Lee, Bae, and Bates 2002; Galt et al. 2002). Conversely, a few students felt that a PDA might disrupt the patient/client relationship and lead to the loss of personal touch (Park 2006).

The Social Computing Intersection (SCI) is the least explored component. Local Area Networks (LANs) and free or inexpensive wireless connectivity address the physical part of this intersection. Students in both the studies of Stroud, Erkel, and Smith (2005) and Park (2006) mention email as the only interactional use of the PDAs. We are now interested in the use of PDAs to help to form a learning community. The connectivity potential of these devices for practice and education has not yet been fully explored.

We conclude from this review that there has been little research on interactional use of PDAs by health care professionals. As well, further research and exploration is required relating to confidentiality and security of data with PDA use. The final issue – cost – will most likely decrease with increased demand and increased wireless capacity.

The Use of Mobile Technologies to Address Challenges in Nursing Practice Education

Changes in health care delivery have impacted nursing practice education and as a result created ideal conditions for the implementation of m-learning approaches. More specifically, care is moving to the community where client complexity and acuity is increasing and where up-to-date information at the point-of-care is critically needed to support practice. This means that care delivery requires physical mobility throughout the community which does not lend itself to more traditional direct teaching supervision models. The instructor is removed from instruction at the point-of-care and the real-time responsibility for instruction falls on practitioners whose focus is necessarily on service delivery rather than pedagogy.

As outlined in the FRAME model (Koole and Ally 2006), the social environment is an essential component to the construction of knowledge by the learner. Mobile learning that provides opportunities for connectivity and interaction has the potential to provide the learner with a meaningful learning environment, one in which the learning is situated in a real life context. Timely and rapid access to practice resources may better support teaching and learning, particularly when practice takes place in the community where the instructor is further removed from the point-of-care, and where opportunities for student-to-student interactions are more limited.

The requirement to provide theory and evidence-informed care to clients (College of Registered Nurses Association of British Columbia [CRNBC] 2000) is also challenging in the context of more isolated care in the community and of a rapidly expanding body of knowledge. Access to current knowledge can be problematic for students in the practice setting because of limited access to text resources, computers, and connectivity to the Internet and library data bases and even more challenging for students whose access is further removed from the point-of-care.

In keeping with Koole's (2005) FRAME model, access to and usability of mobile learning devices is critical to supporting the context of learning and learning interactions. Carefully planned selection of hardware, software (such as decision-making and drug reference programs), and connectivity options that meets the learner's cognitive, physical, and psychological needs in the context of their learning environment is critical in supporting theory and evidenced-informed practice. Together, the resulting educational challenges to changes in health care delivery have created an ideal environment for mobile technologies that provide resources for students at the point-of-care and which enable instruction to be re-introduced in real time.

Guided by the FRAME model (Koole 2005; Koole and Ally 2006), we designed a pilot project and a formative evaluation study to help us to begin to address the gaps in the literature and the challenges in nursing practice education outlined above. This study was exploratory and descriptive in nature and was structured as a two-stage formative evaluation of the use of specific mobile devices, Hewlett Packard iPAQ© PDAs, in nursing practice education. Stage 1 consisted of one-on-one trials with 4th year nursing students and instructors, while Stage 2 was a full field trial in a one month long 3rd year nursing practice course. In the remainder of this chapter, we report of the results of Stage 1 of this study.

Methodology

Research Setting

Stage 1 of the study was designed to test the feasibility of the use of the iPAQs with nursing students before their introduction into a real life nursing class. Two instructors and three volunteer students in the final year of a four year Baccalaureate Nursing Program at a western Canadian community college participated in this part of the study. The mobile device, the HP iPAQ model 6955, they used was a full fledged Pocket PC computer combined with a mobile telephone and a digital camera and provided for both WiFi and GPRS wireless capability. The participants were supplied with selected software programs. These included both those programs built in to the iPAQs (Microsoft Office Mobile©, Internet Explorer©, and Pocket MSN Messenger©) and additional software provided by the research team, including nursing support software (the 2007 Lippincott's Nursing Drug Guide©, and Davis' Lab and Diagnostic Tests©), the Skype© audio conferencing program, and Acrobat Reader Mobile©, which were loaded onto the devices in advance.

Research Questions

This stage of the study was designed to answer the following questions:
1. Can PDA use be implemented and sustained in independent nursing practice education settings?
2. Are PDAs useful in nursing practice education settings?

3. What is the appeal of/comfort-with PDAs for nursing students and instructors in real life instructional settings?

Study Design – Stage 1

Stage 1 consisted of one-on-one trials. Tessmer (1993) indicates that a one-on-one trial involves the evaluator working with one learner/instructor at a time (for example, doing "walkthroughs"). The two faculty members assisted the lead author in setting up the mobile devices and testing them for use. These three researchers then met with the student participants for Stage 1 to provide a two hour initial training session in the use of the devices. The students were then asked to try out specific features of the devices around campus and the community for a two week period; that is, to make use of the devices in a variety of possible ways in order to first test out whether or not the mobile devices can be used effectively and efficiently for the purposes planned for the real-life instructional setting of Stage 2.

Several forms of evaluation data were collected in Stage 1:

- The researcher's written comments during one-on-one observations of student use of the mobile devices and any specific comments directed to them.
- A pre-study demographics survey.
- Semi-structured interviews with the course faculty members and 4th year students, conducted by the lead author.
- Reflective logs kept by faculty and students.

Analysis

The pre-study demographic survey was tallied and descriptive statistics compiled. The interviews were transcribed and coded using AtlasTi© software. Each interview was coded by two research team members independently and then the codes were merged. The code were then discussed by the research team and examined in relation to the FRAME model.

Findings

Prior Knowledge of Mobile Devices

The data and the interviews revealed that, with the exception of one of the instructors (both research team members), this group were novices in m-learning and had had no prior direct experience with PDA use. They had ample experience with mobile (cell) phones and four of five owned one (see Table 3). For most of the participants, this was their first experience with a PDA–style pocket computer. They were all familiar with, and had used, MS Windows,

MSOffice, Hotmail, and Skype on desktop or laptop computers, but not on PDA style devices. They were also aware that there was nursing software for PDAs, but had not used it (except for the one instructor).

TABLE 3 Level of Mobile Device Ownership

Own mobile device	n
Cell Phone	4
PDA	2
None	1
Stage 1: N = 5	

Despite their lack of direct experience with PDAs, all five participants reported that they were very comfortable with these devices. This was a somewhat curious self rating since their prior experience clearly was only with mobile telephones and, to a lesser extent, digital cameras (presumably built into their mobile phones). Table 4 details the participants' prior experience with the functions and software provided in the HP iPAQs. The interviews, however, revealed that this comfort was based on their experience with computing in general and with observations of others using PDAs for some of these functions.

TABLE 4 Prior Expertise with Mobile Devices

Feature / Experience	None	Beginner	Competent	Experienced
Telephone	0	0	1	4
Photography	2	1	0	2
Email	2	1	1	1
Internet	2	2	0	1
Text Messaging	3	1	0	1
Audio Messaging	4	0	0	1
Word Processing	2	1	1	1
Spreadsheet	3	0	1	1
Database	3	0	1	1
Nursing Software	2	1	1	2
Stage 1: N = 5				

Learning the Mobile Device Features

It was not a simple task for our participants to learn to use all the features available on these devices. As reported above, the PDAs provided to the participants were loaded with a relatively wide range of software. The HP iPAQs also provide users with a number of built-in features, including both a touch screen (with stylus) and a thumbing keyboard (see Figure 2) and the capability to transcribe hand writing using the stylus to text. In addition, when appropriate service is available, iPAQ 6955 users can use either WiFi hotspots or GPRS (cell phone and data) wireless connectivity to send email, browse the Internet, or use an audio conferencing program such as Pocket MSN Messenger or Skype. Participants were provided with both types of connectivity. For the study, the iPAQs were set up with local service GPRS connectivity and WiFi was available both on campus and in spots around the community (for example, coffee shops) as well as the home networks of some participants.

FIGURE 2 The HP iPAQ 6955

The two instructors received their devices two months before Stage 1 of the study began. They were oriented to some of the features of the device by the lead author and learned others through reading the manual and exploration. One of the instructors already owned a similar model of PDA and used that in her practice.

The three students were provided with a two hour orientation. In order to allow them to effectively use these devices, we decided that it was necessary to directly introduce the students to a number of these features and provide them with time to practice under supervisions. Features taught during the orientation were: a) use of both the touch and thumbing keyboards, b) cursive to text transcription, c) how to enable wireless connectivity (WiFi and GPRS) for email and Internet browsing, d) use of the nursing drug and lab values software, and e) use of text and audio messaging.

Ease of Use

Despite the apparent complexity of the devices, especially the number of features to learn, our participants uniformly claimed that these devices were easy to learn and easy to master overall. While they found that the two orientation sessions were not sufficient to allow them to achieve full mastery, our respondents found that they only required an additional one to three hours learning on their own afterwards to become comfortable with the use of the iPAQs. In particular, they found that much of their knowledge with desktop computing was transferable. In the interview, "Jane," who regarded herself as a complete novice with PDAs, noted:

> I think that it's a very easy device to use... you can kind of fumble your way through it and find things and kind of work through. Um... I think that it has something to do with how comfortable you feel on a main computer, as to how comfortable you can come and use one of these. Because a lot of the knowledge is kind of um... transferable. I think personally if I had a longer time with the device I would become more comfortable with the Internet and accessing stuff over the Internet.[5]

More specifically, our respondents even found some of the more unusual features simple to use. Referring to the transcriber (touch hand writing to text), Jane commented that:

> I found that to be just amazing, you could write in anything and ... I have pretty messy hand-writing and I could handwrite words in and it would come up and you know, it would print them on the Word document, it was amazing. I found that to be very... kind of fun to use, you know.

Of the various programs on the PDAs, our participants found the nursing software (2007 Lippincott's Nursing Drug Guide and Davis's Lab and Diagnostic Tests) to be user friendly and reported it to be the feature they used most in the trial. Jane also commented on these programs:

> Yes, and I used them probably ten times a day on a daily basis, every time I was in the hospital. I used them a lot, whenever

---

5. "Jane" and other pseudonyms are used in place of participants' actual names.

> I needed to look up a medication or cross-reference a lab test or even looking up the isolation precautions for Meningitis, it was all right there I could just go in and put in the word, it was easy to find, and it comes right up. You put in a few letters and it comes up with a bunch of options.

Barriers to Use

The feature that posed the most difficulty for participants was wireless connectivity. Despite orientation to this feature, none of our student participants were able to make the GPRS data connection work when using the devices on their own. In one case, the student successfully used the WiFi connectivity with her home wireless system, but did not try the GPRS connectivity. The other two appeared to confuse the two features. "Sally," for instance, when asked about using GRPS stated:

> I tried that in the office at Home Community Care, but it wasn't working for me. But I was just trying to see if I could pick out the signal, but I didn't really try … [and then] I turned on the cell phone feature and the WiFi. [The] cell phone lit up, but the WiFi didn't light up.

Our participants also talked about their inability to use wireless connectivity in the hospital. This was a combination of the local hospitals' policies not to allow the use of wireless devices for fear of causing medical equipment to malfunction and the consequent lack of WiFi connectivity. These policies are under debate in the health care community and, in fact, one local hospital modified its policy during the period of our study, so this may become less a barrier to mobile learning in nursing in future.

While the student participants were not concerned with it, during Stage 1 trials, the instructors and research team discovered one other barrier that promised to seriously impact Stage 2 of our study. This was the inability to access the WebCT course website that would be used for communications and for sharing of resources in the nursing course to be used in the field trial. We were able to access the log in screen but not log in to the course. The issue appears to be with Java scripting and, at the time of writing, has not yet been resolved. This highlights the need for the use of learning management systems and websites that have been designed specifically for mobile use (for example, Google Mobile).

Portability

One of the most pervasive arguments for mobile learning is the perceived ready portability of PDAs and like devices. Our participants generally agreed that the iPAQs were portable, but they had somewhat varying opinions on the degree of this. They agreed that they were suitable to carry in purse or pocket or clipped to a belt whenever this was feasible. Two respondents, for instance, carried the iPAQ in uniform pants (leg) pocket in hospital. Alice reported this to be quite useful:

> Alice: It was in my pants pocket down on the side by my knee, right side always 'cause I'm right handed, and I had no issue with it, it was accessible. There was one time where I was on break, reclined and I guess it slipped out of my pocket. So, an eight-hundred dollar device is sitting in your pocket and you think you're going to lose it, you keep a really close eye on it.

> Interviewer: <laughs> Yeah. Even if it's yours. Yeah. So you found it comfortable?

> Alice: Yeah. Yeah it didn't bother... I never noticed it was there, when it was in my pocket. It wasn't bulky, it wasn't clunky. It was clipped right on; I wasn't worried about it just accidentally slipping out.

Jane, however, found the presence of the device in the uniform pocket to be somewhat annoying and chose to place it nearby instead:

> No, I had it in a leg pocket... I found it quite heavy actually... walking around after a twelve hour shift you really started to feel it there and a couple of days I actually took it off and put it in the... narcotics drawer of the med cart, because it was just too heavy and it kind of rubs on your leg a little bit and it was kind of uncomfortable that way.

Visibility

Kukulska-Hulme and Traxler (2005) considered one of the most significant attributes of mobile technologies to be their ability to support learning that is more situated. This implies that mobile devices might be used in a variety of lighting situations, including outdoors or in automobiles. One of the advantages of the iPAQ 6955 is that the brightness of the screen is easily adjustable using a slider on the home screen. Our participants found that the screens were sufficiently bright and that the colour and type size of the text displayed allowed it to be clearly read. Sally, for instance, commented in response to a question about screen visibility:

> Interviewer: Right... How did you react to the visibility of this device in different situations and conditions?

> Sally: I didn't have an issue with them; I didn't really use them outside. I used them in the vehicle and had no problem with them. You can change the lighting of the screen to lighter or darker. Right now at the angle I'm looking at it, it looks dark, but as soon as I pick it up the glare's gone and it's not an issue.

Our respondents also felt that the screen size of the devices was suitable and pointed out that bigger screens also meant heavier, less portable devices. Alice, for example, commented:

> I'd stay that size because... I don't think it's too big or too small... it was easy to ... handle and carry around; I'd probably keep it the way that it is.

Usefulness in Nursing Practice Education

The option to reference nursing software at the bedside was cited as the most useful feature of the mobile devices in nursing practice experiences. All the participants found the devices to be convenient for immediate reference and easy to access when needed. They also noted that the programs allowed them to remain current via software updates and found that they aided in patient teaching by using "layman's" language. For instance, when asked to comment on the usefulness of the Lippincott drug reference program, Sally noted that:

> If there was a question, if I wasn't sure about something I'd have to actually go back to the office and find out more information and you know, either next visit or I could call the person and call them back and give them the information. But it was really handy to have it right there so I could talk to the patient about it. It was probably like a different drug they had been on and they didn't really understand what it was for and what not. So I found it was really great to be able to do that and be able to use it as a reference tool.

Our respondents also commented on the availability on the iPAQs of the option to use either telephone or email to contact their instructors and on the potential of the devices to allow private communications via mobility. Sally, for example, stated:

Yeah. Well I like it because you have the options of connecting to the Internet or the phone... You could use it to talk with your instructor if you needed to... There was one situation in my clinical setting where I had to get a hold of my instructor and get a hold of him now. And so a matter of finding a private telephone in the hospital... It's pretty much near impossible. If you had at least one of these, you could step outside, you could... have access to the telephone.

Our participants also thought that the mobile devices were useful for seeking information and for document storage and access. Sally again noted:

You always want to look something up or a reference... I like that option of having different programs on there you can refer to. Of course the Internet or different sources you can use to connect to. And you know, storing documents on there... if you were gonna send something to your instructor. It saves a lot of time...

Implications for Practice

The focus of this was on the use of mobile learning in Nursing practice education. During Stage 1 of our study, we worked with a small group of five participants and, therefore, cannot with any confidence generalize our conclusions to nursing students in general. However, our data does point to some initial, tentative, implications for the use of mobile devices in this instructional context:

1. Prior knowledge: Students' previous experience with computing is likely a significant factor in their learning to use mobile devices. There may be a need for some level of differentiated instruction (novice and experienced groups) about, and orientation to, the specific mobile devices to be used in a class or program.

2. Time to learn: 3G mobile devices like the HP iPAQ are generally easy to learn, but they are also complex technologies with many features. Despite our participants' claims that they can be learned quickly, some features – especially those associated with wireless connectivity – may take students time and additional instruction to learn to use effectively and completely.

3. Ease of use: Our participants reported that the mobile devices were both readily portable and provided clear visibility in a variety of situations. While battery life may be an issue, it appears that such devices can be readily and comfortably used in nursing practice contexts.

4. Immediate access to information: Our participants uniformly reported how convenient it was to have immediate access at the bedside to reference information such as drug interactions and lab values. It seems likely that, in this way, mobile learning can add to student nurses' level of confidence in their practice and, therefore, to their safety of practice.

5. Improved communications with instructors: Our instructors commented on the difficulties that they experience staying in touch with their students on a regular basis once these students are out in practice experiences. While policies concerning the use of wireless devices in hospital settings are currently a barrier, mobile devices provide a number of options for connectivity that may lead to more flexibility for instructors to contact students and vice versa.

Conclusion

In this chapter, we reviewed the extensive research literature on the use of m-learning in nursing education and reported on Stage 1 of an exploratory evaluation study of m-learning in a nursing practice education setting. We concluded from the literature review that there has been little research to date on the interactional application of m-learning by nursing educators and that this should be the focus of our inquiry. We noted that nursing care is moving to the community where client complexity and acuity is increasing and where up-to-date information at the point-of-care is critically needed to support practice. As a result, we argued that the delivery of nursing education requires physical mobility throughout the community and does not lend itself to more traditional direct teaching supervision models. Instead, guided by Koole's (2005) FRAME model of m-learning, we judged that access to and usability of mobile learning devices is critical to supporting the context of learning and learning interactions.

The purpose of Stage 1 of the study was to test the feasibility of the use of the iPAQs with nursing students before their introduction in Stage 2 into a real life nursing education class. In this stage, therefore, we asked a number of questions.

First, we asked if the use of mobile devices such as PDAs can be implemented and sustained in independent nursing practice education settings. Our participants felt that this was indeed the case. They uniformly reported that they were comfortable with mobile devices in general and that, despite the number of features required to use the iPAQs effectively, these devices were easy to learn and easy to master overall. In particular, they found the nursing software (drug reference and lab values) supplied on the iPAQs simple to learn and to use at the point of care. They also indicated that they found the devices to be readily portable and the screen sufficiently visible in a variety of settings.

Our respondents did, however, point out barriers to the use of the devices in nursing practice education. The availability and use of wireless connectivity is critical for communications with instructors and other students. Despite orientation, none of our student participants were able to make the GPRS data connection work when using the devices on their own. In one case, the student successfully used the WiFi connectivity with her home wireless system, but did not try the GPRS connectivity. It is likely that a more thorough orientation and more practice of these features will be needed before students will feel comfortable with the interactional uses of mobile devices.

Second, we wished to determine if PDAs were useful in nursing practice education settings. Our participants cited the option of referencing nursing software at the bedside as the most useful feature of the mobile devices in nursing practice experiences. They found the devices convenient for immediate reference and easy to access when needed. They also found that they aided in patient teaching. Our respondents also thought it was potentially useful to use the iPAQs for either telephone or email to contact their instructors and, further, because the devices were mobile, to allow such communications to be more readily private. The results of Stage 1, however, do point to the need for further validation of the interactivity and communications aspects of mobile devices in nursing practice education.

Finally, we wished to assess whether mobile devices such as PDAs appealed to, and were comfortable to use by, nursing students and instructors in real life instructional settings. This again relates closely to ease of use of the devices. Our respondents all reported that they were comfortable with mobile devices in general and that the iPAQs specifically were easy to learn and easy to master overall. They did, however, experience some difficulties using the PDAs – particularly the connectivity – and these difficulties appeared more pronounced for those with less successful past experience with mobile devices and even computers in general. Stage 1 results then indicate that nursing students and faculty are attracted to the use of mobile devices in practice education but that sound prior instruction in their use is important.

In conclusion, Stage 1 of our study confirmed that the use of m-learning, at least with the HP iPAQ PDAs, is feasible in actual nursing practice education settings and that this use has the potential to be very effective at least in affording students and instructors with ready access to resources at the point of care. Our results indicate that the interactive uses of mobile devices are also potentially very useful, but this aspect needs to be more thoroughly investigated in the second stage of our study.

References

CACACE, F., M. CINQUE, M. CRUDELE, G. IANNELLO, and M. VENDITTI. 2004. The impact of innovation in medical and nursing training: A hospital information system for students accessible through mobile devices. In proceedings, *mLearn 2004, the 3rd world conference on mobile learning*, Rome, Italy.

CAHOON, J. 2002. Handhelds in health care: Benefits of content at the point of care. *Advances in Clinical Knowledge Management* 5 (April). http://www.openclinical.org/docs/ext/workshops/ackm5/absCahoon.pdf (accessed September 16, 2005).

DAVENPORT, C. 2004. *Analysis of PDAs in nursing: Benefits and barriers.* www.pdacortex.com/Analysis_PDAs_Nursing.htm (accessed September 16, 2005).

DRISCOLL, M. P. 2005. *Psychology of learning for instruction.* 3rd ed. Boston, MA: Pearson Allyn & Bacon.

GALT, K., E. RICH, W. YOUNG, R. MARKERT, C. BARR, B. HOUGHTON, et al. 2002. Impact of hand-held technologies on medication errors in primary care. *Topics in Health Information Management* 23 (2):71-81.

GEORGE, L., and L. DAVIDSON. 2005. PDA use in nursing education: Prepared for today, poised for tomorrow. *Online Journal of Nursing Informatics* 9 (2). http://eaa-knowledge.com/ojni/ni/9_2/george.htm (accessed September 16, 2005).

GOLDSWORTHY, S., N. LAWRENCE, and W. GOODMAN. 2006. The use of Personal Digital Assistants at the point of care in an undergraduate nursing program. *CIN* 24 (3):138-43.

HILL, T., and M. ROLDAN. 2005. Toward third generation threaded discussions for mobile learning: Opportunities and challenges for ubiquitous collaborative learning environments. *Information Systems Frontiers* 7 (1):55-70.

KEEGAN, D. 2002. *The future of learning: From eLearning to mLearning.* Ericsson.

———. 2005. *The incorporation of mobile learning into mainstream education and training.* Paper presentation, *mLearn 2005, the 4th world conference on mobile learning,* October 25-28, Cape Town, South Africa.

KOOLE, M. L., and M. ALLY. 2006. Framework for the rational analysis of mobile education (FRAME) model: Revising the ABCs of educational practices. In proceedings, *Networking International conference on systems and international conference on mobile communications and learning technologies*, 216.

KUKULSKA-HULME, A., and J. TRAXLER. 2005. *Mobile learning: A handbook for educators and trainers.* London: Routledge.

LEHMAN, K. 2003. Clinical nursing instructors' use of handheld computers for student recordkeeping. *Journal of Nursing Education* 42 (10):41-42.

MAYES, T., and S. de FREITAS. 2004. *Review of e-learning theories, frameworks and models.* Joint Information Systems Committee (JISC) e-Learning models desk study. http://www.jisc.ac.uk/uploaded_documents/Stage%2 02%20Learning%20Models%20(Version%201).pdf#s/;earch=%22JISC% 20Mayes%22 (accessed September 21, 2006).

MILLER, J., J. SHAW-KOKOT, M. ARNOLD, T. BOGGIN, K. CROWELL, F. ALLEHRI, J. BLUE, and S. BERRIER. 2005. A study of assistants to enhance undergraduate clinical nursing education. *Journal of Nursing Education* 44:19-26.

NEWBOLT, S. 2003. New uses for wireless technology. *Nursing Management* 22 (October):22-32.

PARK, C. 2006. Survey data on mobile use by nurse practitioner students. Unpublished raw data.

ROSENTHAL, K. 2003. "Touch" vs. "tech": Valuing nursing specific PDA software. *Nursing Management* 34 (7):58.

ROTHSCHILD, J., T. LEE, T. BAE, and D. BATES. (2002). Clinician use of a palmtop drug reference guide. *Journal of the American Medical Informatics Association* 9 (3):223-29.

STROUD, S., E. ERKEL, and C. SMITH. 2005. The use of Personal Digital Assistants by nurse practitioner students and faculty. *Journal of the American Academy of Nurse Practitioners* 17 (2):67-75.

TESSMER, M. 1993. Planning and conducting formative evaluations: Improving the quality of education and training. London: Kogan Page.

THOMAS, B., J. COPPOLA, and H. FELDMAN. 2001. Adopting handheld computers for community-based curriculum: Case study. *Journal of the New York State Nurses Association* 32:4-6.

TRIFONOVA, A., and M. RONCHETTI. 2003. A general architecture for m-learning. *Journal of Digital Contents* 2 (1):31-36.

WAGNER, E. 2005. Enabling mobile learning. *Educause Review* 40 (3):40-53.

Acknowledgments

This research was supported by a Mission Critical grant from Athabasca University and by a Professional Development grant from North Island College. The authors also wish to express their gratitude to Rogers Communications Edmonton for their generosity in supplying GPRS voice and data service for this study, to Lippincott for providing free software, and to Davis for providing a discounted price for their program.

Informal Learning Evidence in Online Communities of Mobile Device Enthusiasts

GILL CLOUGH
ANN C. JONES
PATRICK MCANDREW
EILEEN SCANLON
INSTITUTE OF EDUCATIONAL TECHNOLOGY
THE OPEN UNIVERSITY
UNITED KINGDOM

Abstract

This chapter describes a study that investigated the informal learning practices of enthusiastic mobile device owners. Informal learning is far more widespread than is often realized. Livingston (2000) pointed out that Canadian adults spend an average of fifteen hours per week on informal learning activities, more than they spend on formal learning activities. The motivation for these learning efforts generally comes from the individual, not from some outside force such as a school, university, or workplace. Therefore, in the absence of an externally imposed learning framework, informal learners will use whatever techniques, resources, and tools best suit their learning needs and personal preferences. As ownership of mobile technologies becomes increasingly widespread in the western world, it is likely that learners who have access to this technology will use it to support their informal learning efforts. This chapter presents the findings of a study into the various and innovative ways in which PDA and Smartphone users exploit mobile device functionality in their informal learning activities. The findings suggested that mobile device users deploy the mobile, connective, and collaborative capabilities of their devices in a variety of informal learning contexts, and in quite innovative ways. Trends emerged, such as the increasing importance of podcasting and audio and the use of built-in GPS, which may have implications for future studies. Informal learners identified learning activities that could be enhanced by the involvement of mobile technology, and developed methods and techniques that helped them achieve their learning goals.

Introduction

According to Tough (1979), informal learning is a deliberate effort to gain new knowledge or skills or obtain improved insights or understandings. Livingston (2000) defined informal learning as any activity that involved learning which occurred outside the formal curricula of an educational institution. Livingston went on to make a clear distinction between explicit informal learning and tacit informal learning, which is incorporated into other social or ad hoc activities. Both forms of learning result in the acquisition of new knowledge or skills; however, only the explicit informal learning project is motivated by some immediate problem or need as defined in Tough's definition of informal learning.

Vavoula, Scanlon, Lonsdale, Sharples, and Jones (2005) developed the classification of informal learning by separating out the goals of learning from the processes of learning as illustrated in Figure 1.

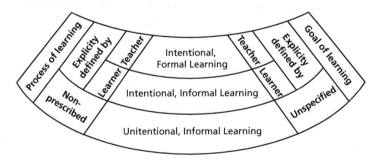

FIGURE 1 Typology of Informal Learning Reproduced from Vavoula et al. (2005)

If both the goals and processes of learning are either explicitly defined by the learner in advance (intentional informal learning) or selected at the point at which the learning opportunity presents itself (unintentional informal learning), then the tools used to support the learning will also be self-directed. As technology advances, so does the range of potential learning tools.

This chapter reports on the results of a study to investigate the informal learning practices of people who owned mobile devices (PDAs or smartphones). Specifically, we asked the question, "Do mobile device owners use their devices to support their informal learning projects, and if so, how?"

Smartphones are primarily communication devices, and many PDAs now offer several communication protocols such as GPRS and/or WiFi. This connectivity supports synchronous communication using voice, voice over IP (VOIP) or instant messaging as well as asynchronous communication via email, weblogs, web forums, wikis, and virtual learning environments. In recent years researchers have investigated the potential of mobile handheld devices to support collaborative learning, devising educational scenarios that make use of their collaborative, interactive, and mobile capabilities. PDAs have been introduced into schools, both inside the classroom (DiGiano et al. 2003) and outside the classroom in support of fieldwork (Chen, Kao, and Sheu 2003). Research has also been conducted in the wider learning sphere, with the use of handhelds as interactive museum guidebooks (Hsi 2003) and as tools to support medical students on hospital placements (Smørdal and Gregory 2003). Roschelle (2003) identified two forms of collaborative participation: "the normal social participation in classroom discussion (for example) and the new informatic participation among connected devices" (p.262). He discovered that in the classroom setting, where the learners were in the same physical space, the normal face-to-face social interaction was supplemented by the wireless interaction between the connected devices. In this context, mobile devices added a new social dimension of participation that was not otherwise available. Given the growing evidence of support for mobile collaboration in more formal learning contexts, this study also asked, "Do informal learners make use of the connectivity afforded by their mobile devices to engage in collaborative learning?"

Vavoula (2004) highlighted some of the difficulties inherent in researching informal learning; it can be intentional or unintentional and people may even be unaware that any learning has taken place. There is also the practical problem of locating a pool of mobile device users who not only engage in mobile informal learning, but who are also willing to provide information about their activities.

PDA and Smartphone enthusiasts were targeted as the community most likely to be using their devices in informal learning and participants were recruited from the active community of web forum users. Web forums are Internet-based, asynchronous discussion groups that are aimed at people who share a specific interest; in this case, mobile devices. Messages were posted in the forums inviting members to participate in a web survey on informal learning with mobile devices. This approach was successful, generating over 200 responses of which over 100 described informal learning with mobile devices.

This chapter describes the methods used in the study and discusses the results, locating them in the context of the wider literature on informal learning. It explores key issues, such as participation in collaborative informal learning that emerged from the findings and outlines research directions arising from the study.

Method

In order to obtain insights into ways in which experienced users use mobile devices to support informal learning, this research needed to plug into existing networks and communities of mobile device users. A method was required that would capture information about participants' informal learning practices and experiences. PDAs and Smartphones are mobile devices and their users may be located anywhere in the world, so a web-based survey method was chosen. This gave access to a wide pool of participants without requiring them to be in any specific geographic location.

Surveys use structured questions to obtain self-reported data from participants. Although surveys are best suited to multiple-choice, quantitative measurements, some of the questions could be adapted to request open-ended, diary-type responses to unearth details of informal learning experiences. By circulating the questionnaire via the Web, additional advantages would accrue. It could be accessed from anywhere in the world, at any time of day, regardless of time-zones, and it could be publicized via email and the Internet.

In order to identify the preferences and informal learning episodes of experienced mobile device users, we needed a group of users with some level of experience in using their mobile device. Internet-based web forums were selected as the best place in which to find them. There is an active Internet-based community of PDA and Smartphone users who participate in a variety of user forums. Membership is free and asynchronous discussion threads allow participants to seek help and discuss a wide variety of device-related issues. Three businesses were also contacted and agreed to circulate an email to employees with a business PDA or Smartphone, inviting them to participate in the research.

The web survey was published over a period of four weeks in summer. During this time, over 200 responses were returned of which over 150 completed all the questions without omission. When asked whether they used their mobile device to support their informal learning, 53 per cent said that they did and provided details. The questionnaire distinguished between informal learning in general and informal learning for which a mobile device was used in some way. There was no great difference in the occurrence of informal learning between PDA users and Smartphone users. However, PDA users were significantly more likely to use their mobile device in support of their informal learning with 61 per cent of PDA users using their mobile device compared to 31 per cent of Smartphone users ($\chi^2_{(3)} = 19.26$, p<0.001).

The responses were classified using a functional framework devised by Patten, Arnedillo Sanchez, and Tangney (2006). This functional framework was designed as a tool with which to analyse handheld learning applications and evaluate their pedagogical underpinning. It therefore seemed reasonable to use this framework to see whether the informal learning activities reported by PDA and Smartphone users fall into the same categories as the mobile learning activities designed by educators.

According to this framework mobile learning applications can be sub-divided into seven categories:

1. **Collaborative applications** that encourage knowledge sharing, making use of the learner's physical location and mobility.
2. **Location aware applications** that contextualize information, allowing learners to interact directly with their environment; for example, collecting environmental data linked to geographical context or accessing contextually relevant reference material.
3. **Data collection applications** that use the handheld device's ability to record data in the form of text, image, video, and audio.
4. **Referential applications** that use dictionaries, translators and e-books to deliver content when and where it is needed.
5. **Administrative applications** that employ the typical scheduling, information storage, and other calendar functions available on mobile devices.
6. **Interactive applications** that use both the input and output capabilities of mobile devices, allowing the learner to input information and obtain some form of feedback which aids the learning process.

7. **Microworld applications** model real world domains to enable learners to use practice in a constrained version of the learning scenario. This category was not found in the informal learning results.

Figure 2 groups the informal learning activities described by the survey participants into categories based on the Patten et al. (2006) functional framework.

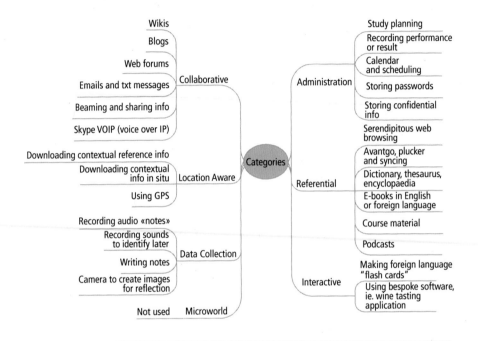

FIGURE 2 Informal Learning Activities

Discussion

Collaborative activities

There was a significant difference between PDA and Smartphone users in the level of communication they engaged in using their mobile device, with 100 per cent of Smartphone users using their device to communicate with others compared to 80 per cent of PDA users. Since Smartphones are first and foremost mobile phones, with their high level of connectivity, this result is predictable. Given these fairly high rates of communication using mobile devices, we might expect high levels of collaborative learning.

When asked to provide details of collaborative learning, only 21 per cent of PDA users and 19 per cent of Smartphone users who used their devices to communicate with others felt that they collaborated. However, in their full-text descriptions, some device users demonstrated that they did collaborate; they just did not always recognize it as such. Table 1 lists the main forms that collaborative learning took:

TABLE 1 Forms of Collaborative Activities

Collaborative resource	How it is used
Blog or Weblog	A form of online diary that is easy to create and maintain, and which can be set to allow updates from more than one person. Some participants cited "downloading blogs" as a collaborative activity.
Wiki	A group website, similar to a collective blog, where members can create collaborative web pages, updateable by more than one individual and contribute to discussion threads.
Web forum	Websites relating to a particular theme that are maintained by a group of administrators, but which have information threads that can be created and added to by members.
Beaming and sharing information	Sharing data between mobile devices using infrared "beam" or bluetooth. Contributing information to a shared database, or one-to-to-one information sharing.

The collaborative activities described generally occurred through the sharing of data in some way, usually by uploading it onto a central server hosting a web forum, wiki, or blog. For example, "Collaborating photos and notes to a central server, i.e. a wiki of sorts."

Web forum users collaborated in many areas, helping each other solve technical problems by posting and answering questions in the forums, building collaborative data bases of information through wiki entries; however, in many cases this collaboration took place via the desktop interface rather than that of the mobile device. At the time of the study, Internet connectivity using mobile devices was still expensive and the interface clumsy.

Location Aware Activities

Patten et al. (2006) looked at location aware learning applications that use Global Positioning Systems (GPS) and sensors to identify geographical context and promote learner engagement. In 2005 when the survey was conducted, GPS-enabled PDAs were just arriving on the market with 24 per cent of survey participants reporting that they used GPS. Given the fact that 60 per cent of participants said that they did not have GPS on their device, this finding may suggest that as GPS becomes more commonly available in mobile devices, informal learners will devise new ways to use it.

Data Collection Activities

In the context of this functional framework, data collection refers to the use of mobile devices for recording data and information about the environment. This data may be recorded for reflective purposes, such as taking notes or pictures, or it may consist of observational data that is combined with the observations of others to produce an information database which may provide further learning opportunities. The survey participants described recording audio, notes and images both for personal reflection and for sharing with others.

Audio Data Collection

The audio recording facilities of mobile devices were used by 54 per cent of participants, with 15 per cent of participants using it on either a daily or weekly basis. Audio was used either as an alternative to writing notes on the device, or as a way of recording ambient sounds. For example, one participant reported: "I use my voice recorder to record magic lectures. I also use the memo application for taking notes at magic lectures, taking down important information such as originators of magical effects, funny lines to remember, names of books, and various sleights to learn."

Taking Notes

PDAs and Smartphones were used by over 90 per cent of participants to record notes, and notetaking was frequently mentioned as a support for informal learning. The reasons for taking notes were varied and included:
- Noting down thoughts and ideas to follow up later
- Making notes whilst learning
- Annotating downloaded material

- Writing lists (topics to research, books to read, events to attend)
- Scanning in handwritten notes to have mobile access to them

The voice recording facility was sometimes used to take notes, and mobility was cited as an advantage of taking notes using the mobile device; for example, "Making notes and keeping information with me so I can revise it often." This activity mirrors the typical handwritten note-taking that most learners engage in. The advantages of using a mobile device (small size, portability, digital notes format that is easily shared with other devices) appear to outweigh any disadvantages of small screen size, slower data entry, and reliance on battery.

Recording Images

The cameras on mobile devices were not used to a great extent. At the time of the research, many mobile devices did not contain a built-in camera. Three participants mentioned taking pictures to use for reference later; others mentioned sharing pictures with other people, but images did not appear to be used extensively in informal learning with mobile devices. This may be due to the lower quality of mobile device pictures compared to those from even quite inexpensive digital cameras. It is also possible that images would be used more often if better software were available to integrate them with the learning project.

Looking up Information for Referential Learning Activities

Many participants accessed the Web to support their informal learning projects. Some used the PC and transferred the content to the PDA or Smartphone for use when away from the PC, with 99 per cent of participants synchronising their device with a computer. Others accessed the web content directly from their devices using GPRS or WiFi whenever something sparked their interest, with 45 per cent accessing the Web from their device on a daily or weekly basis, 30 per cent using it occasionally. In a typical free-text response, one participant wrote, "I do a lot of informal learning through wikipedia. org (and that includes using it on my smartphone). I may be thinking about a subject and then I can quickly get out my phone and look the subject matter up on the Internet"

Podcasting is a method of audio delivery with implications for teaching and learning. Audio broadcasts are published via the Internet, and users subscribe to a "feed" which allows them to download broadcasts in a format that will run on most handheld devices. Two respondents cited listening to podcasts as a form of informal learning that they did with their device, and one respondent described downloading audio books in support of informal learning.

Participants used readily available applications to locate and download text-based information, mentioning tools such as Avantgo, Plucker, and News feeds. AvantGo allows users to register and select from a variety of information services. Information services include newspapers, weather reports, maps, traffic reports, medical details, and foreign language and English dictionaries. Having subscribed to the services, the latest news, weather, etc., gets downloaded to the mobile device automatically when it is synchronized with a PC or laptop. Information obtained in this way varied from reference material such as topic specific web sites and wikipedia (a freely available collaborative web-based encyclopedia) to up-to-date news.

Many of the learning activities described were built around the ability to read the information using the handheld device whilst in some transitory location where other information resources are not readily available. Learners tended to identify a period of time when their usual information sources were unavailable, often when in transit, and load information onto their mobile device in advance. Learners would download e-books, course material, web pages, or papers. These examples illustrate one of the key advantages of mobile devices – their portability and ability to store large amounts of information in a relatively small package.

Some participants described another approach to using the Web. Rather than downloading information that they could read anywhere, anytime, they downloaded information related to a particular place and event. Information could be researched in advance, for example, downloading maps and tourist information before a planned visit. This usage of a mobile device to store reference material for use when visiting places of interest parallels formal research scenarios such as the electronically guided museum visits described by Hsi (2003).

Administrative Activities

PDAs have their origins as organizational devices and Smartphones have inherited this functionality with 84 per cent of survey participants using the Calendar/Contacts functionality on a daily basis.

Interactive Activities

Where software that would support their learning was available, informal learners made use of it. Applications included wine tasting and charting software, as well as applications for tracking diet, fitness, and astronomical charts. Where the software was not available, some learners were prepared to adapt existing applications, or produce new applications themselves. One participant devised an ingenious way to combine the notes application and the voice-recording in order to support his language learning. He first wrote the question on the note or "front side of the flashcard." Then he made an audio recording which he associated with the note as the "back side of the flashcard." The link to the recording was right next to the text so that he could read the text, say his answer, and then check it against the voice-recorded correct answer. Another participant wrote an onboard compiler as well as most of his applications directly on his device, a hobby which he described as "a never ending learning process in programming knowledge." His ultimate informal learning goal was to write a compiler.

Many mobile device users do not have this level of expertise, but it seems that acquiring a mobile device can trigger device-related learning.

Microworld Applications

Microworlds did not seem to be a category well suited to informal learning since it required the creation of an application that models a real-world domain. No informal learning that would fit into this category was described.

Conclusion

The results of this study suggest that this population of mobile device users use their devices to support a wide range of informal learning activities, both intentional and unintentional. The portability, storage capacity, computing power, and convenience of mobile devices emerged as determining factors in learners' decisions to use them to support informal learning activities. The fact that people generally carried their devices around with them meant that they were "on hand" to support serendipitous learning opportunities as well as planned mobile learning activities.

The decision to survey expert mobile device users bypassed many of the device usability issues that characterized previous studies (Waycott 2004), (Smørdal and Gregory 2003), (Commarford 2004). For example, the survey participants did not use any one method of data entry (thumbpad, soft keypad, letter recognition, external keyboard) in preference to the others. Instead, participants adapted to the data entry method that worked best for them, with 64 per cent of respondents reporting that they found it "quite easy" or "very easy" on a five-point Likert scale to enter data into their device. When asked how easy they found it to read from the screen, 95 per cent responded "quite easy" or "very easy." Participants adapted to the mobile interface, and evolved ways to integrate the power, storage, and connectivity offered by their PDAs and smartphones with their informal learning processes.

A more surprising finding was the extent to which some participants adapted their devices to suit their learning needs, writing new applications or tailoring existing ones, and adapted how they learned to suit the functionality available with their devices. These adaptations seem to be a step beyond the simple process of appropriation of PDAs as workplace and learning tools as described by Waycott (2004). Waycott defined appropriation as the integration of a new technology into the user's activities, and her analysis showed that the process of adapting these new tools to every day practice was a two way procedure. Prior expectations and personal preferences shaped the ways that users encorporated the technology into their activities, but the tools also change the user's activities. For example, in Waycott's studies participants who were touch-typists coped with the usability constraints of the PDA by using it with a foldout keyboard or as an adjunct to their desktop computer. This adaptation made it easier for them to enter text into the PDA and enabled them to fit the use of the PDA into their every-day preferred practice. In this study some participants went to great lengths to tailor their use of their mobile device to fulfil their learning goals. The participant who combined text and audio to support his language learning invested a considerable amount of time and effort in adapting the notes application to support his language learning needs. The participants who downloaded material in advance of planned visits had taken the explicit decision to use their mobile device as a learning resource in a mobile context.

The Patten et al. (2006) functional framework was helpful in classifying the responses, but some branches of the framework were difficult to map onto the reported informal learning activities, and some of the activities seemed to fit in more than one branch of the framework. This may be because informal learners have the freedom to explore the learning potential of their devices unconstrained by formal learning goals, or it could be because the survey sample of enthusiastic and successful mobile device users had already overcome technical and usability problems that sometimes inhibit learners in formal mobile learning contexts.

Collaboration emerged as a key theme, although one that was relatively unrecognized as such by the participants. The functional framework defines collaborative applications as those that encourage knowledge sharing. However, some of the data collection, referential and location aware activities described by the informal learners also involved knowledge sharing. This meant that there was some overlap between the categories, with certain learning activities having both an "individual" and a "collaborative" element. The functional framework may need to be adapted to suit the range of informal learning activities evident in the data.

Information sharing and knowledge construction through contributions to web forums and wikis were often described as forms of collaborative learning, with 17 per cent of participants using their mobile device to post and read messages in asynchronous forums or conferences. Other popular ways of sharing information using mobile devices included infrared beam (41 per cent) and bluetooth (33 per cent). Participation in forums and wikis as well as the more diary-like activity of blogging is gaining popularity. As GPRS connection costs fall, as more phones offer WiFi, and as WiFi hotspots become more common, future research into mobile learning needs to take account of the role of mobile technology in supporting collaborative and constructivist learning over a wider geographical and social context.

Location aware activities seemed relatively under-represented in the data. However, more mobile devices are coming onto the market with GPS capabilities, and it is likely that location awareness will play a greater role in informal learning as learners adopt and adapt their mobile device functions to suit their informal learning needs in the future.

Enthusiasm for using mobile devices came across in many of the text responses. The following example is typical of both the content and the length of many of the descriptions of informal learning with mobile devices: "Researching further about geography or science topics I've read about at online sites (Amazon Bore surfing; parasitic creatures). Learning about obscure and/or specific details and terms such as the exact term for a castrated male 'cow' (bullock)... could be classified as 'research related to settling a bet'! Learning new language uses such as urban slang, web chat acronyms, etc. Learning about technology (pdastreet.com forums, MS Windows program shortcuts and how-tos, etc.)." The participants in this survey were selected because they were keen mobile device users, so this finding may not be reflected among less enthusiastic members of the current mobile device using population. However as mobile connected technology becomes increasingly ubiquitous, it is likely that growing numbers of mobile device owners will employ their devices as learning tools.

References

CHEN, Y., T. KAO, and J. SHEU. 2003. A mobile learning system for scaffolding bird watching learning. *Journal of Computer Assisted Learning* 19 (3):347-59.

COMMARFORD, P. M. 2004. An investigation of text throughput speeds associated with pocket PC input method editors. *International Journal of Human-computer Interaction* 17 (3):293-309.

DIGIANO, C., L. YARNALL, C. PATTON, J. ROSCHELLE, D. TATAR, and M. MANLEY. 2003. Conceptual tools for planning for the wireless classroom. *Journal of Computer Assisted Learning* 19 (3):284-97.

HSI, H. 2003. A study of user experiences mediated by nomadic web content in a museum. *Journal of Computer Assisted Learning* 19 (3):308-19.

LIVINGSTON, D. 2000. *Exploring the icebergs of adult learning: Findings of the first Canadian survey of informal learning practices.* http://tortoise.oise.utoronto.ca/~dlivingstone/icebergs/ (accessed November 10, 2006).

PATTEN, B., I. ARNEDILLO SANCHEZ, and B. TANGNEY. 2006. Designing collaborative, constructionist and contextual applications for handheld devices. *Computers & Education* 46 (3):294-308.

ROSCHELLE. 2003. Unlocking the learning value of wireless mobile devices. *Journal of Computer Assisted Learning* 12 (3):260-72.

SMØRDAL, O., and J. GREGORY. 2003. Personal Digital Assistants in medical education and practice. *Journal of Computer Assisted Learning* 19:320-29.

TOUGH, A. 1979. *The adult's learning projects.* 2nd ed. Toronto: Ontario Institute for Studies in Education.

VAVOULA, G. 2004. *KLeOS: A knowledge and learning organisation system in support of lifelong learning.* PhD diss., University of Birmingham.

VAVOULA, G., E. SCANLON, P. LONSDALE, M. SHARPLES, and A. JONES. 2005. *Report on empirical work with mobile learning and literature on mobile learning in science* (No. D33.2).

WAYCOTT, J. 2004. *The appropriation of PDAs as learning and workplace tools: An activity theory perspective.* PhD diss., Open University, Milton Keynes, UK.

M-learning: Positioning Educators for a Mobile, Connected Future[6]

KRISTINE PETERS
FLINDERS UNIVERSITY
AUSTRALIA

Abstract

Mobile learning is variously viewed as a fad, a threat, and an answer to the learning needs of time-poor mobile workers, but does it have a place in delivering mainstream learning? Based on a 2005 comparative research project commissioned by the Australian Flexible Learning Framework, this chapter reports on research into web based information about the use of mobile technologies for commerce and learning, which was then tested through twenty-nine interviews with manufacturers of mobile devices, individuals involved in other businesses, and education providers. The research found that mobile technologies were in common use in some commercial sectors, but their use purely for learning

6. Originally published in the *International Review on Research in Open and Distance Learning (IRRODL)* 8, no. 2. This article is subject to Creative Commons License 2.5 (c) 2007. The original article is published at: http://www.irrodl.org/index.php/irrodl/article/view/348/873. Reproduced with permission of Athabasca University – Canada's Open University.

was rare. However, m-learning lends itself to new methods of delivery that are highly suited to the "just enough, just in time, and just for me" demands of twenty-first century learners.

Introduction

A distinguishing feature of our society at the beginning of the twenty-first century is the rapid rate of technological and social change. Technological advancements that allow fast communications and information processing are supporting new social patterns. As a result, communities are no longer only based on geographical proximity, and new "tribes" (Rheingold 2002) are developing and disbanding according to interest, work patterns, and opportunity.

Mobile information and communication technologies are important enablers of the new social structure. We are experiencing the first generation of truly portable information and communications technology (ICT) with the relatively recent advent of small, portable mobile devices that provide telephone, Internet, and data storage and management in products such as: i-Mate, O2, Palm, HP, and Bluetooth (all registered trademarks) that combine mobile telephony, removable memory chips, diaries, email, Web, basic word processing and spreadsheets, and data input, storage, and transfer.

The communication and data transfer possibilities created by mobile technologies (m-technologies) can significantly reduce dependence on fixed locations for work and study, and thus have the potential to revolutionize the way we work and learn. A mobile, connected society, however, creates new training delivery challenges. Individuals expect training that is "just in time, just enough and just for me" (Rosenberg 2001), and that can be delivered and supported outside of traditional classroom settings (Peters and Lloyd 2003).

In order to support a strategic response to the opportunities and demands of mobile learners, the education and training sector needs to be informed about the actual use of mobile devices at work and in workplace learning, and about potential future trends in mobile learning. This chapter is based on research commissioned in 2005 by the Australian Flexible Learning Framework, which aimed to provide a better understanding of the separation between real opportunities for mobile learning using small electronic communication devices (m-learning) and the hype surrounding the introduction of new technologies. The research provided an overview of popular media coverage of the use of m-technologies and m-learning, and compared this with the findings from a small number of qualitative interviews. A short review of the academic literature was conducted, but the need for a contemporary perspective meant that there were very few research articles on m-learning available and, therefore, limited reference has been made to peer-reviewed academic publications. As the key aim of the research was to separate the hype from the reality, the focus was on providing a snapshot of mobile technologies and their use. Indeed, a completely new generation of mobile communication devices (3G cell or mobile telephones) became available during the six months of research for this project, thus illustrating the challenge of maintaining publishing currency in a fast-moving field.

An Introduction to m-learning

The availability of mobile and wireless devices is enabling different ways of communicating. Mobile communications are no longer restricted to companies that can afford large investment in hardware or specialized software. Individuals now have easy and inexpensive access to mobile telephony, and the cost of mobile access to the Internet is steadily being reduced. Mobile technologies have enabled a new way of communicating, typified by young people, for whom mobile communications are part of normal daily interaction, who are "always on" and connected to geographically-dispersed friendship groups in "tribal" communities of interest.

This research aimed to test the validity of news and information media comment on mobile communications, which indicated that the "always on" generation is, to a large degree, driving the development of consumer communication technologies – as can be seen from the rapid adoption of Short Message Service (SMS). SMS is texting via mobile phones – also known in some countries as cell phones – which was unexpectedly adopted by the "text" generation, and became a pervasive communication tool in its own right. The popular and business press also reported that mobile and professional employees are driving the convergence of Personal Data Assistants (PDAs), telephony, and of "smart" phones (that provide both telephone and Internet services) through their demand for greater integration of online information, data management, and voice, image, and text communications. The same source shows that industries with specialist needs (such as mobile barcode readers in supermarkets and electronic courier delivery confirmations) are another significant driver of mobile product development.

The three drivers described above – consumers (particularly young consumers), mobile professionals, and specialist industries – have created strong demand, which is reflected in the increasing rapidity of development of new mobile communication and data management technologies. The trend toward convergence of applications, the ubiquitousness of mobile phones, and the continuing demand for smaller, more powerful devices indicates that mobile technologies are, indeed, mainstream. Is their use for learning, however, following the same trend?

The advent of mobile technologies has created opportunities for delivery of learning via devices such as PDAs, mobile phones, laptops, and PC tablets (laptops designed with a handwriting interface). Collectively, this type of delivery is called m-learning. While m-learning can be thought of as a subset of e-learning (which is web-based delivery of content and learning management), the emerging potential of mobile technologies tends to indicate that m-learning, while mostly situated within the e-learning framework, also has links directly to the "just enough, just in time, just for me" model of flexible learning (see Figure 1), and is therefore just one of a suite of options that can be adapted to suit individual learning needs.

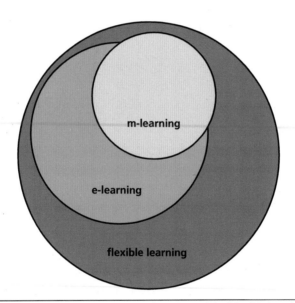

FIGURE 1 The "just enough, just in time, just for me" model of flexible learning.

Literature Review

Much of the documented evidence of m-learning in this chapter has been sourced from www.flexiblelearning.net.au, the Australian website that supports the flexible delivery of, and practice improvements in, vocational education and training. While peer-reviewed academic journals are a preferred source of material, the constraints of this research project (primarily the requirement to find out what was actually happening at the time the research was undertaken), and the funding body perspective (that m-learning projects undertaken under the Australian Flexible Learning Framework should inform the research) determined that the outcome would be a report that provided guidance to future scholarly investigation, rather than one that contributed to the formal literature. The following discussion, therefore, is largely based on the informal literature.

M-learning as a Practical Training Solution in Mobile Workplaces

Klopfer, Squire, Holland, and Jenkins (2002) propose that mobile devices (handheld computers) "produce unique educational affordances," which are:

a) Portability

b) Social interactivity

c) Context sensitivity, the ability to "gather data unique to the current location, environment, and time, including both real and simulated data"

d) Connectivity, to data collection devices, other handhelds, and to networks

e) Individuality, a "unique scaffolding" that can be "customized to the individual's path of investigation"

The 2005 web search found that organizations of all sizes were using mobile devices for learning because technological advances meant that there was no longer the need for large infrastructure and support costs, and even small enterprises could deliver mobile learning simply by structuring learning around web-based content that could be accessed from web-enabled mobile devices.

Work by Marcus Ragus (2004a) for an Australian Flexible Learning Framework New Practices in Flexible Learning Project tested the use of PDAs in four different work environments: botanical gardens, nursing home, food and hospitality, and workplace assessor. The Royal Tasmanian Botanical Gardens trial found that simultaneous personal development for staff in separate organizations was possible, and that such strategies can be designed and targeted for a mixed audience comprising managers, teachers, ground staff, and apprentices. The nursing home trial used integration of PDAs into the general on-site training of the nursing staff through the use of simple resources created with Microsoft PowerPoint (Ragus 2004a). The food and hospitality sector trials grew from a need to develop interesting, interactive resources for use by trainee bar and beverage staff, and demonstrated the application of an existing PDA image program to create a learning resource (the importance of this project was that special software was not required). Workplace assessment practice trials were undertaken within the horticulture sector, the aim of which was to use PDAs and a peripheral plug-in camera to capture evidence of assessment at remote workplaces where it is imperative that both assessors and learners are able to operate with a high degree of flexibility for delivery of learning, and for the materials and equipment required for the work (Ragus 2004a).

Many other m-learning applications were identified, perhaps best exemplified by Deviney and von Koschembahr (2004) who describe a mobile learning program to train new sales associates for a major electronics retailer. In this organization, new employees had previously spent several hours off the job reading materials or accessing a learning portal to study products; because learning was abstracted, the quality and usefulness of this type of learning was limited. Using m-technologies, the retailer was able to equip staff with a handheld PDA and bar-code scanner, and employees were able to learn about products on the sales floor where the learning was situated within the context of their job.

Lundin and Magnusson (2003, p. 19) saw mobile technologies as a solution to the fragmentation of a mobile workforce: "within a distributed and mobile workforce opportunistic meetings with colleagues are naturally less likely to occur than if workers are co-located" (citing Bellotti and Bly 1996). Here mobile technologies provided synchronous communications that enabled connectivity between workers in real time and thus overcame many of the barriers created by mobility.

M-learning and the Teacher-Student Relationship

The digital age has created a new relationship between teachers and learners. Research conducted by the London School of Economics found that children are typically the Internet experts in the family, and described this situation as a "lasting reversal of the generation gap" (Smithers 2003, p. 1). This reflects the challenges facing education and training providers who are steeped in traditional delivery styles when confronted with digitally literate students, where, rather than simply receiving and memorizing the wisdom of their elders, which has been the tradition for millennia, students are now demanding training that meets their specific information needs. Dale Spender, renowned feminist scholar, writer, and consultant, whose work includes exploration of the social effects of new technologies, observed that there is a divide between traditional teaching techniques and the attitudes of contemporary youth. Spender's observation (personal communication, September 30,

2005) reinforces the divide between traditional teaching and the attitudes of contemporary youth. Eight year olds think there's something wrong with their teachers. Don't teachers know that heads are unreliable places? That's what the save key is for. Even if you do store things in your head, you can't ever find them again.

M-learning also creates learning opportunities that are significantly different to those provided by e-learning (at a desktop) or paper-based distance learning. Chen and colleagues (as cited in Bridgland and Blanchard 2005) describe the principal considerations to be taken into account when designing m-learning delivery:

- The urgency of the learning need
- The need for knowledge acquisition
- The mobility of the learning setting
- The interactivity of the learning process
- The situatedness of the instructional activities
- The integration of instructional content

Young people do not experience geographical place and time as barriers (Fannon 2004). Fannon's research found that although some older learners used their mobile phones to arrange face-to-face meetings to work on assignments or discuss learning issues, younger learners were more comfortable with the thought of using mobile phones for learning, and almost half (45 per cent) of the research group were prepared to use Internet-enabled telephones as their only tool for learning. However, the challenges of creating learning to be delivered via mobile phones are not easily solved by teachers, many of whom are recent "migrants" to the digital world (Prensky 2001).

Dale Spender expressed concern about the ability of teachers to understand and respond to digital learning opportunities, citing the aging teacher population and their lack of comfort with digital ICTs, the focus on teaching and memorizing as opposed to learning and seeking information, and reliance on doing it by the book. This approach is fundamentally different to the approach of "digital natives," Prensky's (2001) term for those born in the digital age for whom ICT is second nature, for whom "not knowing is an impetus to find out," and who believe that if you need to use the manual, the product is no good. Spender's position is reinforced by Aquino's (n.d., p. 9) observation: "Teaching has a long established culture of individualism and secretiveness and many teachers are very challenged by the need to work collaboratively with technicians, web developers, instructional designers and programmers to deliver successful web-based education."

Many teachers are interested and able, however, to provide m-learning content, learning management, and support. The following examples illustrate how m-learning is being used and supported:

- Environmental Detectives is an example of an increasing suite of games designed for mobile devices. Students played the role of environmental engineers presented with a scenario in which the spread of a toxin was simulated on a location-aware Pocket PC equipped with a Global Positioning System (GPS). The Pocket PC allowed students to investigate a toxic spill by sampling chemicals in the groundwater and responding to different variables programmed by the teacher (Klopfer et al. 2002). The use of virtual characters within the program allowed students to gain an experience that is close to real life, provided context, significantly reduced abstraction, and resulted in a blurring between the game and real life. For instance, in an unanticipated event, one group stopped in the middle of the game and used Google to search for clues. Not only was the strategy of accessing other outside resources deemed acceptable within the rules, it was perhaps advisable given the time constraints and use of authentic chemicals and historical data. Students were able to locate information quickly and easily on Google, suggesting the role that a tool such as Google can play in transforming an educational experience.

- In designing Melbourne Law School's new building (built in 2002), a key feature was the provision of wireless networking that allowed students with mobile computing devices to access course material and conduct searches of legal databases during class, thus expanding the depth of the discussion and the learning experience for the student (Hartnell-Young and Jones 2004).

- The medical field has applied mobile technology to remote learning in rural health education. Hartnell-Young and Jones (2004) described the use of Tablet PCs that helped students to capture and store confidential patient information, and deliver just-in-time information on clinical problems. Students kept a reflective journal using their mobile device, which was later used as a reference for discussion with their instructors.

- Zurita and Nussbaum (2004) demonstrated the effectiveness of handheld devices in teaching first-grade children to construct words from syllables. In a month-long controlled experiment, children who were supported with technology had significantly higher word construction test score improvements than children who were using paper-based activities.

- These examples of good practice, and of m-learning in the field, are by no means isolated; however, the widespread adoption of m-learning is still some way off, and the application of m-learning requires a new paradigm. Indeed, as Aquino (n.d., p. 5) reflects, learning is "emotionally based and consistently and powerfully influenced by the learner's culture and experience," and traditional teaching methodologies that are "essentially passive, theoretical, text-based and linear" will fail to engage young learners and fail to deliver the skills needed for future social and work environments.

M-learning and Learning Cultures in Workplaces

Is the promise of mobile technologies a trigger to generate learning cultures realistic? And is m-learning any more likely to increase interest in learning than any other form of delivery? Articles about the link between mobile technologies and learning organizations appear to fall into three categories:

1. A database focus that captures organizational knowledge
2. A human systems focus that allows synchronous communication and information sharing at the worksite
3. A learning development focus that suggests that learning about new technologies generates a more general drive for learning

The database focus has, to a large degree, become the accepted wisdom in organizations that use structured processes to collect, codify, and manage knowledge. Mobile technologies have the potential to collect a greater range and percentage of data, through recording of activity on the device (and subsequent analysis of the patterns of access to specific information or information sources) and through the reduction of paper-based records as electronic systems replace paper in the field.

The capacity of mobile technology to deliver synchronous communication and knowledge-sharing can provide benefits to human (or soft) systems. Evidence of these benefits has been reported by Ragus (2004a), who found that m-learning encouraged simultaneous personal development, such as networking and socialisation, outside of normal working groups – an unexpected, and positive result of the m-learning trials.

The "learning tools leads to learning culture" concept is more tenuous and has received limited attention in the m-learning literature. However, the industry participants in Ragus' (2004b) New Practices Project found that m-learning had generated new ideas for the incorporation of technology in the workplace, which indicates an enthusiasm for further learning introduced through the m-learning experience.

Brodsky (2003) looks at drivers in learning organizations and concludes that the trend toward customer self service (such as automated options for telephone enquiries, or online payment or registration of service needs) will result in changes to the nature of customer service training. Brodsky suggests that the automation of routine transactions means that as the role of customer service or sales staff changes, there is greater need to manage complex transactions with a higher level of knowledge and interaction skills. As a result, training technologies will become so intuitive that the technology will no longer be the focus ; instead the focus will be on how the application serves the needs of the business.

The literature described a range of uses of m-technologies for learning, some of which were in the trial stages, and others where mobile devices are in common or daily use, and are accepted as a normal part of learning. To what degree did the experience of Australian businesses and education and training providers reflect the findings from the literature? This question will be answered in the description of research results in the next section.

The purpose of the research was to provide an indication of whether Australian businesses are actually using m-technologies and m-learning in the ways portrayed by the popular media. Originally intended to form the basis of a discussion paper for vocational education practitioners, the research brief did not require rigorous investigation or statistically valid samples. This chapter reports on the findings of that (limited) research, framed by the literature, using interviews to establish the status of m-technology use and m-learning uptake. Interviews were conducted with twenty-nine respondents representing Australian businesses that use mobile technologies, manufacturers of mobile devices and software developers for mobile applications, and educational and training institutions.

The following criteria were used to determine whether devices were within the scope of the research: 1). Capable of providing electronic communication and/ or information functions; 2). Small enough to be easily carried; 3). Can be used (at least part of the time) without a physical connection to fixed power or telecommunications services.

The following section of the chapter describes the method and findings.

Method

Based on the findings from the literature search, three survey instruments were developed: software manufacturer/developer, business, and educational provider. Four manufacturer/developers were interviewed: two working for large international corporations (Nokia and PalmAustralasia), and two developers of software for mobile devices. Six businesses were interviewed, including large national corporations, medium sized firms, and small companies. Nineteen educational providers (n = 19) were interviewed, representing universities, high schools, private training providers, TAFE (the largest public provider of vocational education and training in Australia), and industry skills councils (the organizations that determine the content of national vocational curriculum).

The manufacturer survey instrument contained questions about the use of mobile technologies for business and personal purposes, product uses that were not an expected part of the product design, drivers of new product development (specifically whether designs responded to requests by particular customer demographic groups), future trends for mobile technologies, and whether mobile devices were being produced specifically for educational use. Interviews were carried out by the author's company, KPPM Organisational Strategists, during the period May to July 2005.

The business survey instrument investigated mobile technologies used as part of normal business processes, whether mobile technologies contributed to business efficiencies and greater productivity, the value of mobile technologies to the business, and the use of m-technologies for learning.

Education providers were asked whether m-technologies were discussed by students and teachers, what (if any) mobile technologies were in use as learning aids, whether m-technologies presented opportunities for new types of delivery or management of learning, and the type of student most likely to use m-technologies for a variety of learning purposes (such as communicating with peers or teachers, doing research, or timeshifting lectures).

Results

Business interviews

A search of the print media and Internet revealed a steady stream of new mobile technologies aimed at a wide range of markets. Small mobile communications and storage devices were advertized for applications as wide-ranging as risk assessment, triage, fire inspection, bylaw enforcement, building inspection, city engineering, security, surveillance, and military purposes. These findings were tested through the interviews with businesses, which revealed that (despite the low number of respondents), a range of technologies were used, with the most common being laptops, mobile phones, PDAs, and portable media players.

An example of how m-technologies were being used in business was provided by South Australia's Department of Transport, Energy, and Infrastructure, which was implementing mobile communications for traffic signal maintenance workers. They reported that field staff had previously been using laptops, but had to wait until they were back at the office to update data. The introduction of communications cards enabled real-time communication through automatic redirection of fault logs straight from signal switchboards to field worker laptops. This process also allowed the capture of fault and repair data, which needed to be recorded for legal reasons. Mobile phones were considered for this task, but did not have the bandwidth to deliver sufficient data at the required speed.

Has the use of mobile technologies increased business efficiency? Businesses saw significant benefits from mobile technologies. The following list shows common business efficiencies from the use of m-technologies:

- Flexibility, speed, and more efficient networking, which allows access to large numbers of staff throughout the world
- Provision of efficient customer service
- A more efficient working environment, with less manual paperwork – work can be done faster, more flexibly, and with greater levels of accessibility
- More efficient training, saving time to inform staff about new products and processes
- Improved storage and backup of data, with much of the risk removed
- Saving of time and money
- Creating greater responsiveness to change.

Respondents reported that these outcomes were based on carefully thought-through business cases that considered markets, productivity, professional development, staff morale, risk management, knowledge management, cost, and responsiveness to a dynamic operating environment. For example, one wrote, "If we moved offices again we would commit to 100 per cent wireless network. It makes more sense as we have a lot of core infrastructure already in place. This would also allow flexibility to increase PDA use which would result in increased access to email from outside the office, and automatic synchronising of remote data with the server."

The value of mobile technologies was further tested by asking scaled questions about business benefits in four categories: finance, staff satisfaction, competitive edge, and business culture. The highest ratings were for financial and business culture, but all categories rated at least 4 out of 5 as can be seen in Table 1.

TABLE 1 Business benefits of m-technology use

Category	Mean rating
The value of mobile technologies in creating a business culture that values new knowledge	4,6
The financial value of mobile technologies to the organisation	4,6
The value of mobile technologies to staff satisfaction	4,1
The value of mobile technology in establishing a competitive edge	4,0

Businesses saw the next evolution of mobile technology applications for their businesses to be:

- Greater choice in hardware, resulting in a better fit between commercially available devices and the needs of individual businesses
- More customers using phones, PDAs, Internet, and email to order and make bookings
- Blended training with an increased proportion of learning delivered on mobile devices
- Faster, more efficient technology as part of a normal work environment
- Simulated and interactive training using games to teach problem solving and resolve issues
- Convergence of technologies and increased use of devices that can do more than one thing
- Increase in wireless hotspots to provide improved access to the Internet from outside the standard work environment, so that workers are not restricted when travelling
- 100 per cent mobile

As one responded noted, "It's a great benefit to be totally mobile – efficient and faster – however at this stage it is not a core part of our business. It is important in terms of safety that we get the information out there quickly and efficiently. Moving towards more mobile technologies would be a really good influence in changing the whole culture of this business."

Education and Training Interviews

Interviews with the education and training providers showed that less than half engaged in discussions with students about the use of mobile technologies for learning, despite the high level student use of mobile phones. A public training provider commented, "The topic that is becoming more frequent is how to get access to learning without coming into the classroom, and what mobile technology could be used to receive and store information."

Approximately half of the educational providers said that the use of mobile technologies for learning was a frequent topic of discussion with teaching staff. Some observations expressed in their comments included:

- M-technology is being discussed more because the organization is forcing it to become an issue.
- Change is happening, but the first task is to learn about and understand how to use the technologies.
- The most common discussion is about the development of mobile technologies within industry.

Providers were asked about student readiness for mobile technologies. The most common mobile technology is the mobile telephone, so it was interesting to see what the following seven providers thought about student readiness for using mobile phones for learning:

- Mobile phones are mainly used to SMS parents regarding attendance and other communications.
- Students already have mobile phones and it would be good if they were used more for learning.
- Students have mobile phones although PDAs are not as popular. Providers are less concerned with the device that students use, than with what they do with it.
- Some colleges already use mobile phones for communicating with students using text reminders.
- SMS is already in place but the opportunities to use it for learning have not been considered in great depth – implementation will largely depend on practicalities and cost.
- Resourceful teachers are incorporating SMS because young people are using it anyway, it's a great motivational tool.
- m-learning is ideally suited to adult education if it is used to extend the reach of programs. It allows students to get a response quickly, at all hours, they like the interactivity and the ability to receive a quicker response than they would via email.

A number of educators mentioned that cost is a barrier; the following four quotes are good examples:

- Laptops enable students to dock into the student network, however these are not widely accepted because of cost.
- More students would like laptops and wireless technology, but there is a cost constraint in providing the equipment.

- If all students already owned laptops, PDAs, or mobile phones, it would be easier to use them for learning; but providers cannot ask students to buy them because the cost would exclude some people.
- Teachers would like to use PDAs and laptops, but the problem is resources to develop materials and provide support, and the infrastructure is lacking.

How ready are students for m-technologies other than mobile phones? The five quotes below provide some telling clues:

- Students are already using laptops, but are looking for more wireless options.
- Students are ready for SMS and PDA to access learning objects and assessment pieces.
- PDAs are provided to students to do tests.
- Students are ready for greater use of 3G mobile phones and pocket PCs/organizers, which are already being used for communication because of their flexibility and portability.
- Students use laptops for general learning, mobile phones for downloads from the Internet and general learning, and a few who travel long distances use MP3 players to download lectures.

One regional provider found that students were not ready for mobile technologies, but felt that workplaces were ready. Teacher readiness for mobile learning is seen as a barrier by a number of providers. The following three quotes are examples of this:

- It all depends on the teachers and some have not yet mastered desktop technologies! The teachers are a critical part of this, and some are not ready. Only a small percentage of classroom teachers use PDAs and they are mainly for personal use, although some have used them as a teaching tool.
- A recent survey of our teachers found that 2 per cent had never turned on a PC, 5 per cent could not burn to CDROM and there is no use of ICT for general teaching, although some ICT-based communications are done on an individual, personal basis.
- Not a lot of teachers use mobile technologies. PDA is an executive tool, although mobile phones are ubiquitous.

On the other hand, others found mobile technologies to be beneficial. The following three quotes from workers illustrate this:

- Mobile technologies are being developed for field work, primarily to communicate with the office.

- We use mobile phones to edit our newsletter.
- The availability of m-technologies presented opportunities for new types of delivery and management of learning.

Seven education and training providers reported that m-technologies:
- Make teachers think – the thought process is often hard to change and using new technologies seems to help.
- Overcome geographic barriers; m-learning removes the problem of locality and the requirement that students travel to access learning.
- Offer greater flexibility for staff and students.
- Allow learners to learn in the field, where and when they want. However, mobile phones are not a huge teaching tool, as the students use them mainly for social contact and do not want to use them as a learning tool.
- Force providers to rethink the way that they teach: We need to break down the elements of the course into small packages based on mobile technology so that students can access portable learning, learning activities, and multiple choice games from their mobile units.
- Provide a faster way of informing students (using SMS) and flexible delivery that is not bound to computer so we can engage across physical space.
- Enable situated learning or learning in context, using phones with cameras/video capabilities to enable students to capture their own material and instantaneously transfer to other students and lecturers. Mobile phones are also used as tools for group learning.

Education and training providers were asked about learning outcomes. Their responses show that they understand the pedagogical opportunities provided by m-learning, which is seen to:
- Help to break down the financial and mobility constraints of learning.
- Improve literacy through collection and provision of evidence for assessment portfolios.
- Enable the use of digital story-telling to demonstrate competence.
- Provide faster, more exciting ways of teaching, more flexibility, and more mobility.
- Allow for full qualifications to be delivered via mobile devices.

In many organizations, m-Learning is yet to be structured into the curriculum; the following six quotes illustrate this:
- The uptake of m-learning depends on the teacher and the curriculum coordinator.

- It is experimental at moment, providers are looking at all ways to deliver subjects, so that students can choose how they would like to learn.
- The education of school teachers about m-learning needs to come first. Teachers need to understand the benefits of letting students use mobile devices for learning. At this stage, teachers are still very negative about students using mobile phones in the classroom other than for contacting parents at home time.
- m-learning needs to fit within a whole matrix of curriculum and assessment, the positioning of this mode of delivery needs to be thought through before it is implemented.
- We are just starting to look at mobile technologies, which are regarded as a new area within e-learning.
- The uptake of the technology at the workplace is the prime driver of m-learning.

Only two respondents said that m-learning was already in place in their organizations, and both were delivering learning to remote communities:

- m-Learning is not formally included in courses, but students would experience it in most subjects.
- m-Learning is structured into remote teaching so that all students have access to learning without having to come into the campus. m-learning provides financial savings because we don't have to provide physical space for all students. However, issues such as whether m-Learning allows higher quotas for courses and how to structure lecturers' pay are still to be resolved.

Manufacturers and Software Developers

Because of the limited number of interviews with manufacturers and software developers, the findings have been grouped as follows:

- First, producers of hardware and operating systems often minimize costs and maximize effect through product development partnerships.
- Second, demand from consumers and businesses is the influence on the type of product being developed, with the common requests being: easier to use, smaller, faster, smarter, and greater security. This has resulted in advancements such as multiple security layers, Bluetooth, car and business kits, hands free and infrared data cables. When asked about the future applications or capabilities that are planned for existing products, the response was: "smaller, faster, better, cheaper, and more wireless technology to send bigger files faster."

What percentage of mobile technology is purchased for business purposes and what percentage is purchased for consumer use? The following quote tells the story:

- There is such a cross-over between personal and business use we're unable to tell them apart. Higher end products (i.e., Bluetooth or wireless, products with extra security, or products containing enterprise solutions) are marketed only to business clients, but the simplest phone can be used for business as well as personal purposes.

Much is made of the potential of m-learning, but what is actually happening from a developer perspective? The two following quotes illustrate the developers' insights:

- A Flash-based mobile interface is now being produced for m-learning, so that animated material can be used on mobile phones; the technology is now moving quickly to respond to the increasing speed of m-learning uptake.

- As an add-on to other modes of deliver, m-Learning will increase. But it won't replace other forms of e-education because screens are too small and hard to read, and if you make them bigger, the device isn't as mobile. m-Learning is most useful when it's in a mobile, field environment.

Conclusion

The key features of mobile learning identified in this chapter are its ability to provide learning that is "just in time, just enough, and just for me," learning that is situated (typically in the field or at the workplace), and learning that is contextualized through mediation with peers and teachers. While mobile devices are making some types of learning easier to access, they have the potential to deliver the kind of learning that in past times could only be done with a knowledgeable tutor working on-site, alongside the student. Clearly tutors are too expensive to provide en masse, but mobile technologies provide the capability for training that can be tailored to the needs of the individual learner and diverse worksites.

Is this hype, or is it actually happening? Informal learning using mobile technologies is already embedded in our daily lives. Millions of web-enabled phones are being used by learners (who may not be enrolled in formal courses) to seek information. Use of mobile phones, PDAs, and laptops in organizations is well-established, and interviews with employers indicate that m-learning is occurring at the workplace, although the focus tends to be on business needs rather than the technology used for delivery.

Many education and training providers recognize the benefits of mobile learning, but there appears to be limited adoption for educational use, which was attributed to the age and ability of teachers and trainers, the cost of providing m-learning devices and infrastructure, the slow rate of change in large educational institutions, and that mobile devices are not designed with the education market in mind.

With consumers driving the global uptake of mobile telephony, and the growing functionality of these devices, it appears that m-learning does indeed have a place in mainstream education and training. Managing m-learning as a part of a suite of services that offers greater choice to learners will have benefits for providers, because it can allow teachers to move from delivery to the management of learning, and will help learners to gain specific skills of immediate value in the knowledge-based economy.

References

AQUINO, M. n.d. Something to do, not something to learn: Experiential learning via online role play. *Australian Flexible Learning Framework*. http://www.flexiblelearning.net.au/leaders/fl_leaders/fll04/papers/reviewessay_aquino.pdf (accessed March 17, 2007).

BRIDGLAND, A., and P. BLANCHARD. 2005. *Powerful, portable, personal computing: Is m-learning an opportunity in e-learning?* Melbourne: University of Melbourne. http://eprints.infodiv.unimelb.edu.au/archive/00000889/01/bridgland.blanchard.pdf (accessed March 17, 2007).

BRODSKY, M. 2003. E-learning trends today and beyond. *LTi Newsline* (May 7). http://www.ltimagazine.com/ltimagazine/article/articleDetail.jsp?id=56219 (accessed March 17, 2007).

DEVINEY, N., and C. VON KOSCHEMBAHR. 2004. Learning goes mobile. *Human Resource Executive* (March 21). http://www.workindex.com/editorial/train/trn0402-02.asp (accessed July 22, 2005). Editor's Note: This link is no longer available, but it is cited in D. Keegan 2005. Mobile learning: The next generation of learning. *Distance Education International*. http://learning.ericsson.net/mlearning2/files/workpackage5/book.doc (accessed March 17, 2007).

FANNON, K. 2004. Connectedness: Learner perspectives on learning futures. *Australian Flexibile Learning Network: Flex e-News Newsletter*. http://www.flexiblelearning.net.au/newsandevents/Flexenews/ 41/Kate_Res.pdf (accessed September 27, 2005).

HARTNELL-YOUNG, E., and P. JONES. 2004. Mobile law and e-portfolios. *The Knowledge Tree* (October 6). http://knowledgetree.flexiblelearning.net.au/edition06/html/cr_elizabeth_hartnell-young.html (accessed March 17, 2007).

KLOPFER, E., K. SQUIRE, and H. JENKIN. n.d. *Environmental detectives: The development of an augmented reality platform for environmental simulations.* Los Alamitos, CA: IEEE Computer Society Publications.

LUNDIN, J., and M. MAGNUSSON. 2003. Collaborative learning in mobile work. *Journal of Computer Assisted Learning* 19 (3):273-83.

PETERS, K., and C. LLOYD. 2003. Differentiating needs: Customer demand for online learning. *The National Centre for Vocational Education Research (NCVER),* Australian National Training Authority website. http://www.ncver.edu.au/research/proj/nr2f02.pdf (accessed March 17, 2007).

PRENSKY, M. 2001. Digital natives, digital immigrants. *On The Horizon* (NCB University Press) 9, no. 5. http://www.marcprensky.com/writing/Prensky%20-%20Digital%20Natives,%20Digital%20Immigrants%20-%20Part1.pdf (accessed March 17, 2007).

RAGUS, M. 2004a. Mobile learning: Handheld innovations in flexible learning, case studies. *New Practices in Flexible Learning,* Australian Flexible Learning Framework. http://pre2005.flexiblelearning.net.au/projects/mobilelearning.htm (accessed March 17, 2007).

——. 2004b. Mobile learning: Handheld innovations in flexible learning, project report. New Practices in Flexible Learning, Australian Flexible Learning Framework. http://pre2005.flexiblelearning.net.au/projects/mobilelearning.htm (accessed March 17, 2007).

RHEINGOLD, H. 2002. *Smart mobs: The next social revolution.* New York: Basic Books.

ROSENBERG, M. 2001. E-learning: Strategies for delivering knowledge in the digital age. New York: MacGraw-Hill.

SMITHERS, R. 2003. Children are Internet experts. *The Guardian Online* (October 16). http://education.guardian.co.uk/elearning/story/0,,1064034,00.html (accessed March 16, 2007).

SPENDER, D. 2006. Telephone interview with author, September 30.

ZURITA, G., and M. NUSSBAUM. 2004. A constructivist mobile learning environment supported by a wireless handheld network. *Journal of Computer Assisted Learning* 20:235-43. http://www.blackwell-synergy.com/doi/pdf/10.1111/j.1365-2729.2004.00089.x?cookieSet=1 (accessed May 24, 2007).

PART THREE

● ● ●

Applications of Mobile Learning

Practitioners as Innovators: Emergent Practice in Personal Mobile Teaching, Learning, Work, and Leisure

AGNES KUKULSKA-HULME
JOHN PETTIT
INSTITUTE OF EDUCATIONAL TECHNOLOGY
THE OPEN UNIVERSITY
UNITED KINGDOM

Abstract

Mobile devices have become commonplace tools, yet little is known about how individuals use them in their teaching, learning, work, and leisure. We report on an investigation into personal mobile device use by students and alumni from the global master's degree in online and distance education offered by the Institute of Educational Technology at the Open University (UK). The study identified various types of activity undertaken, and focused on emerging issues in relation to innovative practices. Participants described their uses of four types of device, the frequency of specific uses, and their views on the attractions and disadvantages of mobile learning. The chapter is intended to inform those who are interested in the potential of mobile learning, designing learning for a specific type of device, or who own a mobile device and are simply looking to make better use of it in the future.

Introduction

Mobile learning has reached the stage where the "early adopters" and "early majority" (Rogers 2003) are making the use of mobile and wireless technologies visible across a broad range of contexts and applications. At the same time, the technological and social diversification of the field means that it has become much more open to innovation on the part of educators (i.e., practitioners in teaching and training), whereas in the not too distant past it tended to be largely in the preserve of researchers and specialists. Evidence is provided by the availability of case studies that show how educators are taking advantage of mobile learning to bring about significant enhancements and transformations in their teaching practice (see for example JISC 2005; Manolo 2006). Mobile devices have also become commonplace tools serving a wide array of purposes that may include teaching and learning alongside work and leisure, in both formal and informal settings. Consequently learners, too, are often able to contribute more actively to developing innovative educational uses of the technology as they interweave them with other aspects of their lives.

We were interested to find out more about the ways in which those who are engaged in teaching and learning use mobile technologies, particularly in relation to spontaneous learning and teaching practices and the intersection with daily life and work. We were also intrigued by anecdotal evidence that owning and carrying around one or more mobile devices may encourage users towards experimentation, which in turn could lead to innovative uses. Edwards (2005) suggests that users of various mobile devices should try out activities they haven't tried before (such as subscribing to news, accessing location-based content, viewing video and listening to audio), since "the best place to start is by experiencing first-hand what it's like to get the information you need in the format and location you want" (p. 4). Edwards contrasts this informal and user-driven approach with more conventional, formal learning initiatives that don't take into consideration current trends like mobile working and the constraints on people's time.

The project we report on in this chapter was an investigation of how personal mobile devices are used by students and alumni from our Master's Programme in Online and Distance Education (MAODE), offered by the Institute of Educational Technology at the Open University, UK. Students and alumni of this programme are typically experienced practitioners working in the education sector and many of them are keen users of new technology. In 2001-02, a number of students from the programme enjoyed the opportunity to explore the use of mobile devices as part of a research project aimed at understanding their experiences with PDAs provided for reading course materials (Waycott and Kukulska-Hulme 2003). Whilst we believe, along with Ally (2005), that issues of mobile content delivery are very much alive and need a great deal of attention, our more recent focus has been the complementary activity of investigating emergent practice. By emergent practice we mean the ways in which students and alumni use mobile devices as learners and as teachers – spontaneously and autonomously rather than because they have been asked to. We are also interested in the interplay with other areas of their lives such as work and leisure. Edwards (2005) has noted that it is important to think beyond repurposing content for distribution on mobile devices and to focus more on understanding how people communicate, collaborate, and learn.

Our research aims to contribute to the understanding of innovative practice at the level of the individual empowered by a personal mobile device and social networks that may amplify or modify its use. In our roles as disseminators of innovative e-Learning practice both to colleagues and students in our university and externally (as discussed in Kukulska-Hulme 2005), we also aim to use our research to help inform those who are interested in the potential of mobile learning, who are designing learning with a specific type of mobile device in mind, or who own a mobile device but may not be making the most of it for their own teaching and learning. We would like to see more widespread discussion of how users can best discover and develop the potential of their mobile devices, individually and collectively, and we hope that our research can help raise the profile of that discussion.

Mobile Learning Practices in the Research Literature

In evolving definitions of mobile learning, we are seeing technology-focused approaches being gradually superseded by interpretations that seek to locate mobile learning within broader educational frameworks, taking account of social and philosophical dimensions (Traxler 2005; Laouris 2005). The context for this is the rapidly changing landscape of teaching and learning. The growing importance of lifelong and informal learning has a special connection with the affordances of mobile technologies. Whilst this has long been emphasized by Sharples (1999), it has taken some time to gain momentum.

Scanlon et al. (2005) have been exploring what possibilities exist for science learners in informal settings, and in projects across many subject domains it is not unusual now to find a stated aim of developing systems or materials for informal learning. For example, Fallahkhair et al. (2005) have developed a system to support informal mobile language learning, while Bradley et al. (2005) report on the development of materials for a mobile local history tour. This type of "designed" informal learning may be contrasted with situations where mobile devices are used spontaneously for learning, employing only the device features and software already available for general use, or sought out by users in response to their own needs or interests, perhaps for everyday learning. In connection with the latter, Vavoula et al. (2005) have studied mobile learning as part of everyday learning, in order to uncover "how people learn on the move or outside their normal learning environment, with the technologies that are currently available, such as mobile phones and PDAs" (p. 1). Vavoula (2005) compared episodes of mobile learning (when the learner is not at a fixed location or when she/he takes advantage of mobile technologies) to non-mobile learning, and found "indications that mobile learning is more interactive, involves more 'bustle', more contact, communication and collaboration with people" (p. 17).

Informal mobile learning is also a theme in the work of Oksman (2005), who has reported on research at the University of Tampere exploring mobile communication and Internet use among young people, families, and older people since the late 1990s. Berth (2005) has been studying the use of mobile phones in the intersection between formal and informal learning contexts. There is also growing interest in the new social practices associated with the use of particular mobile technologies such as pervasive image capture and sharing (Spasojevic et al. 2005). However, overall the research literature in the area of everyday informal mobile learning and its integration with daily life is still limited. If we take seriously one of the main conclusions of the Mobilearn project – that "Learning is interwoven with other activities as part of everyday life... Mobile learning is integrated with non-learning tasks such as shopping or entertainment" (Sharples 2005) – then the case for understanding the technology-mediated relationship between learning and other activities is emphasized.

In relation to teaching practices and mobile devices, Leach et al. (2005) have been investigating the impact of new portable technologies on teachers' practices in the context of their professional development. The work shows very clearly that personal uses such as diary and address book functions go hand-in-hand with successful use of the same mobile device for planning teaching and collecting resources for teaching. Wishart's (2006) research in the use of PDAs in initial teacher training gives similar findings concerning the integration of the PDA as both personal organizer and a tool for making notes on information and events as they are encountered. The first year evaluation of Duke University's iPods initiative reported that academic uses consisted of course content dissemination, data capture in the classroom and in the field (capturing discussions, notes, digital assets), study support, and file storage and transfer (Belanger 2005). These studies demonstrate that a multifunctional portable device enables users both to attend to administrative tasks and to develop their practice in a variety of locations. The Duke University initiative continues to encourage the development of practice through "creative uses of technology in education and campus life" (Duke University 2006).

Participants and Methodology

Participants in our research (hereafter referred to as alumni) were drawn from among those who had successfully completed at least one of the courses in MAODE, our global distance learning programme established in 1997. Recent alumni have good or excellent levels of computer literacy (the programme is delivered online and several of the modules explicitly focus on aspects of e-Learning technologies), but even those who completed courses much earlier could reasonably be expected to have at least some knowledge of Information and Communication Technology (ICT). We therefore expected that the alumni would include at least some who had interesting and innovative experience of using mobile devices. Since the MAODE programme is aimed largely at those practising or intending to practise in education and training, it seemed likely that the alumni would throw light on some of the ways in which mobile devices are being used in education and training, and would also reveal how practitioners are using such devices in other areas of their life – in their own learning, social interaction, and entertainment.

Given the geographically dispersed locations of our participants, data for the project was collected by means of an online questionnaire and follow-up interviews by telephone or email with a subset of respondents. The questionnaire contained both quantitative and qualitative questions relating to the use of different types of device (namely, mobile phones, smartphones, PDAs, MP3 players) in five types of activity:
- teaching
- learning
- work
- social interaction
- entertainment (including quizzes and games)

It covered the use of mobile devices as part of user communities and groups, the frequency of specific uses (such as browsing websites, reading e-news, sharing media files, etc.) and users' views on the attractions and disadvantages of mobile learning. It was sent out to 150 alumni and elicited fifty-seven responses.

The main section of the questionnaire focused on the use of mobile devices. Respondents were asked to give one or more examples in detail to show how they used and continue to use the devices for the five types of activity. We were mainly interested in teaching and learning; however, the three remaining categories were included with a view to examining whether the other areas of use might have implications for teaching and learning.

The questionnaire stated that the terms "teaching" and "learning" should be interpreted to include informal uses, for example teaching or learning with friends, family or interest groups – as well as formal situations inside or outside the classroom. For some respondents, "work" equates with "teaching" because of their job. When analysing the questionnaire data we were particularly interested in the types of activity undertaken, innovative or unexpected uses of mobile devices, and issues mentioned by users. The questionnaire results are reported with special regard to those aspects. As a means of data collection, the questionnaire had typical advantages and drawbacks; in particular, the open-ended questions elicited a good array of examples that could not have been anticipated in advance, but they also allowed for a few ambiguous responses that proved hard to interpret.

Nine interviewees were subsequently invited to amplify the responses they had made in the questionnaire a few months previously. Our approach was broadly phenomenological; in relation to the data arising from the interviews, we were interested in gathering individual stories, but aimed not to take these as unsituated accounts. The interviews illustrate ways in which respondents are using mobile devices in diverse situations, and they provide insights into user choices in relation to contexts of use, ergonomic issues, and personal preferences. The nine interviewees were chosen principally because their questionnaire responses suggested they were engaging in interesting or novel applications, but we also took care to include at least some participants from outside the United Kingdom. The interviewees were therefore not chosen as being representative of the cohort; nevertheless, they gave the opportunity to move outside the categories of the questionnaire and to capture details of individual accounts and contexts. The interviewees talked about their choice of device, the content of their activities, and the contexts, both formal and informal, in which they used their devices. All the interviews were carried out by an experienced researcher who was independent of the project. The interviews were transcribed by an administrative assistant and anonymized before being passed on to the authors of this chapter. The interview findings are only covered briefly here; a fuller account is available in Pettit and Kukulska-Hulme, 2007.

Questionnaire Findings

In this section we report the main findings of the questionnaire. About three-quarters of the respondents were aged 35 to 54 and a little over half (55 per cent) were female. Over half lived principally in the United Kingdom, with most of the remainder living in continental western Europe, and five living in Hong Kong, Japan, Peru, and the United States. Nearly all described their profession as associated in some way with education or training.

Almost all respondents reported that they had used a mobile phone, and about half stated they had used a PDA or MP3 player. Smartphones were used by 18 per cent of those who answered this question; a smartphone was defined in the questionnaire as "a mobile phone/PDA in one device."

The findings are reported here firstly in relation to the four types of device and the five areas addressed in the questionnaire, namely teaching, learning, work, social interaction, and entertainment. We believe the most valuable aspect of the findings is the range and variety of activities mentioned by respondents for each type of device, because of our overarching aim to continue using our research to help disseminate innovative practice. For each type of device, we concentrate on listing the activities that were undertaken by respondents rather than the frequency with which they were mentioned. Subsequently we also report on what respondents told us about being part of groups and communities, whether they had undertaken specific activities listed in the questionnaire, their views of what's special about mobile learning and what they perceive to be the single biggest disadvantage.

Mobile Phones

Of those who had used a mobile phone, 96 per cent reported using it for social interaction and 78 per cent for work. Outside these uses, the figures were much lower: 30 per cent for teaching, 19 per cent for entertainment, quizzes and games, and 17 per cent for their own learning. Common mobile phone uses across the categories of activity were contact, scheduling and reminders, and as an alternative means of support, and these were also the main uses of mobile phones in *teaching*. Communication with students by mobile phone occasionally included the use of photographs and short news. In addition, respondents mentioned teaching others about mobile devices, for example how mobiles can be used for more than just voice communication, but in those cases it seems that the phone was used in demonstration mode.

In *learning*, apart from contact, scheduling and learning support, respondents reported browsing the Web, downloading e-books, learning Greek, and receiving the table of contents of journals. One respondent used the phone as a modem for PDA network access.

In the *work* context, contact, scheduling and reminders were again the dominant uses. Some respondents gave more specific reasons (getting taxis, out-of-hours technical support, coordinating location with a colleague), and the uses that might be considered slightly more unusual were text messages in response to correspondence, storing information in Japanese, and conducting telephone interviews for research. The issue of the acceptability of texting was touched upon by one respondent who claimed never to use texting for work.

In *social interaction* the vast majority of respondents used their mobile phone simply for calls and for texting friends and family. Although this majority use was very predictable, there were some interesting comments and examples in this category. One unusual use of the mobile phone was as support for mild visual impairment, namely contacting a spouse when the respondent had lost sight of her in a shop. One respondent emphasized the use of very short messages (to offer congratulations, send football scores, and ask "where are you now?"). Exchanging photos, pictures, jokes, ringtones, and multimedia messages were mentioned, as was checking the time of the next bus. Circumstances of use were sometimes alluded to: using the phone only to leave an important message (and where there is no option of a public phone), using it mainly when on the move, using free minutes only, primarily as an emergency phone, or to be "always available." In four cases running late was a specific reason for use, and one respondent referred to health fears (possible danger of exposure).

In *entertainment*, games, quizzes, and competitions were mentioned, but these were minority pursuits. There were some negative comments regarding the use of mobile phones for entertainment, including the following:

- "Have tried it but not my cup of tea."
- "Did try receiving Virgin bite sized but they were so irritating. Virgin mobile culture seems whacky and crazy and I am neither."
- "Tried – couldn't figure it out."
- "Rarely – too slow."
- "Very rarely, when all other sorts of entertainment have failed."

Photos were mentioned, in one case connected to mobile blogging ("this entertains the community of mobloggers on the site"). Respondents also referred to news as a form of entertainment.

Smartphones

As mentioned earlier, not many respondents had a smartphone, but those who did have one reported some activities that had not been mentioned in connection with mobile phones.

In *teaching* and *work*, use of a smartphone meant access to online documents, a virtual learning environment (Blackboard), a student forum, and other websites. Communication by email was mentioned by a handful of respondents. Learning activities included use of email, accessing resources on the Web, downloading chapters to read, quick access to Alta Vista Babelfish (a translation tool), and groupwork ("participating in groupwork remotely, using handsfree"). It should be noted that each of these uses was typically mentioned by one person, so they were not common activities.

Work activities included note-taking, task listing, presenting Powerpoint slides, web browsing, and share trading, as well as synchronization with a Tablet PC. In *social interaction*, messaging, emails, and voice calls were prevalent; specifically, the use of SMS during videoconferencing was reported by one participant. In the *entertainment* category, mention was made of games on the bus home, taking and sending photos, email, and accessing information such as news.

PDAs

The data relating to the use of PDAs was the most substantial in terms of the range of examples in the work context and the number of spontaneous comments about the experience of using PDAs.

Uses of PDAs in *teaching* included preparing materials, using digital sound files to record progress and achievement, and getting students to take photographs (with text labels). Access to information such as articles, tables of contents, and e-books, was mentioned by several respondents, as was administrative support (lists of talks, tutorials, tasks, and students).

In the context of *learning*, carrying or reading texts (e-books, manuals, and various documents related to courses) appeared to be the most common activity, although note-taking and annotation were mentioned. A small amount of scheduling and web browsing took place, including web access to a discussion forum. This section generated a number of spontaneous comments regarding usability. On the positive side, it was possible to "use time productively while waiting," and to be "always up to date"; but on the negative side, the screen could be "far too small" for reading, and formatting of blogs was considered not to be good enough "at the time."

In relation to *work*, the PDA had many different uses, including various ways of holding or capturing small amounts of information: contacts, action lists, notes, memos, as an "aide-memoire," for "miscellaneous scrappy files," for agenda-setting, and for mindmapping and brainstorming. Larger files were also mentioned, including e-books, full text papers, a drugs database, and medical textbooks. Recording or tracking was another area of use, and this included recording meetings, keeping a record of continuous professional development, and tracking expenses or the amount of time spent on projects. Typical MS Office applications (Word, Excel, and Powerpoint) were also used, email was sometimes accessed, and there was scheduling of appointments and meetings. A world clock was used by one respondent to check time differences. The use of PDAs for work generated a couple of spontaneous positive comments regarding usability, namely that battery life was better than on a laptop and that the PDA was more comfortable to use in airline seats that do not have a proper table – making it suitable for use while travelling.

The categories of *social interaction* and *entertainment* elicited relatively sparse responses but included MP3s, photos, video, e-books, and MSN Messenger. One respondent had tried conferencing but found it "too clunky"; another reported using the PDA to synchronize with various news sites.

MP3 Players

MP3 players, devices that are primarily destined for entertainment (MP3 files were described by one participant as being "perfectly suited to disposable pop music"), were actually used in a wide variety of ways for all categories of activity, particularly in learning.

In *teaching*, they were used to distribute music and sound drills to students, to play files from CDs, and to download interviews for classes. MP3 files were recorded from BBC Radio 4 and the World Service. MP3 players provided background music in workshops, they were used as a voice recorder to record students' spoken reflections on their learning (subsequently included on a spreadsheet or in Powerpoint), and for gap fill and listening exercises. Several issues were brought up by respondents, namely that the microphone was not good enough to record music, cheaper devices have controls that are "extremely awkward and unfriendly," and that audio can be good when working with adults with learning difficulties or in practical classes.

In the context of *learning*, respondents downloaded e-books, copied audio courses onto an iPod (and listened when travelling by bike, train, and plane as well as at home too), listened to podcasts, pre-recorded lectures, and recorded conferences, created MP3 files from Real Media lectures, and recorded lectures and conferences. MP3 players were used in connection with a foreign language – to understand Spanish better (with listening materials downloaded from the Web) and for recordings of Japanese language drills and dialogues. They were used as a storage device between work and home or when otherwise travelling. Another reported use was recording and playback for conversation analysis. For one respondent, the iPod was their "favourite personal learning device."

For *work*, the devices were used as a backup for contacts; to transfer files between home and work, to carry a kiosk version of Firefox browser, to carry presentations, to share audio, video, and photo materials; used with speakers to play sample music to clients, and on business trips ("when can't sleep").

In *social interaction*, they were used (with speakers) on holiday to play music to friends, for iPod parties, and for photos. In *entertainment* they were used for pleasure during journeys, in the office, for walks and jogging, to play solitaire, to hold a database of an entire DVD library and important contacts, to download BBC documentaries, and for "audio books." One respondent saw music as a potential distraction when concentration at work was needed.

Being Part of Groups and Communities

In this part of the questionnaire, we aimed to find out whether participants had used a mobile device to be part of a group or community. Only nine respondents answered this question. Two types of group were mentioned: traditional and online. Traditional communities or groups were teachers, a group of students, colleagues in the same department, a work group, former clients, family, community groups focusing on historic preservation, and a residents' association. Two online communities were a gaming community and moblogging, the latter involving sharing and discussing photos ("the moblogging community are more rewarding and reinforcing than family/friends").

General benefits that respondents derived from group or community activity were keeping abreast of developments, keeping in touch, a sense of satisfaction from fulfilment of civic responsibility, support from peers, and being able to offer support back to others. The online gaming community enabled meeting people from around the world ("my partner doesn't like computer games so the community is important to me"); the moblogging community was an occasional distraction from the respondent's job.

Specific Uses for Mobile Devices

In this section of the questionnaire, participants were asked about suggested specific activities they may have undertaken using their mobile device, and to indicate the frequency of use by choosing one of six options ranging from "at least once a day" to "never." Twenty-three specific activities were proposed in the questionnaire, such as browsing websites, reading an e-book, taking a photograph, making a video clip, recording their voice, using a location-based service, etc. More unusual and more overtly interactive activities were also included; for instance, "linking your device to someone else's to play a game," making a video-phonecall, sending a sound file, or sending an image. In this section, the activities were not related to the use of any particular type of device.

The most frequent activities, performed "at least once a day," were:

- text messaging (38 per cent)
- browsing websites – both "ordinary" and set up for mobiles (20 per cent)
- listening to an audio file (13 per cent)
- reading e-news (9 per cent)
- using a mobile device to make notes (7 per cent)
- taking a photograph (6 per cent)
- viewing a photograph or other image (6 per cent)

When uses occurring "at least once a day" and "a few days a week" are combined, the most frequent activities were (Figure 1 shows a chart representing the above activities):

- text messaging (57 per cent)
- browsing websites – both "ordinary" and set up for mobiles (35 per cent)
- using a mobile device to make notes (29 per cent)
- moving files between a mobile device and a PC (28 per cent)
- listening to an audio file (23 per cent)
- reading e-news (23 per cent)
- viewing a photograph or other image (21 per cent)

All twenty-three activities had at least one person indicating that they had undertaken that activity on a mobile device.

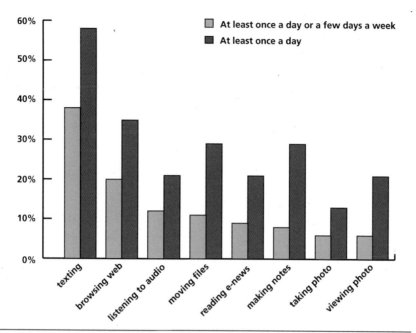

FIGURE 1 Most frequent activities

What's Special, What's a Problem?

When asked about what they considered to be *new* and *innovative* about their experience of learning with mobile devices, respondents mentioned that the devices were always available, flexible, convenient, portable, inexpensive, easy to check again and again, and they mentioned the sense of being in control. Other aspects highlighted were as follows:

- Access to online data to support fieldwork
- Immediate contact with parents of disruptive pupil
- One can retrieve the most up-to-date material
- Learning while on the move
- Multimedia modules on the fly
- To be able to read blogs while travelling
- Ability to carry different types of media
- Using "dead time/hostage time"
- Could log thoughts electronically
- To keep up with email and online discussions
- With headphones, more immersive than a book or video

When asked about the single biggest *disadvantage* that mobile devices bring them in relation to their learning, respondents mentioned issues of cost, privacy, and security or confidentiality of one's mobile number. Technical or ergonomic issues were:

- Battery problems, lost files
- Device is unreliable, it jams, speakers are poor
- Lack of WiFi in many locations
- Fiddly small screen, tasking on the eyes; best used as audio devices

Interaction issues were also signalled:

- Easy to get distracted
- Text-based message lacks inflection
- Lacking interactive multimedia
- Interaction can be clumpy and stilted
- Everything has to be short and small making meaningful interaction difficult
- Limit to the depth of thinking and learning

Interview Findings

As mentioned earlier, a report on the follow-up interviews can be found in Pettit and Kukulska-Hulme (2007). One of the distinctive contributions of the interviews was to illustrate how the participants wove particular devices and practices into their daily lives, especially when travelling. The interviews indicate the particular importance of travel periods for study, for informal learning, or for engagement with news and other material. They also highlight dependence on factors often outside the control of the individual. When participants chose or rejected a particular device, they cited a number of unpredictable factors such as changes to the design of buses or train seats, improvements in typing skills, whether or not a device "looks stupid," or individual trade-offs about the value of carrying a larger device in order to gain a keyboard.

The interviews provided a particularly vivid account of the use of a moblog – where photographs were uploaded, news captured and discussions initiated. The interviewee spoke of the satisfaction of receiving positive feedback on photographs, and highlighted the role of individuals in capturing powerful and almost immediate images of a major incident.

Summary and Interpretation of Findings

In this project, we were particularly interested in the types of activity undertaken, innovative or unexpected uses of mobile devices, and any issues mentioned by participants.

Our findings show that mobile phones were largely used for interpersonal activities including contact, coordination, interviews, as an alternative means of support, and a means to motivate learners; they also appeared to be personally useful as a practical tool and a reference tool. They could support some multimedia content and some forms of entertainment. Having additional functionality in a smartphone was associated with more options for communication, online resources and tools, the possibility to create and share simple content, and to synchronize with a PC.

PDAs came across as highly versatile tools that enabled access to a wide range of information, the preparation of materials, and keeping records of progress and achievement. They seemed to encourage various ways of holding or capturing small amounts of information, mind mapping and brainstorming, whilst also being suitable for larger files and databases. They supported administrative tasks and the use of typical Office applications, music files, multimedia content, and news. Communication was a lesser feature of PDA use but there was mention of email, MSN Messenger and Web access to a discussion forum.

MP3 players were widely used for entertainment but also turned out to be useful in a much wider range of activity, particularly in learning. In terms of receptive use, participants reported downloading podcasts, audio books, documentaries, lectures, conferences, interviews and other listening materials from the Web. In more active mode, they recorded conversations, lectures and conferences, with the BBC being a common source of material. With MP3 players, materials and listening exercises were sometimes distributed to students, and the voice recorder facility was used to capture students' spoken reflections on their learning. A connection with PC applications could be made by subsequently including audio files in a spreadsheet or Powerpoint. Participants were quite active in transferring files to other media, perhaps for the sake of convenience. They copied audio courses and CDs onto their MP3 player and created MP3 files from Real Media lectures. The MP3 players were used as a backup storage and transfer device and a means of sharing audio, video, and photos. Although a favoured personal device, the MP3 player was also used in social ways, with the addition of speakers, to provide background music in workshops, to play sample music to clients and to play music to friends.

It seems that compared to other devices, the MP3 player was particularly conducive to creative and social uses that may not have been anticipated when we started this project, when MP3 players were largely perceived to be personal entertainment devices for private listening. Some activities are easily identified as new, for example a teacher using mobile devices to capture students' reflections on their learning, or the person who posts photos to a mobile blog and gets feedback from an online community. The "newness" of the activity of course depends on whether it has been heard of before, which may be difficult to verify in relation to informal uses that frequently go undocumented. Other activities may be new, but in a less obvious way. From the nature of our data, it is difficult to determine the extent to which an activity performed with a mobile device might have been transformational, for example in that it constituted a new way of working for the individual concerned. Note-taking or mind mapping may seem like ordinary activities, but the possibility to perform them on a personal device that is used in situations involving mobility may significantly change the nature of what is noted and how. Unexpected uses include ways in which mobile devices may be used in conjunction with other technologies, for example, the use of SMS during videoconferencing, or as an alternative medium when other avenues of support are (perhaps temporarily) unavailable.

In this project sample, the use of mobile technologies in connection with groups or communities was not at all widespread. Although the project participants would all have had experience of online collaboration within the MAODE programme, the idea of using mobile devices to be part of a group or community was still relatively new in 2005. How rapidly this may change would be worth tracking through ongoing research. The extent to which mobile devices were already being used to browse websites was a slight surprise to us. The presence of activities relating to a foreign language (Greek, Japanese, and Spanish) suggests that this may be a fruitful area for informal learning with mobile devices.

Issues brought up by questionnaire respondents related to some social aspects of use, travel, and technical problems. Depending on the context of use and the individuals concerned, texting may or may not be socially acceptable, and people may prefer to use their mobile phone in exceptional circumstances only or to remain always switched on and available. There appeared to be a clash between emerging mobile cultures (i.e. Virgin mobile) and the preferences of a group of participants who may not see themselves as belonging to that culture. Mobile phone messages are typically very short and social, which may need to be considered when introducing more formal communication, as between learners and an education provider. Spontaneous comments relating to use of PDAs were largely positive, with the devices keeping their users up to date and enabling productive use of time.

Technical issues surfaced in responses relating to PDAs (small screen, difficulties with blogs and conferencing) and MP3 players (poor microphone, awkward controls). Battery problems, lost files, reliability issues and lack of WiFi in many locations were among the issues highlighted as disadvantages of mobile learning. These seemed to inhibit making best use of the devices but we did not ask specifically whether the problems were perceived as major ones or whether they had been overcome.

If we were to look for evidence, in common with Vavoula et al. (2005), that mobile devices were being used in ways that are more interactive and involve more contact, communication, and collaboration with people, the high usage of text messaging is clearly important. Beyond that the most frequent uses out of those proposed in the questionnaire were those that were largely self-contained, such as browsing websites, making notes, listening to audio, and reading news. Participants expressed some reservations about the quality of interaction in mobile learning. Perhaps the fact that these are distance learning alumni with experience of high-quality online interaction contributes to their behaviours and views.

Implications for Practice

Is it possible to say on the basis of this research that the ways in which participants are using mobile devices in work, social interaction, and entertainment might have implications for teaching and learning? There were certainly many instances of general activities that participants may have mentioned in relation to one sphere of activity but that could easily be transposed into another. Mobile blogging was mentioned under "entertainment," but blogs are general purpose tools that are currently being exploited in education. An entertainment tool such as an MP3 player was used for the more serious task of recording and playback for conversation analysis. It seems that for an individual, it is largely a matter of coming up with the ideas and perhaps making the mental leap that takes one from seeing a device in one light to being able to use it in a different way altogether.

Educators need to exercise similar mental agility with regard to diverse possible uses for a single device. Furthermore, if they want to use mobile devices to exploit learners' commuting time, they need to examine its patterns carefully – not only periods of actual travel, but unexpected delays, waiting for connecting flights, or time spent waiting for buses and trains to arrive. We have seen in our research that learners want to use time productively while waiting, and that they will try to find ways of adapting learning materials given to them to suit their particular lifestyle needs.

A broader question is how do we enable people to discover the full potential of any mobile device in relation to teaching and learning? We may be moving away from a world in which the use of any new technology was associated with going on formal training courses in order to become proficient at its use, towards a world where more informal learning will happen among colleagues and friends. Is a high level of comfort with mobile technology associated with increased personal innovation? And what are the best mechanisms for sharing with others ideas for new ways of using mobile devices in teaching and learning? Future research must try to address these broader issues. We are currently running a project in which we are investigating how academic and support staff can use smartphones to support their own learning, within a semi-formal community structure, and with a focus on personal and professional development (Kukulska-Hulme and Pettit, 2007).

Conclusion

Our research confirms than amongst the participants of this study, mobile devices have indeed become commonplace tools serving a wide array of purposes that include teaching and learning alongside work and leisure. The education practitioners in this sample come across as active and sometimes experimental individuals who are taking advantage of the capabilities of mobile devices to meet their own needs and the needs of their colleagues, clients, and students. Our research connects with current interest in tracking teacher-led innovation, the focus of the UK Futurelab Teachers as Innovators Project, which has set out to investigate where innovation is occurring in UK schools, and examine the factors contributing to innovation and methods for sharing and disseminating innovative practice with digital technologies (Sutch 2006).

Thanks to mobile devices, learning appears to be occupying a new space that gives individuals the capacity to make use of electronic resources and tools in flexible ways that suit their circumstances and lifestyles. We have uncovered a vast range and diversity of ways in which a mobile device can be used to support different aspects of an individual's teaching and learning, and interactions with others. Since the devices are so personal, we think it is both challenging and important for educators and learners to find out how others are managing to use their mobile devices to help them in their teaching and learning. To enable this to happen, we need to find good ways of sharing and disseminating information about making effective use of the capabilities of mobile devices in education.

References

ALLY, M. 2005. Use of mobile devices in distance education. Paper presentation, *mLearn 2005*, October 25-28, Cape Town, South Africa.

BELANGER, Y. 2005. *Duke University iPod first year experience*. Final evaluation report. http://cit.duke.edu/pdf/ipod_initiative_04_05.pdf (accessed March 29, 2007).

BERTH, M. 2005. Mobile learning: Methodologies for the study of informal learning with mobile devices. Paper presentation, *mLearn 2005*, October 25-28, Cape Town, South Africa.

BRADLEY, C., R. HAYNES, and T. BOYLE. 2005. Adult multimedia learning with PDAs: The user experience. Proceedings, *mLearn 2005*, October 25-28, Cape Town, South Africa.

Duke University. 2006. iPods enter Duke classes. *Center for Instructional Technology website*. http://cit.duke.edu/ideas/newprofiles/ipod_faculty articles.do (accessed March 29, 2007).

EDWARDS, R. 2005. Your employees are increasingly mobile, is your learning? Proceedings, *mLearn 2005*, October 25-28, Cape Town, South Africa.

FALLAHKHAIR, S., L. PEMBERTON, and R. GRIFFITHS. 2005. Dual device user interface design for ubiquitous language learning: Mobile phone and interactive television (iTV). Paper presentation, *IEEE international conference on wireless and mobile technology for education (WMTE)*, Tokushima, Japan.

JISC. 2005. Innovative practice with e-learning. *Case Studies*, JISC website. http://www.elearning.ac.uk/innoprac/index.html (accessed March 29, 2007).

KUKULSKA-Hulme, A. 2005. Case studies of innovative practice. *JISC-funded project outcomes*, JISC website. http://www.jisc.ac.uk/whatwedo/ programmes/elearning_innovation/eli_oucasestudies.aspx (accessed March 29, 2007).

KUKULSKA-HULME, A. and J. PETTIT. 2007. Self-service education: Smartphones as a catalyst for informal collective and individual learning. Paper accepted for conference, *mLearn 2007*, October 16-19, Melbourne.

LAOURIS, Y. 2005. We need an educationally relevant definition of mobile learning. Paper presentation, *mLearn 2005*, October 25-28, Cape Town, South Africa.

LEACH, J., T. POWER, R. THOMAS, X. FADANI, and A. MBEBE. 2005. 4D technologies: Appropriating handheld computers to serve the needs of teachers and learners in rural African settings. Proceedings, *mLearn 2005*, October 25-28, Cape Town, South Africa.

MANOLO. 2006. Guidelines for integrating e-, w- and m-learning. *Project Deliverables*, Mobile Case Studies. http://130.37.78.10/Projecten/Manolo/ (accessed March 29, 2007).

OKSMAN, V. 2005. Young people and seniors in Finnish mobile information society. Paper presentation, *Symposium on portable learning – learner and teacher experiences with mobile devices*, June 15, The Open University, Milton Keynes, UK. http://kn.open.ac.uk/public/index.cfm?wpid=4378 (accessed March 29, 2007).

PETTIT, J., and A. KUKULSKA-HULME. 2007. Going with the grain: Mobile devices in practice. *Australasian Journal of Educational Technology (AJET)* 23 (1):17-33. http://www.ascilite.org.au/ajet/ajet23/ajet23.html (accessed August 31, 2007).

ROGERS, E. 2003. *Diffusion of innovations.* 5th ed. London: Free Press.

SCANLON, E., A. JONES, and J. WAYCOTT. 2005. Mobile technologies: Prospects for their use in learning in informal science settings. Special issue, *Journal of Interactive Media in Education*, ed. A. Jones, A. Kukulska-Hulme, and D. Mwanza. http://jime.open.ac.uk/2005/25/ (accessed March 29, 2007).

SHARPLES, M. 1999. The design of personal technologies to support lifelong learning. Proceedings, *CAL '99 conference on computer-assisted learning*, London.

——. 2005. Re-thinking learning for the mobile age. *Kaleidoscope Network Viewpoint* (posted October 5). http://www.noe-kaleidoscope.org/pub/ lastnews/default-0-read159-display (accessed March 29, 2007).

SPASOJEVIC, M., M. ITO, N. VAN HOUSE, I. KOSKINEN, F. KATO, and D. KABE. 2005. Pervasive image capture and sharing: New social practices and implications for technology. Position paper, PICS workshop, *Ubicomp 2005*. http://www.spasojevic.org/pics/papers.htm (accessed March 29, 2007).

SUTCH, D. 2006. Teachers as innovators. Futurelab project, October 2006. http://www.futurelab.org.uk/showcase/teachers_as_innovators/teachers_as_innovators.pdf (accessed March 29, 2007).

TRAXLER, J. 2005. Defining mobile learning. Proceedings, *IADIS international conference on mobile learning, Malta.*

WAYCOTT, J., and A. KUKULSKA-HULME. 2003. Students' experiences with PDAs for reading course materials, *Personal and Ubiquitous Computing* 7 (1):30-43.

VAVOULA, G. 2005. D4.4: A study of mobile learning practices. MOBIlearn project deliverable. http://www.mobilearn.org/download/results/public_deliverables/MOBIlearn_D4.4_Final.pdf (accessed March 29, 2007).

VAVOULA, G., M. SHARPLES, C. O'MALLEY, and J. TAYLOR. 2005. A study of mobile learning as part of everyday learning. Userlab document. http://kn.open.ac.uk/public/document.cfm?docid=7199 (accessed August 31, 2007).

WISHART, J. 2006. Personal Digital Assistants: Teachers prefer the personal. Paper presentation, mLearn 2006, October, Banff, Canada. http://telearn.noe-kaleidoscope.org/open-archive/browse?resource=469_v1 (accessed August 31, 2007).

Design and Development of Multimedia Learning Objects for Mobile Phones

CLAIRE BRADLEY
RICHARD HAYNES
JOHN COOK
TOM BOYLE
CARL SMITH
LONDON METROPOLITAN UNIVERSITY
UNITED KINGDOM

Abstract

This chapter discusses the design and development of a series of prototypes of a multimedia learning object for the mobile phone. It begins with the rationale for this development, and the underlying design and development principles of our learning objects. It then presents the iterative development process that ensued in creating four prototypes for the mobile phone, each of which was refined in light of use and feedback. The design issues and solutions are discussed in the process, documenting the development route that was taken. Student evaluation data is also presented, and this has informed the further development of the prototype. The development sections are followed by a discussion about the implications of this work, and the chapter concludes with where it is going in the future.

Introduction

The ability to produce effective multimedia learning applications for technology that is ubiquitous is very appealing. Mobile phones are becoming more technically sophisticated. They can create and play multimedia content; they have larger high quality colour screens; many models can now capture, edit, and play back video, audio, and photographs; many models can also run Flash-based interactive applications (through Flash Lite). They also have greater storage capacity, and networking connectivity with PCs the Internet with Bluetooth and WiFi. Surveys conducted with university students show that they own mobile phones that have multimedia and connectivity capabilities in increasing numbers (Cook et al. 2006). Harnessing the use of these devices for multimedia learning resources which are known to engage and motivate students could be a powerful way of providing learning materials to students who need more flexible learning solutions because of other time demands in their life (Boyle 1997). Specifically, multimedia learning objects can provide multimodal channels that enable students to build up their own knowledge representations of the task in hand. If used in a collaborative way they can help students in identifying the gaps in their own knowledge and hence assist successful task comprehension and performance (Soloway and Norris 2005). Indeed, Nyíri (2002) points to potential enhancement of communication and knowledge that multimedia mobile devices can offer:

> Mobile communication is enhanced everyday communication; and just as our everyday conversation is indifferent towards disciplinary boundaries, so, too, is m-learning. Situation-dependent knowledge, the knowledge at which m-learning aims, by its nature transcends disciplines; its organising principles arise from practical tasks; its contents are multisensorial; its elements are linked to each other not just by texts, but also by diagrams, pictures, and maps (p. 124).

Thus our approach to developing mobile multimedia learning objects taps into the desire to communicate and crosses disciplinary boundaries. The organizing principles of our learning objects arise from practical tasks but use multisensorial elements to link the knowledge construction together.

This chapter discusses developmental work being carried out as part of the Centre for Excellence in Teaching and Learning in Reusable Learning Objects (RLO-CETL) at London Metropolitan University. It builds on our previous work in developing multimedia learning objects for the PC and for the PDA (Bradley, Haynes, and Boyle, 2005a). It explores the next step on the continuum, in designing learning resources for a more ubiquitous and portable device, the mobile phone. An existing web-based learning object on Referencing Books was selected for adaptation for the phone. This was chosen as it was a small and self-contained learning object that could be worked through in a few minutes, and was thus considered suitable for mobile learning, where short, bite-sized resources are most effective. The content development had already been done, and this simplified our task to re-design this content so that it was appropriate for and took advantage of the characteristics of the phone. Our aim is to develop multimedia learning content for mobile phones which is interactive, highly visual, engaging, and effective for the learner, using Flash Lite for authoring and delivery (Flash Lite is a version of Flash for mobile phones). Such learning objects can easily be used by the student whenever they have the desire or opportunity to engage in some learning, wherever they are, taking advantage of this "always there, always on" technology.

This chapter outlines the underlying design and development principles of our learning objects, and then presents the iterative development process that ensued in creating four prototypes for the mobile phone, each of which was refined in light of use and feedback. The design issues and solutions are discussed in the process, documenting the development route that was taken. The third prototype was evaluated with students, and some of their feedback is included. This led to the development of a fourth prototype that rectifies some of the issues that the students raised. The process has been lengthy (spanning about ten months), involving many tests and the creation of different design options. This is illustrated with examples from each of the prototypes, along with references to useful sources of help and information that were used to inform the work. The development sections are followed by a discussion about the implications of this work, and the chapter concludes with where it is going in the future.

The PC-based Study Skills Reusable Learning Objects

The team has designed and evaluated a suite of high quality, interactive, multimedia Reusable Learning Objects (RLOs) for learning study skills. The suite of learning materials developed for the project included RLOs on how to reference a book, a journal, and a website. They were all designed to encourage first year students to actually have a go at referencing their work. The whole approach to these objects was mapped out after a significant student observation (in a participative design session) that students don't reference their work "because they [the students] think that tutors will think they don't know enough ... and it will lower their grades."

With RLOs we place pedagogy at the heart of our concerns, and focus on the need to deal with different types of users (students and teachers). Team Enhanced Creativity (TEC) is an approach to the design of RLOs developed by our team (Cook et al. 2006b; Holley et al. 2007; Smith et al. 2007). Our approach is partly based on Boyle's (2003) notion of decoupling and cohesion. Internally cohesive means the RLO meets a single learning objective and decoupled means that it has no link-outs to external resources. It is also heavily influenced by notions of user-centered and participative design (Norman and Draper 1986). The TEC approach feeds into the wider RLO-CETL Development Methodology (Boyle et al. 2006). TEC enables teaching staff, multimedia developers, and students to become involved in an iterative and highly creative process of reusable learning object design, implementation, evaluation, and reuse. The starting point of the design process is that a number of designs are storyboarded and prototyped. These prototypes are then thoroughly tested for the next iteration of design. One of the main design considerations is to ensure that all the navigation content and controls are easily accessible without overcrowding the interface or overloading the user. Adobe Flash is used for the software development of all our RLOs because it enables the design and development of rich interactive multimedia applications.

Each of the referencing RLOs has a number of sections that are intended to be used in sequential order on the first occasion. However, on subsequent visits the menu system can be utilized to allow users to access sections according to their learning need or indeed what they consider to be the most useful sections at that moment in time. Each RLO starts with a visual splash screen. This proved popular as a means of drawing in the audience. Next is a section that highlights the reasons why the user should reference their work. This was designed to be as simple as possible as it was the first page and, again, the emphasis was not to overload the user. The next section is a tutorial on how to create a reference from either a book, journal, or website. A screen shot from the Referencing Books RLO is shown in Figure 1. This is typical of a guide section, which contains a number of small steps (a tutorial) that allow the user to deconstruct the learning process at their own pace. This is followed by a reference checklist and the final reference list with the newly constructed reference dynamically loaded into place.

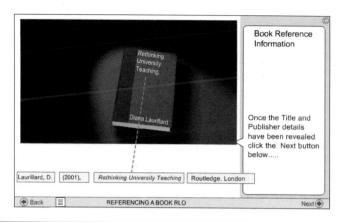

FIGURE 1 A screen from the Referencing Books RLO PC version

The RLOs all conclude with a set of activities to test your knowledge. They have been designed to achieve scaffolding and interactivity by the incorporation of questions, based on presented information that the learner is required to answer. Students are thus scaffolded (Wood et al. 1976; Holley et al. 2007; Smith et al. 2007) into a deeper appreciation of fundamental concepts that may be further developed via a blended learning approach to teaching. The first activity is a set of multiple choice questions, where answers are met with feedback that indicates whether the answer is right or wrong, gives the correct answer, and any additional tips relating to the particular question. The second activity involves the student creating a reference from clicking on given components to assemble them in the correct order. If they do not get it right first time, they are suggested to try again. If they get it wrong a second time, they are recommended to go through the resource again to improve their understanding. In this way the RLOs are designed to allow individuals to construct knowledge by working to solve realistic problems. They can also be used at a later stage for revision or refreshing the memory of a particular concept without having to work through the same problems.

The Development Process for the Mobile Phone

We started developing learning objects for the mobile phone by adapting the RLO on Referencing Books. We chose to develop for popular Nokia series 60 phones (N70 and then N91), which can run Flash Lite 2 (the latest version at the time). This helped us to see what is feasible and effective on the mobile phone. It meant we could research the development and design issues involved, and find solutions without needing to become involved in the wider technical issues inherent in developing applications that will work on a range of phones with different technical specifications and operating systems. This section describes the iterative development process that ensued, from initial research and testing on the mobile platform to the development of the three prototype versions that were created before conducting student evaluation.

Initial Concerns

We were aware that designing for mobile devices is very different to designing for desktops (Baird and Whitear 2006), and we had some initial concerns about how the nature of the mobile phone might compromise the design of our RLO. Compared with a desktop PC, the Nokia N70 phone screen is small: 176 × 208 pixels, about the size of a matchbox. Input devices are limited: there is no keyboard, mouse, stylus, or touch screen. Input and selection has to be controlled by the phone's keypad. The N70 phone has two soft keys at the top left and right, directly under the screen, a five-way scroll key with navigation buttons in four directions (up, down, left, right) and a selection button in the centre, and a grid of alphanumeric keys. Figure 2 shows the available keys on the Nokia N70 phone.

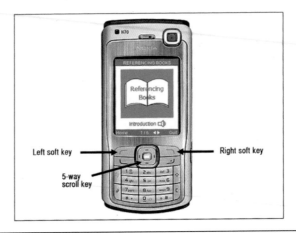

FIGURE 2 The Nokia N70 phone and keypad and the opening screen of Referencing Books

We anticipated further issues in transferring the content of the existing learning object to the mobile phone. Changing the content and structure might be necessary which could compromise the pedagogic integrity of the original learning object. We also had concerns about the ability and performance of Flash Lite on the mobile. Could the mobile phone play the media used in existing learning objects? Could it dynamically load media (as the movie is playing) such as XML text, video, and MP3 audio?

However, we were confident that we would be able to resolve the concerns we had, having tackled similar issues in developing learning objects for the PDA. To address them we took three simultaneous steps. Firstly, we took time to learn Flash Lite. We began by following the practical guidelines in the Macromedia Flash Lite 2 Content Development Kit (CDK) (Adobe website A), and searching for and learning from online tutorials, forums, and developers' blogs (see the reference list for URLs). We carried out functional tests, and soon became confident that Flash Lite 2 would be able to handle the required media components and that we could achieve the desired levels of functionality and performance on the mobile phone. We discovered, for example, that in order to load assets dynamically, file formats would commonly need to be changed. Text could be loaded in an XML format, graphics were most effective when converted to PNG format, video to 3GP (a format specifically developed for mobiles), and that audio could remain in an MP3 format. We found that free software is available for converting video files into the 3GP format, such as the Nokia Multimedia Converter 2.0 (Forum Nokia website). Adobe has produced a useful document "Optimization tips and tricks for Flash Lite 2," with sections on optimizing multimedia assets and animation performance (Duran 2006). We also learned that Flash Lite can be made to interact with the phone. The two soft keys accept commands. The five-way scroll key could be used to shift "focus" between buttons on a screen. For example, pressing the down navigation key will move focus to the next button below the one with the current focus. The centre key could then be used to select and activate the button. Extensive tests confirmed that Flash Lite 2 supports ActionScript 2. This meant that much of the existing functionality, for example the original self-test multiple choice questions with feedback, could be ported to the mobile.

Secondly, we looked at other Flash Lite examples to identify emerging conventions and design trends. Examples of Flash Lite movies are available from the Adobe Flash Lite Exchange (Adobe website B), and are discussed in the Nokia white paper, "Flash Lite for S60 – An Emerging Global Ecosystem" (Nokia 2006a) and the Nokia "Flash Lite: Visual Guide" (Nokia 2006b), which has tips on emerging Flash Lite solutions. Although many of the Flash Lite movies available at the time were games, they pointed to trends in screen and interface design, navigational techniques, and interactive functionality which were helpful. We found with regards to the two soft keys for example, that the left key is often used for options or home to take the user back to the start of the application, and the right key often has a quit or exit function.

Thirdly, we developed a set of design templates for the component parts of the object and assembled a code library of Flash Lite 2 ActionScript functions. This code library was a combination of found third-party scripts that were reused or adapted and home grown scripts, and included many functions for commonly used procedures; for example, to manage navigation sequences, button focus, and the loading of external assets. Many of these functions were added to the Flash Lite template as the code library expanded, and it gradually became more robust, and streamlined the development process of the prototype movies. Both the template and code library were created to save time during the development of this and future learning objects as they enabled common object features and functionalities to be reused.

The Development of Prototype 1

Following this initial period of research, we moved into the development of a first working prototype, during which time many key design decisions were made. We wanted to retain the structure, modularity and the linear page structure of the original learning object in the Flash Lite prototype. The first step therefore was to thoroughly analyze the existing PC-based learning object and decide how the content and pedagogic approach could most effectively be adapted to the mobile phone, and just as importantly, be effective for use in mobile situations.

Rethinking Problems

In many areas the learning object content and the interactive devices used within it needed rethinking for the mobile phone. We had learnt from our work in designing learning objects for the PDA that smaller screen sizes are not necessarily a design constraint (Bradley et al. 2005a). You just have to rethink any problems that arise, consider available options, and find creative solutions. One example of this was the use of text in the existing learning object. We decided to replace lengthy pieces of text usually used for instructions and explanations with short audio clips. This substitution of text with audio not only alleviates screen overcrowding, but is easier for people to assimilate in mobile situations. Our research has also shown that some students find it easier to learn from audio (Bradley et al. 2005b).

A detailed storyboard was developed, that showed how each of the content screens would be adapted. The storyboard contained the wording for all the text elements to be included, which were often edited and simplified from the existing text for the mobile. It also contained the scripts for the audio clips that would replace the lengthy text-based instructions and explanations, and these were recorded on an MP3 player so that they could be quickly incorporated as guide tracks into the Flash movie as authoring began.

The next design decisions tackled the issues of methods for user interaction, user navigational controls, and the design of the user interface, and these were incorporated as test content screens were developed. Different solutions for user navigation and interaction were required for the mobile version, controlled solely by the keys on the phone. For user interaction, a two-step "focus and select" method was adopted for the user to be able to click on or activate on-screen buttons. This meant that first the user had to give a button focus by navigating to it, whereupon it would become highlighted, and then use the select key to activate it. This approach was used for both interactive on-screen buttons and content elements, and for navigation from one screen to another. Screen to screen navigation was controlled by two arrow-shaped buttons. To enable additional user control of the resource, conventional commands were assigned to the two soft keys: the left was used as the Home key, and the right as the Quit key to close the learning object.

The user interface design can be seen in Figure 3 below. On each screen a horizontal bar at the top housed the name of the learning object. A bar at the bottom of the screen provided navigation controls and orientation information. On the left and right were the labels for the two soft keys, Home and Quit. In the middle was the screen number and its position within the resource (e.g., two of six), and the navigation controls to move forwards and backwards through the resource (two simple arrow buttons). Directly above the bottom bar was the title for the screen or section, along with an audio icon to play the introductory audio clip. The audio icon was given focus on entering the screen (highlighted in green as in Figure 3), as the first thing we wanted the user to do was to listen to this audio introduction. Navigation within the content of a screen thus began at the bottom, with the user moving upwards to access other content elements. In part this was because of the interface design of the PC-based learning object, which also had the orientation and navigational controls at the bottom of the screen, and was retained for the mobile version. Because the screen orientation information was at the bottom, it seemed natural to place the screen title there too, and the audio icon as well. From there, if there was other content to access on the screen, as there is in the example in Figure 3, the user would move upwards, using the up navigation key. A deep red colour scheme was chosen for the orientation and navigation bars and for the headings. Elements on the top and bottom bars were white. This colour scheme was chosen in an effort to provide strong contrasting colours to improve readability on the phone's screen, especially important when devices are used outdoors.

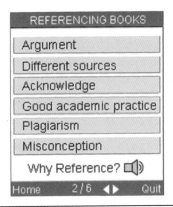

FIGURE 3 The test your knowledge Why Reference? screen in Prototype 1

Creative Adaptations

A number of key adaptations were made from the original learning object as the development of the mobile prototype progressed. One example is the "Why Reference?" screen (see Figure 3). The original used text keywords that were clicked on to reveal a text-based explanation. This would be difficult to transfer to the mobile, as it would require an easy method of selecting the text keyword, and then enough space on the screen to be able to display the text explanation. Our solution was to retain the mood of the original by keeping the text keywords, each of which can be given focus and then selected to play an audio explanation of it.

Another technique used to avoid overcrowding on the screen, was to divide content into smaller bite-sized chunks, so it was "split over a number of screens" (Baird and Whitear 2006) than are found in the existing learning object. For example, questions and feedback are on separate screens in the quiz at the end of the learning object.

The "Making a Reference" section of the original learning object has a series of 3D animations over a number of screens that explain the process. For the mobile this was adapted into a step-through series of simple animations with audio commentaries (see Figure 4). To navigate through the steps the user has a sub-menu row of square numbered buttons. The navigation design in this section was influenced by the Making Coffee step-through animation (Flash Lite: Visual Guide v1.1, Nokia 2006b).

The self-test activities at the end of the object also needed adaptation, in particular the second activity which required the user to click on components to assemble a reference in the correct order. This would be difficult to reproduce on the mobile, and it was felt that the activity could effectively be tested in

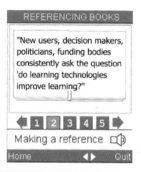

FIGURE 4 The Making a reference section from Prototype 1

another format. The two activities were therefore combined into a quiz, containing six multiple choice questions with answers and feedback. Scores were also added to the mobile version at the end, which actually led to an enhancement over the original version. This type of multiple choice assessment task is perfect for the mobile phone, as questions can be answered easily and quickly without the need for complicated user input, and the presentation format fits effectively within the dimensions and portrait orientation of the mobile screen.

The Development of Prototype 2

The first prototype was tested with peers (the multimedia development team and colleagues), and they did not like the navigation system. The two-step process of navigation between screens wasn't thought to be intuitive, and was slow to use, as the user first had to navigate to the button to give it focus, and then press the select key to activate it. The "click investment" required slowed the user down (DotMobi Mobile Web Developer's Guide 2007). Users found that it was not easy to use the learning object with one hand, and that it needed the attention of a dexterous user.

Finding a better method was influenced by the tutorials loaded onto the Nokia N91 mobile phone (we purchased some N91 phones part-way through this development work). In these tutorials, horizontal screen to screen navigation uses only the left or right navigation keys on the phone, and follows the observation made by Ulm that "all mobile navigation is linear" (Ulm 2005).

A revised design attempted to simplify the navigation process, and used the left and right navigation keys to navigate between screens. Only a single action was needed to the right key to advance a screen or to the left key to go back. As well as being easy to use, this also reserved the up and down navigation keys for vertical navigation within the content of a screen.

At this stage we did not change the design of the user interface. We did however experiment with different colour schemes. The aim was to visualize a number of contrasting colour schemes, and see how this affected clarity and legibility on the mobile screen. The main interface elements were changed to what was considered by the designer to be a more widely acceptable blue colour scheme.

Figure 5 shows the "Reference Checklist" screen from the second prototype, and the revised colour scheme. The checklist acts as a reinforcement of what was covered previously, namely how to construct a reference for a book to include in a reference list. The audio clip explains the process step by step, and is accompanied with animations that visually illustrate each piece of information or component that makes up the reference. Thus the component being described in the audio is simultaneously highlighted on the screen, in this example the second component, the date of publication. Beneath the numbered components, the book reference is constructed, and scrolls across the screen from right to left in real time with the audio clip. This scrolling technique was adopted as a solution to not being able to display a complete book reference clearly and legibly across the width of the screen.

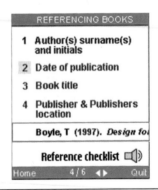

Figure 5: The reference checklist screen from Prototype 2

The Development of Prototype 3

Feedback from a further round of tests by peer users confirmed that the simple one-step navigation technique adopted to move between screens had greatly improved usability. As a result the navigation process was less confusing, and allowed "the user to interact without thinking too much about it" (Lettau 2005). Users found it was more intuitive to use the navigation keys on the phone to go right or left (forward or backward) through the object. It also improved one-handed device operation as you didn't have to concentrate so hard on the navigation process.

However, users highlighted that there were problems with the navigation of the step-through "Making a Reference" sequence, particularly now that the screen to screen navigation had been changed. It was criticized for not being obvious and for being slow, so a better, more intuitive and usable solution was sought.

It was decided to adopt a simplified sub-menu, which would use a small button in the form of a page with a number in its centre. Once the graphic button has focus, the up or down keys on the phone will increase or decrease this number, from 1 through to 5. The centre key when pressed loads that numbered section of the animation, together with its accompanying audio file. Text-based instructions to use the up and down keys were added at the bottom of the screen, next to the audio icon. The resulting overall interface and sub-navigation system for the "Making a Reference" sequence can be seen in Figure 6 below, which shows Part 3 of the sequence. On the bar at the bottom of the screen the two arrows pointing left and right have been retained from previous versions to indicate to users that there is horizontal, linear navigation, and that navigation between screens is done by pressing the navigation keys to the left or right.

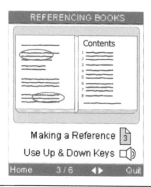

FIGURE 6 Step 3 in the making a reference sequence from Prototype 3

With the completion of the third prototype, we felt that we had reached a stage where the overall design of the learning object, the user interface and the navigation system were sufficiently refined and effective. The next stage was to evaluate the prototype with students, to get their valuable feedback, and to confirm if our design was effective for them.

Student evaluation of the third prototype

The refined third prototype was evaluated with students to get their feedback. We particularly wanted their views on the mobile learning object, and to know if they found it easy to use and navigate through it. We also wanted to get their views more generally on mobile learning and on learning materials for mobile phones. Evaluation was conducted in three separate sessions, and involved seven students. Each was given a Nokia N91 mobile phone with the learning object pre-installed, and they were asked to work through it and make any comments they had as they did so. They were only given a short briefing that told them what they were going to be looking at and how to use the keys on the mobile phone to navigate and select and execute actions. They were not given any instructions on how to navigate through the learning object, as this was one of the main functionalities that we wanted to test to see if our design was intuitive and easy to learn how to use. Afterwards they completed a short questionnaire, and this was followed by an informal discussion about their experiences.

All the students owned a mobile phone, so they could not be described as novice mobile users. There were five females and two males, and they represented a broad age range, with one student between 18-20, three between 21-25, one between 26-30, and two between 36-45.

The first question they were asked was what they thought about the Referencing Books resource, and all the feedback was very positive. One described it as "refreshing," two said it was "a very useful tool," two said it was "helpful," three mentioned that it was "concise," and one commented that it "could have contained more in-depth information." One of the students said, "I think it's a really useful tool – referencing is important and often overlooked. It's clear, concise, and easy to use. I wish I had this in my first degree."

In terms of usability, they all thought that the object was easy to use, with four rating it "very easy" and three rating it "easy" (ratings were on a 3-point scale, from "very easy" to "not easy"). We specifically asked if they had any problems navigating through the object, to test their views on the navigational system we had chosen. One said, "no not really once you're familiar with your phone," and another said, "occasionally unsure when a section had come to an end." Another said it "took a while to work out how to go backwards." However, none of the students reported significant navigational problems, with most saying that once they had become familiar with what they had to do, they were fine, "because it's really short and organised in that way, if you do make a mistake and mess up where you want to be you can get back to where you were really quickly." One student did, however, raise an important usability issue. "After playing the audio on each page I naturally felt compelled to scroll down, instead of up... I think it's natural that I want to scroll down first." None of the students raised concerns about the size of the learning object on the mobile phone, or had problems reading or understanding the text or interface elements. Two students did comment that the Nokia N91 phones were quite large and chunky compared to some phones, and wondered what the experience would be like on a phone with a smaller screen.

On the visual design of the resource, four students used the word "clear" to describe it. Comments included "Uncluttered and clear," "Basic but efficient," "Great. Simple and clear," and "It was clear and easy to follow." No mention was made about the colour scheme, so we can assume that no-one had concerns with it.

We asked if they would like the university to provide them with resources like this, and the six students that answered the question all said yes. The same six students also said that they would be prepared to use their own mobile phones within their university course. One student commented afterwards that he was already using his mobile and his PDA for learning purposes. Two questions were asked about their attitudes towards using mobile phones for teaching and learning, and the results are shown in Tables 1 and 2 below.

TABLE 1 How useful would it be to access learning materials via your mobile?

Rating	Extremely important	1	2	3	4	5	Not at all important
N		1	4	1	0		
%		16,7%	66,7%	16,7%	0%	0%	

They all consider it to be important to be able to access learning materials via their mobile, 83 per cent, if you combine the responses to "1" and "2," although one rated "3" in the middle so could be undecided, and one did not answer the question (see Table 1). We have received a much more positive response to this question from these students than when we asked 101 first-year students the same question in a mobile phone survey a few months earlier, when only 46 per cent thought it was useful to be able to access learning materials on their mobiles, and 29 per cent were undecided, rating "3." This could be because the students in this evaluation study have had an opportunity to see and use learning materials on a mobile phone, whereas the others had not, and therefore couldn't visualize the types of learning materials that could be created. This question was pursued in the informal discussions that followed the questionnaire completion by asking if they would have imagined having something on their mobile that they could learn from before being involved in this exercise today. Most of the students answered no, with one saying "No I wouldn't have thought about it but I don't see why not because you can get everything else. I mean, you can get mobile phones which are like PCs and you can carry your entire life in your mobile phone." Another said "I can see so many different uses." A couple of students asked how we intended to make such resources available to students, and this is something that we have not tackled yet.

For the second question, they all thought it was positive if the university contacted them via their mobile phone for learning purposes (again one did not answer the question). The full results are in Table 2. Their responses suggest that students are becoming more open about their personal mobiles being used for learning tasks, and that they do not see this as an infringement upon their personal devices or space.

TABLE 2 How would you view the university contacting you via your mobile for learning purposes?

Rating	It would be a positive aspect	1	2	3	4	5	It would be a negative aspect
N		2	4	0	0	0	
%		33%	67%	0%	0%	0%	

Many of the comments made by students in the informal discussions afterwards reinforce the positive responses given in the questionnaire. Some of these are included in Table 3.

Many of the comments made are very emphatic. One student describes it as "cool," another "brilliant," and one said "I love it." One said "I really enjoyed using it." Two students commented on the potential of the mobile learning object, saying "I think it's got a lot of potential," and "I think it's a great idea."

TABLE 3 Student comments about the Referencing Books mobile learning object

"I really enjoyed using it."
"I thought it was great and really handy."
"I think it's brilliant."
"I think it's got a lot of potential. I would definitely use it if it was applicable to my course."
"It's cool."
"I love it."
"I think it's something that's really useful."
"You can go home on the tube or the bus and just read it."
"I think it's a great idea."
"I think it's really good."

A frequent topic that was raised by students was the notion of wanting to have learning resources that are convenient for them. Resources that could make use of what was referred to as "dead time," for example, while traveling on the tube (subway), bus, train, or coach to and from university or going home to visit parents, or in any environment where you did not have access to a computer, such as whilst having lunch in a cafe. They like the fact that mobile learning resources have the added advantage that they can be used anywhere, anytime, because they are designed for small devices that are carried everywhere, and can be used whenever its convenient, especially in cramped environments (such as when on public transport as one student noted) and in situations when it would be more difficult to study from bulkier text books or course notes.

The Response to Student Evaluation

Student feedback confirmed that some aspects of the design were not intuitive and could be improved. This led to another development cycle and the creation of Prototype 4.

The Development of Prototype 4

In the light of student feedback, and discussions with colleagues from another multimedia development team, further changes were made to the presentation of content on the screen and navigation through it, the overall interface design, and to the Making a Reference step-through sequence.

The biggest problem with the screen design was that peer users and students did not like navigating through the content within a screen from the bottom upwards. They did not find this intuitive, so this was changed.

This in turn led to changes in the overall interface and screen design. The title of each screen or section was moved to the top horizontal bar and replaced the title of the learning object, which was considered to be superfluous and removed. Because mobile learning objects are likely to be short for completion in just a few minutes, it was considered that it was not necessary to include the title of the object beyond the first screen. At the same time, the audio button was moved to the top bar, next to the title, because as the audio clip introduces each screen, it suited being in the same place. Moving the audio button also benefited the focus order. The audio button has focus when the user enters a screen, and pressing the down navigation key on the phone moves the focus down the button list, resulting in a more straight-forward top to bottom focus path. These changes had the effect of freeing up space below the central content area, and made the overall screen design less crowded.

A better solution for navigating through the Making a Reference step-through sub-menu was also required. Operating the step-through was still a slow two-step process. Our test users and some of the students had found this problematic. Users suggested making use of the number keys on the mobile to control each step. By clicking a keypad number from 1 to 5, the appropriate step in the animation sequence is played. This was a totally different approach to any of the other navigational techniques we had used to date, and made use of the alphanumeric keys on the keypad of the phone for the first time to navigate to content screens. Instructions on how to navigate through the step-through were included within the introductory audio clip, thus removing the need for textual instructions to be placed on the screen. The revised design is shown in Figure 7.

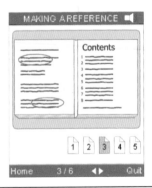

FIGURE 7 Step 3 in the making a reference sequence from Prototype 4, showing the revised user interface and sequence navigation

Summary of the Key Design Decisions

To summarize, this fourth prototype has gone through a number of key changes in its iterations, influenced not only by input and feedback from the development team, but also from peer users and from student feedback.

The overall navigation system from screen to screen was simplified, from a two-step "focus and select" process to using the left and right navigation keys on the five-way navigation key to move forward and backward through the object. This has proved to be more intuitive to users, is an easier and simpler process, and improves the ability to use the learning object on a mobile phone with one hand.

The design of the user interface was refined in light of the revised navigation technique, and to improve overall usability and clarity. When the arrows on the bottom bar were used to navigate between screens, it seemed natural to access content on the screen from the bottom upwards, starting with the audio introduction. This did not prove to be intuitive with users, and once navigation through the object was changed to using the left and right navigation keys, there was no reason why you couldn't navigate downwards through a screen, from top to bottom. The screen title and audio icon were therefore moved to the top bar, and the learning object title was considered to be superfluous and removed.

The navigation of the Making a Reference section has proved to be the most difficult to find a solution to. Having a sub-section is in itself problematic in what is only a short learning object, and maybe the storyboard needs revisiting to break down the content of that sub-section into a series of discrete screens, which would remove the need for an additional navigation system. The current prototype makes use of the alphanumeric keys on the phone to select the appropriate section.

We have found that user interactivity and the use of multimedia have not been compromised in the mobile version. Users still control what they look at, and the pace in which they work through the object. All of the multimedia elements from the original have been retained, except for the 3D animation which was replaced with a 2D cartoon strip type animation. Most of the graphics used in the prototype were deliberately kept simple, so that we could concentrate on the more fundamental design and development challenges. In some places the use of multimedia has enhanced the mobile version, for example the addition of audio commentaries aids understanding, and simple animations can accompany them providing visual illustration.

In this first learning object that we have developed for a mobile phone, how to navigate and execute user interactions using the available keys was a major challenge. We are confident that we have arrived at an effective navigational system, making use of the available, common device keys. The five-way navigation key is used to move backwards and forwards through the learning object, and up and down through the content elements of individual screens. Number keys on the keypad are used to access numbered screens within the sub-section, and clearly this technique could be more widely utilized, for example to navigate to specific screens or to select parts of content, such as in a numbered list, or a menu.

Discussion

A significant issue at the beginning of this project was the extent to which the Mobile Learning Objects (MLOs) can retain the pedagogical richness of the original desktop based resources. The original learning objects were developed to tackle a series of pedagogical challenges, such as facilitating learner engagement, and aiding students in dealing with problems of abstraction and complexity. These learning objects for the PC used a number of constructivist principles. They provided, for example, rich interactive visualizations, learner controlled pacing, and used scaffolding to assist learners in the transition to real-life use of knowledge (Boyle 2003; Holley et al. 2007; Smith et al. 2007). Given the constraints of the mobile phone device, a significant question was to what extent this rich functionality could be retained.

The underlying conceptual approach to tackling this problem is based on the idea of Generative Learning Objects or GLOs (Boyle 2006). In this approach the concrete realization of the learning object is separated from its underlying design. The underlying design, or pedagogical pattern, is viewed as providing the true basis for reuse. In this approach the mobility of learning objects is viewed as another presentation level of the same learning object. This work has allowed us to explore the extent to which this approach works. The pedagogical structure of the learning object is represented in the GLO approach as a network of pedagogical choices. This network is independent of any particular concrete realization. Mapping the pedagogical choices to the mobile device thus involves two main considerations.

The first is the transformation of media elements: text, graphics, animations, and so on, so that the presentational richness of the original PC objects can be captured in the mobile devices. The bulk of the chapter has dealt with this issue, and demonstrated that this was largely achieved. The second issue is the extent to which the richness of pedagogical intent of the original can be captured in the mobile version. Do the navigational limitations and small screen size of the device provide significant obstacles to achieving this pedagogical richness? The feedback from the study points strongly to the ability to capture this pedagogical richness on mobile devices. The navigation system has to be transformed into basically a two-dimensional navigation of page forward and backward, and tab up and tab down the selected screen. However, this provided no major barriers to achieving rich interaction. In fact, work on this and other learning objects has shown that quite rich techniques, such as fading from video to schematic representations, can be achieved quite naturally within this apparently limited navigation structure. A further insight is the extent to which transforming text to speech, especially when mediated through headphones, produces a more intimate feel for the learning objects. This, in fact, enhances the engagement level of the learning objects over and above the PC-based learning objects.

The outcome of the study, and our explorations to date, indicate that very rich pedagogical techniques can be achieved on mobile phones. This often requires adaptation at the media level, for example replacing explanatory text with speech. However, these presentation level adaptations do not detract from the pedagogical richness of the learning object, and in some instances, enhance it. MLOs obviously have certain other features, such as the ability to produce situationally-specific learning, which provides opportunities not easily made available on desktop devices. The future for developing pedagogically rich, constructivist learning resources on mobile devices thus looks very promising.

Conclusion

We have reached the stage where we have developed four iterations of a prototype with refinements made at each stage in the light of peer testing and student feedback. We now have a fully functional prototype, and in the process we have researched and tackled a lot of the issues involved in developing multimedia Flash Lite 2 learning objects for Nokia Series 60 phones. Student feedback confirms that multimedia mobile learning objects are desirable, and this work is now developing in a number of parallel strands.

A key issue now is how we can integrate MLOs and students' own mobile phones into campus-based teaching scenarios in a coherent manner. We are already beginning to develop new MLO prototypes in different subject areas, and will conduct more extensive trials on these with students. There are also opportunities to embrace the strengths that the mobile phone can bring to learning, for example in combining multimedia learning content with scenarios for learners to capture and contribute media files (user generated content), dynamically upload content on the move, and communicate with peers and/or tutors. The possibilities for incorporating multimedia learning resources into sociable learning scenarios on mobile phones is achievable and could be very powerful, and that is one of the directions that we are interested to pursue in the next phase of development.

We also have to investigate and tackle a number of issues associated with how we could make such learning objects available to students. Since we embarked on this work, licensing deals with mobile device manufacturers are making Flash Lite available on more phone models, and in most cases freely, making Flash-based learning objects a more viable proposition. So far we have limited our work to developing solely for Nokia Series 60 phones, and in particular the N70 and N91. There are issues around how content would be presented on phones with different screen display sizes and resolutions (which currently varies widely). We have to determine how we can best package up the learning objects for easy transfer onto the phone (the current prototype consists of one SWF file, and a series of external assets for the audio and text files). And then determine how we could make available the packaged files for users to have on their phone (for example, by providing pre-installed SD or memory cards, or by downloading from the Internet, which is a cheap option if it can be done via WiFi), sending them via Bluetooth, or transferring them via a PC (if students' phones permit this).

Another area we are working towards is streamlining the production process of our learning objects, so that once the creative design phase is over, the Generative Learning Object (GLO) tool can be used to instantiate versions for the Internet, mobile devices and further down the line for ubiquitous devices such as wearables.

Having a refined working prototype has been vital in helping us to get meaningful feedback from students, and has helped them to visualize what the future of mobile learning could look like. Student feedback on this learning object has been extremely positive, and is very encouraging. A high percentage of them (83 per cent) think it would be useful to be able to access learning materials on their mobile. Students can not only see the potential for multimedia MLOs, but they see them as being "cool" and "brilliant." They can also identify ways in which they would use them, saying that they're "really handy" and "really useful," and can see the benefits of using them in periods of dead time, when traveling in cramped spaces, and in environments where there is no access to computers. Such comments suggest that multimedia MLOs can engage students into learning, and provide an interesting and enjoyable experience. We are constantly surprised by the positive student reaction towards mobile learning, and the fact that they say the kinds of things that we would be aiming for, summed up by one student who said, "I think it's got a lot of potential. I would definitely use it if it was applicable to my course." Such feedback indicates that students are receptive towards multimedia MLOs, and that there is therefore great potential in continuing with this direction in mobile learning, providing that materials are well designed and based on sound pedagogic principles.

References

Adobe. 2006. Website A: Macromedia Flash Lite 2 Content Development Kit (CDK). http://www.adobe.com/devnet/devices/flashlite.html (accessed March 27, 2006).

——. 2006. Website B: Adobe Flash Lite Exchange. http://www.adobe.com/cfusion/exchange/index.cfm?view=sn310#loc=enus&view=sn310&viewName=Adobe%20Exchange&avm=1 (accessed November 9, 2006).

——. 2006. Website C: Getting Started Developing for Flash Lite. http://www.adobe.com/devnet/devices/flashlite.html#cdk (accessed November 14, 2006).

BAIRD, P., and C. WHITEAR. 2006. Mobile charting with Flash Lite 2: Designing for the mobile device interface. Adobe mobile and devices developer center. http://www.adobe.com/devnet/devices/articles/fl2_charting_components.html

BOYLE, T. 1997. *Design for multimedia learning.* London: Prentice Hall.

——. 2003. Design principles for authoring dynamic, reusable learning objects. *Australian Journal of Educational Technology* 19 (1):46-58. http://www.ascilite.org.au/ajet/ajet19/boyle.html

——. 2006. The design and development of second generation Learning Objects. Proceedings, *Ed-Media 2006, world conference on educational multimedia, hypermedia & telecommunications,* June 26-30, Orlando, Florida.

BOYLE, T., J. COOK, R. WINDLE, H. WHARRARD, D. LEEDER, and R. ALTON. 2006. An agile method for developing Learning Objects. Paper presentation, *ASCILITE conference,* Sydney, Australia, December 3-6.

BRADLEY, C., R. HAYNES, and T. BOYLE. 2005a. Design for multimedia m-learning: Lessons from two case studies. In *Exploring the frontiers of e-Learning: Borders, outposts and migration,* ed. J. Cook and D. Whitelock. Research proceedings of the 12th Association for Learning Technology Conference (ALT-C 2005), September 6-8, University of Manchester, England.

———. 2005b. Adult multimedia learning with PDAs – the user experience. In proceedings, *mLearn 2005*, October 25-28, Cape Town, South Africa.

COOK, J., D. HOLLEY, C. SMITH, C. BRADLEY, and R. HAYNES. 2006a. A blended m-learning design for supporting teamwork in formal and informal settings. In proceedings, *Mobile Learning 2006*, July 14-16, Dublin, Ireland.

———. 2006b. Team enhanced creativity: An approach to designing user-centred reusable Learning Objects. Paper presentation, *4th international conference on multimedia and ICTs in education (m-ICTE2006)*, November 22-25, Seville, Spain.

DotMobi. 2007. *Mobile web developer's guide.* http://www.blueflavor.com/blog/mobile/dotmobi_mobile_web_developers_guide.php (accessed March 27, 2007).

DURAN, J. 2006. Optimization tips and tricks for Flash Lite 2. Adobe mobile and devices developer centre. http://www.adobe.com/devnet/devices/articles/optimization_tips.html

HOLLEY, D., J. COOK, C. SMITH, C. BRADLEY, and R. HAYNES. 2007. Getting ahead at university: Using reusable Learning Objects to enhance study skills. In proceedings, *Ed-Media 2007, world conference on educational multimedia, hypermedia & telecommunications*, June 25-29, Vancouver, Canada.

LETTAU, T. 2005. Design for devices. http://weblogs.macromedia.com/xd/archives/mobile/index.cfm

Nokia. 2006a. Flash Lite for S60 – an emerging global ecosystem. http://www.s60.com/pics/pdf/S60_Flash_Lite_May.pdf (accessed March 27, 2007).

———. 2006b. Flash Lite: Visual Guide v1.1. Forum Nokia website. http://www.forum.nokia.com/main/resources/documentation/s60.html (accessed March 27, 2007).

———. n.d. Nokia Multimedia Converter 2.0. Forum Nokia website. http://www.forum.nokia.com/main/resources/tools_and_sdks/listings/media_tools.html (accessed November 14, 2006).

NORMAN, D., and S. DRAPER, eds. 1986. *User centered system design: New perspectives on human-computer interaction.* Hillsdale, NJ: Lawrence Erlbaum Associates.

Nyíri, K. 2002. Towards a philosophy of m-learning. In proceedings, *IEEE international workshop on wireless and mobile technologies in education* (WMTE '02).

Smith, C., J. Cook, C. Bradley, R. Gossett, and R. Haynes. 2007. Enhancing deep learning in sports science: The application of rich media visualization techniques in mobile and reusable Learning Objects. Paper presentation, *Ed-Media 2007, world conference on educational multimedia, hypermedia & telecommunications*, June 25-29, Vancouver, Canada.

Soloway, E., and C. Norris. 2005. Using handheld computers in the classroom: Concrete visions. Podcast of keynote address, *mLearn 2005, 4th world conference on mlearning.* http://libsyn.com/media/digit5th/SolowayNorris.mp3 (accessed February 2006).

Ulm, J. 2005. Mobile UI animation, Part 2. http://weblogs.macromedia.com/xd/archives/mobile/index.cfm (accessed March 27, 2007).

Wood, D., J. Bruner, and G. Ross. 1976. The role of tutoring in problem solving. *Journal of Child Psychology and Psychiatry* 17 (2):89-100.

Flash Lite websites and blogs worth visiting:

http://www.biskero.org/

http://flash-lite-tutorial.blogspot.com/

http://chiaotsu.wordpress.com/

http://www.flashmobilegroup.org/

http://richardleggett.co.uk/blog/index.php

http://www.flashdevices.net/

http://www.flashmobilegroup.org/

http://justin.everett-church.com/index.php/

http://casario.blogs.com/mmworld/

http://www.christianhalbach.de/blog/

http://www.blueskynorth.com/

Adobe Mobile and Devices Forums: http://www.adobe.com/cfusion/webforums/forum/index.cfm?forumid=68

Nokia Developer Discussion Boards: http://discussion.forum.nokia.com/forum/index.php

Yahoo Group: http://tech.groups.yahoo.com/group/flashlite/

Acknowledgments

The Centre of Excellence in Teaching and Learning in Reusable Learning Objects is funded by the Higher Education Funding Council for England. London Metropolitan University is the lead site, in partnership with the universities of Cambridge and Nottingham.

From E-learning to Mobile Learning: New Opportunities

MICHELLE PIERI
DAVIDE DIAMANTINI
UNIVERSITY OF MILANO-BICOCCA
ITALY

Abstract

This chapter focuses on an experience of blended learning that is still ongoing for the training of managers of Technological Transfer (TT), who work in an Italian Scientific Technological Park (STP). Their main activity is linked to technological transfer. In the STP the technological transfer manager is the key figure in the management of the transmission of scientific knowledge from the research world to the industrial dimension. The aim of this project is to conduct an experiment in a "Training course for the TT manager" in order to satisfy their training needs. The course is based on a blended learning model, with the use of combined traditional educational methodologies: (1) e-learning methodologies and face to face and (2) m-learning methodologies and face to face. This chapter will focus on the blended m-learning experience.

Introduction

This chapter focuses on the ongoing experience of blended learning (e-learning and m-learning) for the training of managers of Technological Transfer (TT), who work in an Italian Scientific Technological Park (STP).

With the term mobile learning we refer to a modality of distribution of any learning content with portable devices such as the Personal Digital Assistant (PDA), Tablet PC, e-book, and mobile phones. More generally, it is possible to call mobile learning any form of learning through devices which are very small, autonomous from the electrical supply, and small enough to accompany people anytime and anywhere (Roschelle 2003; Trifonova and Ronchetti 2003; Liang et al. 2005).

Since 2000, literature on mobile learning has been increasing more and more every day. Many researchers from all parts of the world have been researching and are still working on this new learning methodology. Mobile learning is different from e-learning, since it is not just electronic, it is mobile (Shepherd 2001). Mobile learning is seen as the natural evolution of e-learning, according to Hoppe, Joner, Millard, and Sharples (2003), "m-learning is e-learning using a mobile device and wireless transmission." In Harris's (2001) opinion, "m-learning is the point at which mobile computing and e-learning intersect to produce an anytime, anywhere learning experience."

With mobile learning the learning phase is not bound to a location with specific characteristics, potentially becoming omnipresent learning. For example, delays during commuting and travelling on the underground become potential learning moments. In general, any moment which would otherwise be "wasted," or that before now could not be enriched with didactic contents, has now become a potential learning moment thanks to mobile learning.

The main activity of the STP is linked to technological transfer. STP is a structure where companies can find valid support in terms of space, technologies, and financing. STP is a privileged access channel for innovation and applied research, thanks to a system of integrated services available for companies situated inside the park, and also for those in the entire surrounding territory. Until 1995 there were only three STPs in Italy; at present there are thirty-three.

In the STP the technological transfer manager is the key figure for the management of the transmission of scientific knowledge from the research world to the industrial dimension. The TT manager has various levels of competencies and is able to talk to the research world as well as to industry. The TT manager has the task of turning the functions/objectives of the research world towards the demands of industry and of government and also of simplifying the knowledge transfer from the research world to the business one (Diamantini 2004).

The dynamics of innovation, even if they are very important for the national socio-economic system, are a circumscribed phenomenon (Lundvall 1992; Patel and Pavitt 1994). Because of the limited number of interested subjects and of the necessary high profile of excellence and of the enormous quantity of competences involved, these training processes are for the training of a highly specialized elite.

From the training of TT managers, various difficulties emerge when designing models for specific training situations. A first difficulty is tied to the formalization level of the highly specialized expertise, which constitutes the central nucleus of the competencies on which the activity of the TT manager is based. Some of these competencies can be based on knowledge linked to a concrete know-how, others on an abstract and theoretical knowledge. However, it is clear that knowledge which is based on strictly academic educational processes, characterized by a high level of abstraction, translates into highly specialized training models which is often far away from the concept of problem solving. Instead, in the everyday scene the TT manager has to solve concrete problems, where not only academic-theoretical knowledge is required, but also practical knowledge. Therefore, the knowledge that TT managers need for their work must be composed of a complex mix of theoretical competencies acquired from study and a set of practical competencies, along with experience and know-how accumulated in a professional ambit.

In Italy there are various initiatives for the training of the TT manager, from universities and other public agencies not referable to the academic institution in a strict sense. These projects, even though they are relevant in the Italian framework, do not satisfy the training demand of TT managers. First of all, the training model used in these experiences is still the traditional face-to-face lesson, and possesses an extremely abstract character. Secondly, there is the problem of time. Typically, the TT manager does not have long periods of time to spend on training during the work day.

The Blended Learning Course

After an analysis of the complex situation illustrated in the previous paragraphs, it was decided to conduct an experiment for the "training course for the manager of technological transfer" in order to satisfy the training needs of the TT manager. This experience, which began in January 2005, is still ongoing.

In the Italian framework, the methodologies that were used are the novelty of the course. The course is based on the blended learning model. Blended learning is a combination of different approaches and strategies to teaching with the objective of making learning more effective and personalized. In this view future training programs are oriented towards an integration of different educational methods and creating equilibrium between the traditional face to face classroom and distance learning. This trend is in a prospective of lifelong learning and also brings the valorisation of individual knowledge, not only formal but also informal knowledge.

In this training the following educational methodologies were used:
- e-learning methodologies and face to face
- m-learning methodologies and face to face

It was decided to use the blended learning methodologies since it is believed that both e-learning and m-learning present a series of pros and cons, as in all new applications. Therefore, the forms of blended learning are able to take advantage of the benefits of the technological innovation without having to sacrifice the strong points of the more traditional and consolidated modalities of a classroom setting.

The Sample

The sample was chosen according to two main criteria, the subject of the sample must:
1. Have a role and organizational function relative and coherent with the objectives of the course.
2. Show a real need for the training.
3. Be motivated to participate in the training, as a fundamental component for a positive outcome.

To reach the first two objectives it was necessary to choose high level employees and not office clerks.

The sample is made up of fifteen people, five men and ten women, between twenty-nine and forty-three years old (average age = 39.7). These people who not only have a university degree, in some cases (six) have a master's degree and in other cases (two) are working on their doctoral degrees.

Blended E-learning Experimentation

The experimentation of the blended e-learning model was made on four levels:
1. Needs analysis. In this step the company indicates the organizational and individual shortages. The analysis of needs is supported by

competency models which indicate learning and competencies to be developed, through subsequent educational processes.

2. Design of the interventions. Educational interventions are designed after the training objectives, which are intended to be followed and the modality of transmitting the competencies of the models that have been selected.

3. Delivery of the training. Education processes are delivered, and they are structured in further evolving cycles that make the creation of new learning effective.

4. Assessments. In this conclusive phase new elements which are produced and interiorized are integrated. They become part of the organization which codifies and assimilates them by making them part of the common patrimony shared by its members.

The experience of blended e-learning will not be described here in detail, but this chapter will focus on the results of the assessment phase, since these results were the starting point for the design of a blended m-learning experience.

Critical Factors That Emerged in the Course of the Blended E-learning Experimentation

There were three instruments used to analyze the results obtained from the blended e-learning experimentation. There was the double objective of understanding the qualities and characteristics of the sampling and the positive and negative aspects of the course:

1. A questionnaire about the correlated competences for a personal development plan (PDP), in which the objective was to show aptitudes and competency of the students.

2. Assessment forms of the learning modules taken, used to identify the strong and weak points of the modules.

3. In depth interviews of the students to integrate with the questionnaires in order to finish the profiles.

The assessment shows that on one hand, the students judged the contents positively; on the other hand, there is a limit created by the mental representation of a desktop computer, which is seen only and exclusively as a work instrument and not as a lifelong learning instrument.

The students had difficulty becoming familiar with the computer instrument as a training and communication instrument and not only as a work instrument. The first level of analysis is to represent the work instrument; all students work on a personal computer, but none of the students had taken an online course. Therefore, representing the work instrument as a training instrument requires the structuring of an appositive learning path. For example, a pre-course would be useful to help the student become familiar with the instrument. According to the students an entry test would be useful, as a means to understand how the learning instrument could be effectively used.

Furthermore, as was shown by the tracking of the platform accesses, almost all the students came on the platform during the work day at precise times. This lets us understand how the computer instrument is not viewed as a training instrument and how the training is not perceived as a continuative process, but is still seen as a moment in itself that must not go beyond precise times during the day.

The Blended Mobile Learning Course

It is thought that m-learning can make up for the critical factors that characterized the blended e-learning experience. In the blended m-learning we decided to:

1. Administer a pre-questionnaire in order to understand how the learning instrument could be best used.
2. Familiarize the students with the instrument through a first face to face meeting of the course where the Pocket PC is presented and distributed to the students; the fruition of a learning unit on mobile learning and a second face to face meeting to share doubts about the new learning typology.

In particular, it is thought that the mental representation of a mobile device is different from a desktop computer for the following multiple reasons:

1. The versatility and the wide use of the mobile device for teaching, a palmtop for example, easily becomes a multimedia screen for listening to music, looking at pictures, and viewing films.
2. As suggested by Graham (1997), Steinberger (2002) and Figg and Burston (2002), it is so easy to learn how to use a mobile device that normally an instruction booklet is not even necessary. In less than half an hour a new user is able to become familiar with the main functions of a new device and to acquire familiarity with its software in order to autonomously attend a course. This is due to the fact that most of the users are using similar devices everyday, such as mobile phones. This consideration is not true for a personal computer where the lack of knowledge of the computer environment requires training sessions for at least one day for someone who does not have familiarity

with a computer. It may require more time for the use of application software.

3. The mobile device, different from the desktop computer, which for many people is bound to the work and the office environment, now accompanies the majority of Italians practically all the time and everywhere.

The experience of blended mobile learning can be divided into the following phases:

1. Face to face meeting with the students, during which a pre-questionnaire is administered and the Pocket PC is presented and distributed to the students.
2. Completion of a learning unit on mobile learning.
3. Face to face meeting with the students to discuss the new learning methodology.
4. Completion of the didactic module on one of the topics taken from the needs analysis made in Phase 1.
5. Face to face meeting with the students for the discussion of their observations and the administration of the assessment questionnaire about the experience.

As previously reported, the experience is still ongoing. After having explained the model and the teaching strategies used, a brief explanation will be made of the didactic modules, the pre-questionnaire, and the assessment questionnaire.

The Model and Didactics Strategies

The transformations in the current didactics used for mobile learning are mainly linked to the fact that the learning activity takes place through a new tool – the mobile device. And, just as online didactics differ from face to face didactics, didactics via mobile devices must also take into consideration some elements that differ from face to face and online didactics.

Obviously, these elements are not linked exclusively to the mobile device in itself, but to the peculiarities of mobile learning: the time gaps and places of its use. Just as online didactics cannot be a simple transposition of personal didactics in the most traditional sense, the same is also true for didactics via mobile learning – it cannot be a mere transposition of online didactics.

We decided to structure the course using learning object approach. From the tests and studies carried out so far, it seems that the mobile devices are very flexible technologies which can support various models, from those based on the transmission of contents to those based on interaction, experience, and the building up of knowledge.

Starting with these considerations, in each Mobile Learning Object (MLO) we decided to let the transmission of contents be followed by a topic for reflection or by homework, the results of which were shared during the next face to face meeting.

To create this didactic unit, the guidelines of Steinberger (2002) and Figg and Burston (2002) have been taken into consideration. According to them (as quoted by Trifonova and Ronchetti 2003):

> Modules should be short, and last no longer than five to ten minutes. Users should be able to use small fragments of time spent waiting or free time for learning, by reading small pieces of data, doing quizzes or using forums or chats. Simple, fun and added value functionality. The computational power and other properties of mobile devices make it difficult in most cases to use complex or multimedia content, although devices of the same size are used for entertainment with great commercial success. It should be possible to use an m-learning system without reading a user manual, and the experience of studying with the help of such devices should be interesting and engaging.

When introducing the contents to promote learning, we followed the guidelines by Mayer (1999) who suggests:

- Underline the most significant information using titles, italics, bold, underlining, font sizes, icons and images.
- Explain the didactic goals in order to orient the participant's attention towards the main contents
- supply short summaries.
- Take out redundant information and adopted a concise style in order to reduce "noise."

To make it easier for the student to organize and process the new information, and help the student to connect the selected representations in order to create a coherent mental representation, we have tried to:

- Structure the text in a clear and comprehensible way; in particular we have explained the conceptual relations among its parts (cause/effect, confrontation/comparison, classification, and so on).
- Supply an "outline" of the key points.
- Indicate the key words.
- Supply graphic representations to correlate the new concepts (i.e. schemes).

The Pre-questionnaire

The pre-questionnaire was created by selecting thematic areas from a survey made on scientific literature regarding mobile devices in general, and mobile learning in particular. It is divided into four parts.

In the first part, several free associations are requested (maximum five) for four stimuli: mobile telephones, desktop, notebook, and handheld computer. In the second part, participants are asked to give their opinion about the associations they gave: positive (+), neutral (0), or negative (−) ratings.

In the third part, they had to answer questions about their own mobile devices and their use.

In the last part, social-personal questions were asked, such as sex, age, residence, education, profession, average time spent to reach their place of work, and their use of Internet.

The goal of this questionnaire is to understand how the learning instrument can be used, something which was not done in the blended e-learning experience. For this, it is necessary to understand what mobile devices our subjects have, how they use them and how they are willing to use them.

The Didactic Modules

The didactic modules, in text format and audio, constitute the learning objects which last approximately ten minutes each. Every MLO has a contents part followed by tasks to do (for example: "Try to reflect on one of the topics that was just presented to you," or "Collect material on one of the topics which was just presented"). The results of the reflections and the tasks will be shared with the participants of the course in successive face to face meetings which will lead to the co-construction of common knowledge.

The Assessment Questionnaire

The areas to be investigated in the assessment of the quality of the mobile learning experimentation have been identified also in the literature about mobile learning. In particular we have considered:

- The benefits of mobile learning, such as the chance to access the training contents anywhere and anytime.
- The features of the mobile device in itself, in this case the Pocket PC, both in terms of hardware and software.
- The way the user feels the mobile device is as a learning tool.
- The structuring of the course both in terms of content organization, the stimuli and the homework assignments proposed.

The results obtained from the analysis of the data from the various areas had the objective of identifying the areas of the training process where action should be taken in order to improve the participants' satisfaction of the training processes.

Regarding the features of the mobile devices in themselves, if subjects have never used a PDA before, they were asked if they had any problem using the Pocket PC. They were also asked to assess the following aspects using a five-point Likert scale:

- readability of the contents on the screen
- use of the pen
- surfing and menu changing
- screen colours
- battery life
- audio

As for the characteristics of use, the space and time gaps in which the mobile device was used for the didactic unit have been investigated. Students were also asked if using the Pocket PC in public has been easy and accessible, or if it has been difficult. If some difficulty was experienced, the student had to specify if it was caused by lack of concentration, reception, reading of the screen, or by some other factor.

With regards to the course content and organization, after a question about the general assessment of the course, the students were asked to assess the proposed topic and its relationship to their training path with another five-point Likert scale. The students were asked to assess the stimuli and the homework assignments proposed at the end of each single MLO, and they also have a final meeting with the trainer.

Finally, they had to indicate the three positive and the three negative points of the module and also the main problems they had found, making suggestions regarding the development of the module offered to them.

Implications for Practice

To obtain good results from the course it is important to have a first face to face meeting with the students in order to familiarize them with the mobile device, where they are loaned the Pocket PC and trained in its use.

From the evaluation questionnaire it was seen that the subjects were afraid of losing the pen or having the Pocket PC stolen. At the final meeting it was seen that the emphasis they put on the fear of theft or loss was tied to the fact that the Pocket PC was not theirs. In light of these elements, it was thought that it would be useful to promote the purchase of the mobile device by the company/subject so that it would become 100 per cent part of the subject's daily life for work and after work. It is important that the mobile device is seen from the start not as an instrument limited to a temporary experience, but as a permanent instrument of life-long learning.

Conclusion

From this experience of blended m-learning still in progress, it seems that blended m-learning training method suits the needs of TT managers better than blended e-learning. Mobile learning allows trainees to use time and spaces formerly "lost" from training activities (for example, the time spent on the bus from the city to the STP) by blending it with e-learning.

Among the positive elements of this experience, subjects mentioned the ease of use of the mobile device, its usefulness to fill up empty moments like traveling on the train, and the fact that taking a course via a mobile device was engaging and fun. This last point is a further confirmation of what has emerged from other numerous international experiences: Learning with a mobile device is enjoyable for students (Prensky 2001; Seppälä and Alamäki 2003; Savill-Smith and Kent 2003; Schwabe and Göth 2005).

The work with blended m-learning also shows that there is the need to develop teaching strategies that focus on those experiential elements which can strengthen learning by building what in contemporary literature is called "learning experience."

References

DIAMANTINI, D. 2004. *Il Manager dell'innovazione. La Formazione nelle Professioni del Trasferimento Tecnologico.* Milano: Guerini e Associati.

GRAHAM, B. 1997. The world in your pocket: Using pocket book computers for IT. *Social Science Review* 79 (287): 45-48.

FIGG, C., and J. BURSON. 2002. PDA strategies for preservice teacher technology training. Paper presentation, *14th world conference on educational multimedia, hypermedia and telecommunications,* Denver, CO.

LIANG, L., T. LIU, H. WANG, B. CHANG, Y. DENG, J. YANG, C. CHOU, H. KO, S. YANG, and T. CHAN. 2005. A few design perspectives on one-on-one digital classroom environment. *Journal of Computer Assisted Learning* 21, no. 3:181-89.

LUNDVALL, B. 1992. *National systems of innovation: Towards a theory of innovation and interactive learning.* London: Printer Publisher.

MAYER, R. 1999. Design instruction for constructivist learning. In *Instructional design theory and models*, ed. C. Reigeluth, 141-59. New York: Lawrence Erlbaum Associates.

PATEL, P., and K. PAVITT. 1994. Uneven (and divergent) technological accumulation among advanced countries: Evidence and a framework of explanation. *Industrial and Corporate Change* 3: 759-87.

PRENSKY, M. 2001. *Digital game-based learning*. New York: McGraw-Hill.

ROSCHELLE, J. 2003. Keynote paper: Unlocking the learning value of wireless mobile devices. *Journal of Computer Assisted Learning* 19:260-72.

SAVILL-SMITH, C., and P. KENT. 2003. *The use of palmtop computers for learning: A review of the literature*. London: LSDA.

SEPPÄLÄ, P., and H. ALAMÄKI. 2003. Mobile learning in teacher training. *Journal of Computer Assisted Learning* 19:330-35.

SHEPHERD, M. 2001. M is for Maybe. Tactix: Training and communication technology in context. http://www.fastrak-consulting.co.uk/tactix/features/mlearning.htm.

SCHWABE, G., and C. GÖTH. 2005. Mobile learning with a mobile game: Design and motivational effects. *Journal of Computer Assisted Learning* 21:216-40.

STEINBERGER, C. 2002. Wireless meets wireline e-learning. Proceedings, *14th world conference on educational multimedia, hypermedia and telecommunications*, Denver, CO.

TRIFONOVA, A., and M. RONCHETTI. 2003. Where is mobile learning going? Proceedings, *World conference on e-learning in corporate, government, healthcare & higher education*, November 7-11, Phoenix, AZ.

MobilED – Mobile Tools and Services Platform for Formal and Informal Learning

MERRYL FORD
MERAKA INSTITUTE
SOUTH AFRICA
TEEMU LEINONEN
HELSINKI UNIVERSITY OF ART AND DESIGN
FINLAND

Abstract

MobilED is a South African initiative aimed at designing teaching and learning environments that are meaningfully enhanced with mobile technologies and services. The deliverables are the development of a set of scenarios and guidelines on how mobile technologies could be used for teaching and learning within and outside the school context. The applicability of mobile phones in an educational environment is examined, with a specific focus on the differences and similarities between the developing and developed worlds. The first phase of the project in South Africa focused on the use of low-cost mobile phones, which are readily available in the developing world, and the second phase examined the use of more advanced mobile phones with multimedia capabilities. Pilot projects in South Africa are being replicated in Finland, India, and Brazil to explore the cultural, social and organizational context of the utilization of mobile phones in and out of school in a developing and developed world context.

Introduction

Mobile technologies, particularly the mobile phone, are set to play a major role in the development of the information society in developing countries. According to the International Telecommunications Union (ITU), Africa's mobile cellular growth rate has been the highest of any region over the past five years, averaging close to 60 per cent year on year. The continent-wide total number of mobile phone subscribers at the end of 2004 was seventy-six million (ITU Report 2006). The economic and social benefits of mobile phones are evident at all socio-economic levels of society and the penetration rate of mobile phones is significant, especially given the fact that access to these devices is often shared.

Contrary to trends in the developed world, where PC and Internet connectivity is almost ubiquitous, mobile phones are currently the most important networked knowledge-exchange technology used in the developing world. From a developing country perspective, features such as limited or no dependence on permanent electricity supply, easy maintenance, easy-to-use audio and text interfaces, affordability and accessibility are the most important considerations for using mobile phones as potential learning tools (Masters 2005; Mutula 2002; Stone et al. 2003). The contention that a "socially and educationally responsible definition (of mobile learning) must view the learner as the one being mobile and not his/her devices" (Laouris and Eteokleous 2005), and the ability for "anytime, anywhere" learning is still applicable in the developing world, but more as a positive side-effect. If we separate "mobile learning" into "mobile" and "learning," the learning aspect is the most important concept in the developing world. The computing device just happens to be mobile.

These mobile devices are becoming increasingly powerful computers, with built-in advanced multimedia facilities. It is interesting to note that today's high-end mobile phones have the computing power of a mid-1990s PC – while consuming only one-hundredth of the energy (Oelofse et al. 2006). Even the simplest, voice-only phones have more complex and powerful chips than the 1969 on-board computer that landed a spaceship on the moon (Prensky 2005). In addition, if we have a closer look at the whole mobile phone infrastructure, we will realize that the actual device can be seen as a terminal for using several computers in a network. When making a simple call or sending an SMS message we use (1) the "computer" of the mobile phone, (2) the server computers of the operators, and (3) the "computer" of the receiver's mobile phone. When mobile phones are perceived as terminals for using computers, we open up a new perspective for the design and development of practices relating to how mobile phones could be used in different human operations and processes, including formal and informal learning.

Context: ICT in Education in South Africa

South Africa's education system has undergone a dramatic change over the past ten years, with the introduction of "outcomes-based education" (OBE). Spady (1994) defines OBE as a "comprehensive approach to organizing and operating an education system that is focused on and defined by the successful demonstrations of learning sought from each student. Outcomes are clear learning results that we want students to demonstrate at the end of significant learning experiences and are actions and performances that embody and reflect learner competence in using content, information, ideas, and tools successfully." South Africa's education policy is thus one of the most forward-thinking in the world. However, the implementation of this policy has put tremendous pressures on the education system, and especially on teachers. This focus, combined with a lack of infrastructure and insufficient funds, has resulted in very little use being made of modern technologies in South Africa's government schools (Oelofse et al. 2006).

In order to drive a strategy for implementing ICTs in South African schools, the Department of Education published the national e-education white paper in November 2004. In this context, e-education is defined as the use of ICTs to accelerate teaching and learning goals, particularly in a developing world context. ICT is seen as an enabler rather than an end in itself. It enables teachers and learners to connect to better information, ideas and to one another via appropriate and effective combinations of pedagogy in support of learning goals (White Paper on E-education 2004).

There has been a concerted attempt to introduce computer technology into schools in South Africa, with mixed results. Many have been PC-specific, sporadic, and have often adopted unsustainable models. Hence, scalability is a major consideration. Issues that are prevalent include (White Paper on E-education 2004):

- Lack of ICT literacy at a general level amongst teachers.
- Stringent and structured forms of teaching with little or no scope for lateral thinking.

- Realization of the importance of technology but inability to incorporate this due to lack of training, adequate infrastructure and integration with the current curriculum. This is more apparent as we move from the urban to the rural centres.
- In most places, there is a gender skew in access to education and this gets reflected in access to information technology.

Even in developed countries where computer technology has been used for educational purposes for several decades, the delivery has rarely met the expectation. Teachers have used computers for drill and practice, automated tutoring and instruction and only lately as a tool for communication, collaboration and problem-solving (Statham and Torrell 1996). The use of technology or media does not in itself improve learners' learning achievements. Learning is influenced more by the instructional strategy than by the type of medium used (Clark 1985).

There is thus a desperate need for a new approach to integrating technology into the classroom, particularly in the developing world environment. The model needs to take into account issues of usability, accessibility, and affordability, while ensuring that appropriate pedagogical models are adhered to.

MobilED Philosophy and Principles

Currently, mobile phones do not play an active role in formal education in South Africa. In fact, most schools ban the use of mobile phones during school hours. In an informal learning context, however, mobile phones are widely used. We call our colleagues and friends to seek information and reciprocally help them with their knowledge acquisition and problem-solving. Simultaneously, we build up our social networks and strengthen the links that are considered very important in modern theories of learning (see Senge 1990). In African traditional culture, "Umuntu ngmuntu ngabantu" means literally, "a person is a person because of other people." In other words, "you are who you are because of others." Expressed variously as "Botho" in Sesotho and "Setswana" and "Umbabtu" in the Nguni languages, this concept is about a strong sense of community where people co-exist in a mutually supportive lifestyle.

The idea of the MobilED project is to create technology that supports existing social infrastructures and increases the potential of current practices with mobile phones by introducing new opportunities for knowledge-sharing, community-building, and shared creation of knowledge in the authentic context of studying and learning. With this technology the participants may be encouraged to increase the value of their current practices through knowledge-sharing and collaboration across boundaries of time and place. Freedom from the constraints of time and place enables the timely use of technology wherever knowledge acquisition and problem-solving are situational and contextual.

The approach of the MobilED project is to integrate research-based ideas of using mobile technologies in teaching/learning with active scenarios of real learning programmes. The project includes the design, development, and piloting of prototype applications where multimedia and language technologies (voice, text, images) will be used via the mobile phone as tools in the learning process. In order to work within a contextual framework, the project will rely on the advances made in the psychology of learning, which emphasize the collective nature of human intellectual achievements and the use of local languages in the learning process. The aim will be to enable all members of society (especially those in the developing world) to become active participants in the information society by being contributors to, and not just passive recipients of, information.

From a technology perspective, all tools and platforms developed will be made available as Open Source Software (OSS) in support of the collaborative, knowledge-sharing philosophy of this project. Probably the most important benefit of OSS is that it stimulates the local IT sector in a country, which is crucial in developing countries to ensure full participation in the information society. From the social angle, OSS is highly beneficial because it allows software to be customized to local conditions by the communities themselves.

MobilED Objectives

The MobilED project has four key scientific, technical, and developmental objectives:

- To explore and comprehend the cultural, social, and organizational context of young people in and out of school in three developing countries (South Africa, India, Brazil) and in a developed country (Finland) in their utilisation of mobile technologies, particularly mobile phones.
- To develop research-based models and scenarios of how mobile technologies could be used for teaching, learning and empowerment of students within and outside the school context.
- To develop concepts, prototypes, and platforms that will facilitate and support the models and scenarios developed.

- To test, evaluate, and disseminate the scenarios, models, concepts, prototypes, and platforms in the four countries.

The project aims to contribute to scientific and technical know-how by learning about how groups of young people in and out of school environments are using mobile devices in their everyday knowledge-acquisition and problem-solving situations. It also aims to uncover user innovations and concepts relating to mobile devices through a participatory design process with users. Within the research work that the project implements will be several prototypes that can be tested and disseminated in real environments, which includes schools, youth clubs, and other informal groups.

Project Participants

The current principal partners of MobilED are the Meraka Institute of the CSIR, South Africa, and the Media Lab of the University of Art and Design in Helsinki, Finland. The network of associated partners and advisers includes Nokia (Finland), the Centre for Research on Networked Learning and Knowledge Building, University of Helsinki (Finland), the Tshwane University of Technology (South Africa, the University of Pretoria (South Africa), the Escola do Futuro Universidade de São Paulo (Brazil), the WikiMedia Foundation (U.S.A.), and the Centre for Knowledge Societies (India). For the pilots, handsets were donated by Nokia and airtime was donated by MTN (a South African network operator).

MobilED Research Framework and Process

The strength of the multidisciplinary nature of the consortium, as well as deep roots of participants in cognitive, learning, and design sciences, lends a multi-pronged perspective to this initiative. In order to ensure cohesion and understanding between the different disciplines (including teachers, educational researchers, educational psychologists, designers, and technologists), a research framework was developed and is shown in Figure 1.1.

Each intervention needs to be grounded in the local context. Central to the intervention is the design process, which is fed by both the appropriate pedagogical models and the potential of the technology itself. Since South Africa is a developing country, any intervention needs to take cognizance of the developmental and societal outcomes. The outcome mapping methodology (as designed by IDRC in consultation with Dr Barry Kibel of the Pacific Institute for Research and Evaluation as an adaptation of the outcome engineering approach) is being employed here, and this methodology looks at

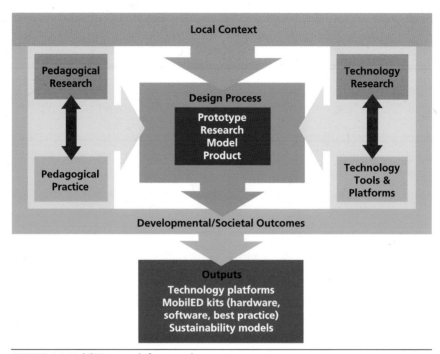

FIGURE 1.1 MobilED research framework

the results of an intervention as a behavioural change in the project participants. Outcomes are seen as desired changes indicating progress towards large-
scale development goals. At the heart of outcome mapping is documenting
contribution rather than attribution, and seeking to understand the ways in
which communities contribute to change rather than trying to attribute
change to a single intervention (Smutyo 2001).

Technology Used

The basic technology components being used in the project are:

- Mobile devices and network(s): GSM/SMS phones, multimedia
  phones, Internet tablets, PDAs, the US$100 laptop (OLPC project of
  MIT), etc.
- Wikipedia: The free encyclopedia.
- Social software: Mediawiki, blogs, knowledge-building tools, etc.
- Open Source language technologies: speech interfaces, audio usage,
  etc.
- Open Source telephony and software frameworks and platforms.

MobilED Pilots

The first phase of the project included the design, development, and piloting of a prototype platform in which multimedia and language technologies (voice, text, images) are used via the mobile phone as tools in the learning process. A scenario-based approach was adopted to develop potential uses of the technology in formal learning environments. One of the main problems in South African schools is access to learning and reference materials for both learners and teachers. The focus was on how to use low-cost mobile phones, which are readily available in the developing world, while ensuring that participants not only access information, but also contribute information. Based on these prerequisites, we developed the concept of a mobile audio wikipedia, using SMS and text-to-speech technologies to enable access to information, as well as the contribution of information using voice. The mobile audio wikipedia works as follows:

1. A user can search for a term by sending an SMS message to the server.
2. The server then calls the user.
3. A speech synthesizer will read the article found in the wikipedia.
4. If the term is not found in the wikipedia, then the user can submit his/her contribution by dictating it to the system.

Prototype Platform

Based on the scenarios developed, the technology development team built the version 1 MobilEd platform. MobilEd employs three main technology platforms to achieve its goal:

1. An SMS communication interface/gateway, such as Kannel (http://www.kannel.org) or Alamin (http://www.alamin.org/) to send and receive SMSs.
2. The Asterisk Open Source PBX (http://www.asterisk.org/) for audio telephony communications.
3. A media wiki (http://www.mediawiki.org/) server with suitable content, such as http://www.en.wikipedia.org (Leinonen et al. 2006)

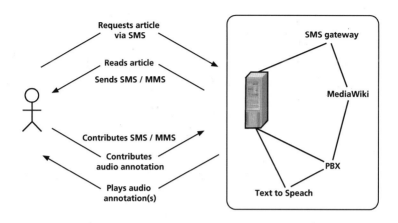

FIGURE 1.2 Simple high-level usage scenario (user's perspective) (Leinonen et al. 2006)

A typical case of a high-level use of the system is provided in Figure 1.2.

Pilot 1

The first pilot was conducted at a private school, Cornwall Hill College, in South Africa. The learners ranged from age fifteen to sixteen. The theme of the pilot was HIV/AIDS. The project followed the principles of the "jigsaw cooperative learning technique" (Aronson et al. 1978), where each learner is a member of two types of groups. The first kind of group is the "home group"; in our case we called them the "audiocasting groups," referring to the idea of podcasting. The second kind of group is the "thematic expert group." Each thematic group consists of one member from each home group.

The thematic group discussed different aspects of HIV and used the MobilED server with the English wikipedia content to search for information related to their theme.

Learners could navigate through the audio of the article as follows:
- *Fast forward*: skips ahead one sentence in the same section.
- *Rewind: skips* back one sentence in the same section.
- *Next section*: skips to the next section of the article.
- *Previous section*: skips to the previous section of the article.

Pause: pauses playback – if any other DTMF key is then pressed, playback continues from where it was paused. Figure 1.3 shows the use of the audio wikipedia.

FIGURE 1.3 Using the audio wikipedia

The results of the information retrieval and discussions were reported back to each audiocasting group. The audiocasting group then discussed the most relevant issues of HIV/AIDS for their own age groups and communicated the results to the school community as an audiocast recorded via MobilED onto the wiki. To access the audio encyclopedia and the audiocasting service, the students used shared Nokia 3230 phones with speakers.

The learners from Cornwall Hill College were all from affluent homes and most already owned a mobile phone. They were also fully ICT-literate. It was decided to test the service with these learners before testing with learners from disadvantaged backgrounds so that we could improve the platform based on their more experienced input. The learners were given very little time to experiment with the phones before the pilot started, and although they supported each other and figured out all the main functions of the phones in a short period of time, they felt they needed more time to "play" with the devices. It was not necessary to "teach" the learners how to use a phone – it was an everyday skill that they had already mastered. In addition, these learners did not like the fact that the phones were shared in the group – each said they would have preferred their own phone. However, the use of shared phones with speakers supported collaboration in the shared task. Based on the observation and the video data, it was obvious that the use of the shared phone made it possible to distribute the cognitive load related to the use of the technology and to fulfill the study tasks. Peer support and learning were obvious.

We also noted that the boys tended to dominate the technology usage. During the pilot there were a few technology hiccups, and at one stage a temporary measure was instituted to record their audiocasts onto an analogue tape recorder – it was most interesting to note that more learners were challenged figuring out how to use a tape recorder than how to use the MobilED service. Other input we received from these learners was that the "voice" used for the text-to-speech engine was very difficult to understand and that the speakers did not work very well. Overall, however, there was overwhelming official support and student enthusiasm for using mobile phones in the classroom.

An unexpected consequence of the first pilot was that the school requested another pilot. Although this was not planned as part of the original intervention, an additional pilot (Pilot 1A) was run. In this pilot learners went on a trip to a theme park as part of a science lesson on energy. All interactions between the teachers and learners were via SMS. Some content was "seeded" on the wiki and the MobilED platform was expanded to include information retrieval via SMS as well. The learners used their own mobile phones and there was spontaneous sharing of mobile phone capabilities (such as photos, audio, and video). Once again, there was much excitement about and support for the concept by the learners (Botha et al. 2006).

Pilot 2

Pilot 2 was run at a local government (or previously disadvantaged) school, Irene Middle School. The learners were from very poor backgrounds and most travelled long distances from outlying rural areas on a daily basis to get to school. Most learners did not own their own mobile phones, and many had never used a mobile phone. Although the school did have a computer lab, the computers had been stolen and the learners were not at all ICT-literate. The learners do not speak English as a home language, but are educated in English from Grade 4.

The MobilED platform was significantly enhanced and upgraded to version 2, based on the results of Pilots 1 and 1A. The Irene Middle School learners had a lesson on HIV/AIDS based on the same lesson plan developed for Cornwall Hill College, but here the learners were given a longer period of time to familiarize themselves with the mobile phones, and they were also given a printout of a typical wikipedia article. Since very few articles exist on wikipedia in their home languages (Sepedi, Setswana, and isiZulu), the lesson was given in English. They were divided into groups as with the first pilot.

This MobilED pilot was once again a success, with wholehearted support from both learners and teachers. Learners were motivated and energized and clearly enjoyed the learning process. In fact, the server logs showed that many of the learners spontaneously used the service to get information about many other topics (particularly World War II and Adolf Hitler, which was the current topic in their history lessons). Figures 1.4 and 1.5 below show the groups "playing" with the mobile phone and accessing the MobilED service.

FIGURE 1.4 Trying out the MobilED service

FIGURE 1.5 Hard at "play"

Although the learners were not ICT-literate and very few had access to mobile phones, they took only a very short time to familiarize themselves with the technology. Since many mobile phones are shared in their culture, they did not have a problem with sharing the mobile phone during the lesson and enjoyed the collaborative aspects of the tasks. In addition, it was interesting to note that the boys did not dominate the technology as in the previous pilot – there was equal use by both sexes.

They were also less critical of the artificial voice (which had been improved in the interim). When asked about their language of choice for learning, every group chose English – they see English as the "academic" language and the gateway to opportunities later in life. It was interesting to note that interactions between participants were in their home languages, but most produced audiocasts in English. They were excited that their contributions could potentially reach a huge worldwide audience. It was obvious, though, that using English as the language of instruction was a major problem for some of the learners, as evidenced by the written responses to some of our questionnaires, which were in poor and broken English.

During this pilot there were very few technology problems and this contributed to a much better experience for these learners. The audiocasts were passionate and uninhibited and included spontaneous harmonizing of songs, including rap songs. As part of the outcomes mapping methodology, some mobile phones were left at the school for the teachers and learners to use, with the idea of monitoring the use of the service over the next few months.

Pilot 3

In pilot 3 we wanted to observe the collaborative behaviour of groups of children from different cultural and socio-economic backgrounds when using the mobile phone as a tool for learning. We also wanted to introduce and test the use of MMS/SMS technology as part of the MobilED platform. Another aim was to test the platform with younger children. The first part of the pilot consisted of ten learners (aged thirteen to fourteen) from Irene Middle School and from Cornwall Hill College who were invited to the Meraka Institute as part of a learning activity to create a reusable multimedia slide show about three technology projects developed by the institute. The photo in Figure 1.6 shows some of the learners who were involved in the pilot.

FIGURE 1.6 Learners from Cornwall Hill College and Irene Middle School

The learners were divided into groups of two comprised of one learner from each school, and an icebreaker activity was used to familiarize the learners with each other. Thereafter they were given a short period of time to "play" with the mobile phones and experiment with sending SMS and MMS messages. Their task was to use the mobile phone for the following purposes:

- capturing information
- taking photos
- recording and storing
- compiling a slide presentation with all the above and MMSing to the server

The learners seemed to enjoy the activities and were extremely creative with their photographs. There was a marked difference at the beginning of the pilot with regard to usage of the mobile phones, but the less-experienced learners soon "caught up" and were able to do most of the tasks with ease. Most pairs worked well in their groups, although there were instances of incompatibilities. On the whole, the girls tended to work better in their groups and there was spontaneous sharing of knowledge in these pairs. This pilot is still incomplete and data is in the process of being analyzed. Figures

1.7A and 1.7B shows the good spirit of cooperation that existed between the participants.

FIGURE 1.7A Collaboration and peer learning

FIGURE 1.7B Collaboration and peer learning

Discussion

Will the MobilED technology transform the way in which teaching and learning can take place in schools, particularly in Africa and the rest of the developing world? It certainly has the potential to enhance existing practices and extend the capabilities of currently established forms of technology without any special redesigning of the basic tool. It also extends the use of mobile phones to incorporate a particular learning project – this was accomplished with relative confidence and ease (Ford et al. 2007).

The results of the pilots show that the use of a mobile phone as technology tool to aid the learning process can work extremely well. The barrier of entry was very low – the learners themselves were very open to using the technology and the teachers could focus on facilitating the learning process, rather than having to grapple with new, unfamiliar technologies (as is the case with traditional computers). Thus both learners and teachers felt empowered and confident in using the phones as learning tools. In addition, a mobile phone is a portable device and can be used anywhere, anytime – the teacher does not need to take her learners to the technology (as per the computer lab model), but is able to take the technology to the learner. A mobile phone also opens up the possibility of using the technology on field-trips and out of typical classroom environments, thus demonstrating again the potential to use the mobile phone as a complementary tool to a traditional computer.

The concept of a mobile audio-wikipedia is particularly of interest in Africa, where the access to information, both paper-based and electronic, is limited. It also supports the strong African oral tradition. Since the mobile phones used were basic models and only needed to support the ability to send an SMS, the cost factor for the handset was small. However, the network costs (sending an SMS and providing the content via a phone call) could become prohibitive if the service were to be provided widely in South Africa and Africa more broadly. The issue of sustainability and affordability will need to be clearly understood and various models explored as part of subsequent phases in years two and three of the MobilED project. It seems obvious that some kind of support would be needed from the mobile network operators in the various countries where MobilED could be implemented (Ford et al. 2007).

With regard to potential models for making the technology of practical use in schools, especially in the light of many schools in South Africa banning mobile phones, some initial ideas have been developed by the MobilED team. One such idea is the creation of a MobilED "kit" – a secure and rugged box that contains a set of mobile phones with places for charging them, speakers to attach to them, pedagogical guidebooks with descriptions of learning events, some reusable physical "learning objects" (for example, laminated paper sheets) that will help teachers and learners implement mobile learning events, and a DVD with video footage of example projects. The MobilED kit could be part of the school's facilities, just like blackboards, overhead projectors, computers, etc. When a teacher wants to implement a mobile learning project it will be easy to take the MobilED kit to the classroom and when the project is over to return it to a secure environment (such as the teacher's room or school library).

Further development of MobilED will include the integration of more advanced technologies (such as MMS and data services) and the development of additional scenarios, concepts, models, and processes for formal learning environments. It will focus on massification strategies to cost-effectively implement the platform in as many schools as possible in South Africa, and exploring what would be needed to expand into the rest of Africa. This will include a strategy to collaboratively develop a set of lesson plans for teachers to include in their teaching activities, using the open source model for content creation.

Conclusion

The MobilED consortium will be reflecting on the results of these pilots and will use the results to develop future strategy. Some of the ideas that have been suggested in South Africa include:

1. Using the service to disseminate ideas and lesson plans to teachers by creating slide shows of lessons with audio narrations in all eleven of South Africa's official languages. A teacher could send an SMS with the title of the lesson to the server and this would be sent the slideshow (if they have an MMS-capable phone) or he/she would be phoned back and the audio played. The teacher could add an audio/video annotation to add his/her ideas to the lesson plan.
2. Making existing educational video/animation "bytes" available to teachers and learners via MMS and data services.

Worldwide interest in the project has been overwhelming: Brazil will start its own MobilED pilots in the near future, and Colombia and Mexico are also planning pilots. Even comparatively wealthy countries like New Zealand are showing interest. For more information on the status of the project and future plans, refer to the MobilED website (http://mobiled.uiah.fi).

Despite this enthusiasm, however, a major problem being faced in trying to institutionalize the use of mobile phones is the current negative publicity regarding their illicit use in schools. There is no question that currently there is a lot of "under the table" use of mobile phones in classrooms and that they can be distracting influences. This came out very strongly in many of the interviews held while we were collecting data for MobilED. After the pilots, Cornwall Hill decided to champion the use of mobile phones in their school and started developing a strategy for institutionalizing the phones. Additional work needs to be done, but some of the results are discussed below.

Because mobile phone use is difficult to monitor in a classroom setting, the appropriate use of these instruments can be encouraged through values-based principles, instead of managing it on a rules-based system. Values must be clearly defined, understood, communicated, and practiced. Individual responsibility and accountability can be stipulated and its acceptance is to be encouraged amongst all stakeholders. Well established communication channels can also help ensure proper participant behaviour.

Developing a clear strategy for the formal use of these instruments to facilitate learning is paramount to the success of adoption, and this strategy can be divided into three different phases. The first phase focuses on creating awareness amongst the various stakeholders in a school setting. This can be achieved by creating an atmosphere of informed curiosity by running pilots and publishing the results in a local and global context. The second phase consists of an adjustment and developing period where competencies are identified and policies drafted. It is crucial at this stage to offer support to those who want to come on board to keep the momentum and growing interest going. The final phase involves the identification of mentors to coach and form ongoing relationships with those already involved in the initiative. Their role is to have a clear understanding of organizational context and to give advice on how to move forward. The crucial factor in determining successful implementation of new strategies is to create cause champions in the process. It is the role of the champion to demystify the mobile instruments and to create an environment in which it can be viewed as just another tool in the toolbox of the educator to help them in their efforts to facilitate lifelong learning (Ford et al. 2007).

The MobilED technology developed in the first year of the project (the mobile audio encyclopaedia) has many different possible applications beyond that of education. Since the basic content source in the pilots is a wiki (specifically the wikipedia implementation), this mobile audio wiki can be seen as a community information system that can be used with a mobile phone, which would be of tremendous importance in places where there is a strong culture of mobile phones, but where the Internet and World Wide Web are not widely used (Leinonen et al. 2006). Thus, the platform could be used for e-government, e-health, NGO support, SMME support, etc., in developing countries – all aspects integral to socio-economic growth.

The MobilED platform enables all people in the developing world not only to access information, but also to contribute information back – thus becoming active participants in the information society. It is making a significant step towards bridging the "digital divide."

References

ARONSEN, E., N. BLANEY, C. STEPHIN, J. SIKES and M. SNAPP. 1978. *The jigsaw classroom*. Beverly Hills, CA: Sage Publishing Company.

BOTHA, A., J. BATCHELOR, J. CRONJE and F. AUCAMP. 2006. When wikis grow up and go for outings. Paper presentation, *mLearn 2006, 5th world conference on mobile learning*, Banff, Canada.

CLARK, R. 1985. Evidence for confounding in computer-based instruction studies: Analyzing the meta-analyses. *Educational Communication and Technology Journal* 33:249-262.

FORD, M., and A. BOTHA. 2007. MobilED: An accessible mobile learning platform for Africa? Paper presentation, *IST Africa conference*, May 9-11, Maputo, Mozambique.

FORD, M., and J. BATCHELOR. 2007. From zero to hero: Is the mobile phone a viable learning tool for Africa? Paper presentation, *Educational and information systems, technologies and applications (EISTA) conference*, July 12-15, Orlando, FL.

ITU Report. 2006. *What's the state of ICT access around the world?* http://ww.itu.int/newsroom/wtdc/2006/stats/index.html

LAOURIS, Y., and N. ETEOKLEOUS. 2005. We need an educationally relevant definition of mobile learning. Paper presentation, *mLearn 2005, 4th world conference on mobile learning*, Cape Town, South Africa.

LEINONEN, T., E. RATNA SARI, and F. AUCAMP. 2006. Audio wiki for mobile communities: Information systems for the rest of us. Paper presentation, *Mobile HCI conference*.

MASTERS, K. 2005. Low-key m-learning: A realistic introduction of m-learning to developing countries. Paper presentation, *6th conference on communications in the twenty first century: Seeing, understanding, learning in the mobile age*, Budapest, Hungary.

MediaWiki. 2006. http://www.mediawiki.org

MUTULA, S. 2002. The cellular phone economy in the SADC region: Implications for libraries. *Online Information Review* 26 (2):79-91.

OELOFSE, C., J. CRONJE, A. de JAGER, and M. FORD. 2006. *The digital profile of the teenage mobile phone user.* Paper presentation, mLearn 2006, *5th world conference on mobile learning*, Banff, Canada.

PRENSKY, M. 2005. What can you learn from a cell phone? *Innovate online magazine.* http://www.innovateonline.info/

Republic of South Africa. 2004. *White paper on e-education.* Pretoria: Government Printer.

SENGE, P. 1990. *The fifth discipline: The art & practice of the learning organization.* New York: Doubleday.

SMUTYO, T. 2001. *Crouching impact, hidden attribution: Overcoming threats to learning in development programs.* Toronto: IDRC.

SPADY, W. 1994. *Outcome-based education: Critical issues and answers.* Arlinton, VA: American Association of School Administrators.

STATHAM, D., and C. TORRELL. 1996. *Computers in the classroom: The impact of technology on student learning.* Boise, ID: Boise State University.

STONE, A., K. LYNCH, and N. POOLE. 2003. A case for using mobile Internet and telephony to support community networks and networked learning in Tanzania. Paper presentation, *ICOOL 2003, international conference on online and open learning.*

Exploring the Challenges and Opportunities of M-learning Within an International Distance Education Programme

JON GREGSON
UNIVERSITY OF LONDON EXTERNAL SYSTEM
UNITED KINGDOM

DOLF JORDAAN
UNIVERSITY OF PRETORIA
SOUTH AFRICA

Abstract

This chapter provides a case study of a mobile learning project, involving postgraduate distance learning students based in the Southern African Development Community (SADC) region. The project explores ways of enhancing the programme design and delivery, within the broader context of a global programme with students in over one hundred countries. The use of e-learning tools alongside traditional print-based approaches has created a more connected learning community that makes increasing use of interactive learning resources. However, new challenges have emerged in providing equivalent access and support to students based in developing countries. The authors outline the practical ways in which mobile learning tools help address the problems identified, and provide opportunities for innovation in design and delivery of distance learning. The approaches explored provide insights and not a prescriptive solution, since they are contingent on diverse and dynamic contexts, the student profile, and the nature of the problems arising.

Introduction

The Wye Distance Learning Programme (DLP) has offered postgraduate distance education degrees awarded by the University of London since 1987, and runs programmes for the School of Oriental and African Studies (SOAS)[7] and Imperial College London.[8] In August 2007 it was transferred from Imperial College to form part of the newly established SOAS Centre for Development, Environment and Policy (CeDEP). The DLP has over one thousand students located in over one hundred countries, with many students based in Africa and other developing regions. The spread of students is illustrated in Figure 1 below. The courses offered have an emphasis on social science, and relate to the following thematic areas: "Sustainability and Development," "Environment and Biodiversity," and "Applied Economics and Business." DLP students are typically mid career professionals, with more than 75 per cent of the student body in the 30-50 year age range, and approximately one third being female.

There are currently over forty course modules, and most of these are supplied to students as printed study guides accompanied by text books and bound sets of copyright cleared reading materials. In the late 1990s the DLP took on a pioneering role by developing an Online Learning Environment (OLE) for distance learning students to use, which was adopted by the University of London External Programme. More recently it has been creating interactive CD based versions of the study guides, and fifteen course modules now exist in this format.

7. www.soas.ac.uk/cedep
8. www.imperial.ac.uk/dlp

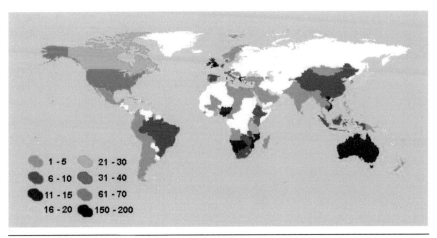

FIGURE 1 World map showing DLP student distribution

The growth of e-learning approaches across the DLP's courses has meant that many students can enjoy more interaction with other students and with their tutors. Learning materials are being enhanced by new features including self assessment quizzes, animations, and quick search facilities that support revision. However, the e-learning model has its limitations, as many of the DLP's students are based in countries where Internet access is still not widely available and students do not typically have much access to computers outside their workplace. Some students have to travel two to three hours to the nearest town simply to access emails via a cybercafé.

For these reasons the DLP has pursued a strategy of using e-learning tools to enhance and complement rather than completely replace the established methods of delivery and support. Participation on the OLE has been optional and printable PDF file alternatives to content designed for the CDs are always provided.

The rapid global diffusion of mobile technologies presents exciting new opportunities for the DLP to explore in addressing some of the constraints experienced with the e-learning model. This potential for mobile learning (m-learning) within the DLP is seen as providing:

- Scope for enhancing the learning model.
- A solution to access issues faced by students in Africa and many developing countries, moving eventually towards a global delivery that supports learning anytime and anywhere.

In October 2005, the DLP successfully applied for a "teaching and development grant" from the University of London Centre for Distance

Education (CDE), and commenced work on a two year m-learning project titled "Developing an educational model for delivery and support of post-graduate distance learning in Southern Africa that incorporates m-learning." The project is being implemented in close collaboration with the Department for Education Innovation (EI) at the University of Pretoria, and directly involves DLP students based in the Southern African Development Community (SADC) region in contributing to the design and testing of suitable m-learning approaches.

This chapter provides a case study telling the story of our experience so far. This is illustrated with qualitative data drawn from interviews, country visits, and direct feedback. The primary focus is on piloting of m-learning approaches in the Southern African context that complement and enhance existing distance learning approaches. We take the reader through the steps followed in the design and implementation of the project, highlighting some of the important considerations and challenges and suggesting areas where further research would be useful.

The study covers an investigation of the context and potential value added of mobile learning, considering the pedagogic and practical models being used by the DLP. An initial phase where four students were identified and became involved in the planning of the project is outlined. Work is currently being undertaken (2007) involving a larger group of students testing out course materials, activities, and tutoring approaches that have been designed for the mobile phone. The instructional design and pedagogical approaches being followed are described, and some of the initial outcomes and feedback are discussed, together with preliminary ideas on the development of a holistic learning environment to support mobile learners, as well as incorporating the strengths of e-learning and traditional distance learning approaches.

Background

We will start this background section by providing more insight into the design of the study environment and learning materials, as this is important in providing an understanding of the nature of the problems we seek to address through m-learning approaches. This is followed by a review of literature related to educational theory of relevance to mobile learning design, and reference to project examples and experiences that we have learned from in relation to m-learning in the developing country context.

i) The Current Status of E-learning
Within the DLP Programme Design

Until the advent of the Internet in the 1990s, most communication with students was by airmail and then increasingly through email. At the time all Tutor Marked Assignments (TMAs) that students submitted for marking and feedback were optional, due to the unreliability and slowness of the postal system and difficulties in authenticating the work.

As the Internet became more widely available in the late 1990s, the DLP quickly saw the opportunity for creating an online community. At the time commercial and open source learning environments were not particularly advanced, and did not meet the requirements of a widely dispersed student community with slow Internet access. For this reason an in-house OLE (subsequently called Effect) was developed and subsequently adopted by the University of London External Programme.

The OLE homepage is illustrated in Figure 2, and from the outset design features have taken account of the developing country context of many of the students. These features include (a) limited use of graphics with minimal file size to facilitate fast download, (b) attempts to design a single click access to most of the key areas of the OLE to speed up access, and (c) offline synchronisation of content (though this has proved problematic to implement).

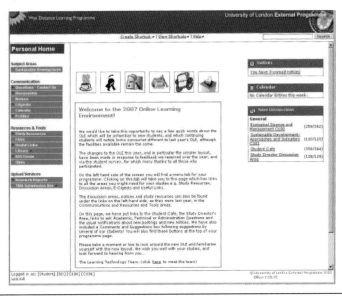

FIGURE 2 Screenshot of the DLP's 2007 Online Learning Environment homepage

The OLE has acted as a repository for downloadable learning materials and programme documentation, but has been primarily used to support academic discussions among students and tutors. The reality is that roughly one-third of the student community make regular use of the OLE, one-third uses it occasionally, and the remaining third never login. There are a wide range of reasons for this, with some students simply preferring not to participate in the learning community, and students based in developing countries do not find it easy to access the OLE regularly. Reasons for this will become clearer later in the chapter.

Since the introduction of the OLE, the DLP's investment in tutoring has grown considerably, and has reached the point where the teaching alongside the design and delivery of study materials is becoming the frontline activity and a major selling point for the programme. Interaction with tutors is no longer an occasional occurrence based around optional assignments. All DLP students now have an expectation of access to tutoring irrespective of their location or quality of Internet access.

The second major initiative within the DLP has been a move over the last five years to make the study materials available digitally. The driver for this was pedagogic innovation, but there was also a financial motivation to keep fee levels affordable and invest more in educational technology rather than printing and dispatch. Initially this process involved providing PDF or Word format copies of the study guide to students via the OLE, but a more ambitious agenda to enhance the materials also began to be implemented.

This involved developing ways to make the content more interactive, and developing a flexible authoring model that would support reusability of content and ease of maintenance. Due to the type of subject matter, which is typically narrative or economic models, there needed to be a careful assessment of what would add value to the student experience. This leads to a focus on interactive content that helps explain difficult concepts, self assessment questions, and search features to support revision. There was also the hope that in time greater use would be made of audio visual learning materials and live weblinks to further study resources.

Due to the diverse location of the students, it was decided to distribute the materials on CD-ROM. Figures 3 to 5 provide illustrations of the CD courseware linking together ten units of content, interactive materials, and quizzes. The content was actually designed using HTML, Flash, and Java-Script to enable viewing with common web browser software. This means it could also be set up easily as web based e-learning material, but the CD format enables large files (images, audio, and video) to be accessed more readily by students not connected to the Internet.

FIGURE 3 CD courseware front page

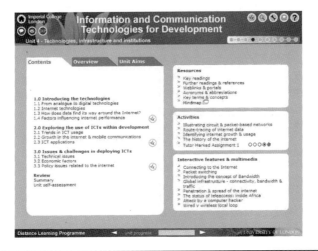

FIGURE 4 CD Unit 4 index page

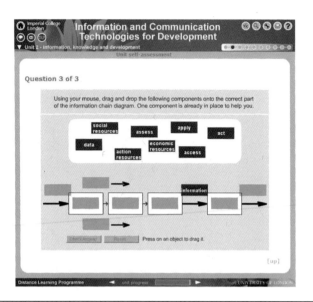

FIGURE 5 CD courseware example of interactive content

ii) Review of Relevant Literature and Examples of M-learning in the SADC Context

We will now briefly consider relevant educational theory and review experience and examples drawn from the SADC region context where the students involved in the pilot project are mainly based. Before commencing with any specific development work we sought to answer three further questions:

- What insights can we gain from relevant literature in relation to the context, educational and pedagogic approaches, and technical alternatives?
- What can we learn from the experience of others who have sought to develop m-learning approaches, particularly in the southern African context?
- What can we learn directly about the context that might influence our project approach?

The third question will be addressed when we provide an overview of the project. The first two questions are considered at this point.

LITERATURE REVIEW

In examining relevant literature, we sought to explore the evidence of mobile phone diffusion in Africa, gain insights into the type of mobile device and the application environments and standards, identify suitable models for m-learning, and examine the pedagogical and instructional design approaches that would be suited to the DLP piloting of mobile learning.

Barker et al. (2005) state that Africa is lacking technological development and that this has a negative effect on education there. In contrast with the diffusion of other technologies the continent is experiencing very rapid growth in mobile phone usage. Various sources confirm this growth which can facilitate the integration of mobile learning within educational models used in the region.

It has become increasingly difficult to make a clear distinction between the different mobile devices as the functions of mobile phones, smartphones, and PDAs integrate and share characteristics (Kukulska-Hulme and Traxler 2005). Whilst mobile devices may have different operating systems, most recent models now support similar application development tools and standards including WAP, Java, WML, and XHTML (Extensible HyperText Markup Language). Mobile users are often used to accessing the Internet from their desktop or notebook computers, and phones that use XHTML have an advantage (compared to WAP) of working well with mobile versions of web browser, giving access to a fast growing variety of services and academic content likely to be useful to distance education students.

Various m-learning models have been designed and proposed for adoption in Africa. One of these models was designed by Andreas Barker and colleagues from the Department of Information Systems at Rhodes University in South Africa. They describe this as follows:

> A model for m-learning adoption contains an m-learning environment, which is underpinned by the traditional learning environment and also supported by effective m-learning policies and guidelines. Within the traditional learning environment, as indicated in the model, learning can still take place through desktop PCs. The proposed model demonstrates that the mobile devices can be used as academic support for learners via online assessment, providing course content and access to the Internet. The mobile devices in the proposed model for m-learning adoption enable learner-to-learner communication, as well as learner-to-teacher communication. (Barker et al., 2005)

A range of studies, reviews, and reports have been published suggesting frameworks or models for the integration of mobile devices in learning at various levels of education across the world. Attempts are being made to find suitable learning theories or models for m-learning that try to find new teaching and learning practices for the new mobile technologies and apply existing learning theories to the findings. In most instances learning theories such as behaviourism and constructivism were investigated along with collaborative, informal, and lifelong learning methods. The integration of mobile technologies within the DLP activities described in this paper specifically draw on the integration of constructivist, situated, collaborative, and informal learning theories and activities. Drawing on Naismith et al. (2004), these can be described as follows:

- Constructivist activities enable learners to actively construct their own new ideas or concepts based on both their previous and current knowledge.
- Situated learning activities takes place in an authentic context. Mobile devices are well suited to authentic context-aware applications.
- Collaborative activities promote learning through interaction. Mobile devices can support Mobile Computer Supported Collaborative Learning (MCSCL) by providing another means of coordination without attempting to replace human-human interactions.
- Informal and lifelong learning activities support learning outside a dedicated learning environment and formal curriculum.

Ally (2004) indicates that the use of mobile devices for learning has direct implications for instructional design. He proposes the following principles for designing m-learning materials:

- It is important for designers to use presentation strategies that enable learners to process the material efficiently due to the limited display capacity of mobile learning devices.
- Information should be organized or divided into smaller pieces to facilitate processing.
- Information should be organized in the form of a concept map identifying the important concepts and showing their relationships.
- As information is presented in small pieces it is important to use advanced organizers to allow learners to make sense of the new content.
- The interface must coordinate the interaction between the learner and the learning materials and must include good navigational strategies.
- Learning materials should take the form of learning objects which are electronically available and reusable.

The University of Pretoria Experience

Many of the DLP's students in the SADC region are Commonwealth Scholarship students, and, under the terms of the scholarship funding, the DLP has been collaborating with the University of Pretoria (UP). Over the last five years strong links have developed between UP's Department for Education Innovation (EI) and the learning technology team within the DLP. EI has an established reputation in m-learning, so a useful starting point for this project has been to learn from the UP experience, which is now briefly described.

The use of mobile phones in distance education in Africa has been implemented with success at the University of Pretoria since 2002. The Faculty of Education presents a postgraduate diploma in education through distance education. The integration of SMS messaging with a paper-based programme resulted in an increase in attendance for contact sessions and a better response to information provided in SMS messages. Mobile support to the students was implemented to provide administrative and motivational communication to both large and small groups of students.

The university proceeded to investigate the possible use of SMS messaging with academic functions in 2004. A task team investigated the integration of bulk SMS and Instant Voice Response (IVR) as well as development of an SMS assessment tool. A pilot project investigated four categories of asynchronous SMS academic interventions which included the IVR system through which the student can phone a FAQ number and receive answers from a pre-programmed system. Students also receive Multiple Choice Questions (MCQs) to which they can reply via SMS. They can also ask questions about a pre-selected topic and receive answers automatically based on the comprehensive programmed text database.

The UP pilot proved highly successful in establishing that most students had access to mobile phones. Students were comfortable using their own phones to make use of these new SMS related services and for academic purposes. Increased commitment of students exemplified by timely completion of tasks by a greater percentage of students was also noted. The first generation handsets available to students supported text and voice calls at the time of the UP pilot in 2004, and three years later the potential uses of the more recent smartphone and 3G handsets for supporting a broader range of academic activity within education in Africa are considerable.

The Pilot Project: Developing an Educational Model
for Delivery and Support that Incorporates M-learning

Before making any major investment in a new approach to tutoring or course authoring, it is important for the DLP to carefully review the practicalities and benefits, since the update of learning materials is a major task with significant cost implications and requiring implementation against the background of five year student registration periods. A pilot project approach therefore has many advantages, and as we introduce and describe this project, we will move through the following stages:

1. Identification of some of the major challenges and problems the DLP faces.
2. Review of baseline information gained from a survey of students living in the SADC region.
3. Description of in-country visits to gain direct insights from context.
4. Feedback from initial activities tested with a small group of students.
5. Overview of the design and development of learning materials and m-learning approaches for two course modules, including some preliminary student feedback.

1. CHALLENGES TO BE ADDRESSED

The growing emphasis on the use of e-learning tools worked well for a good proportion of the DLP's students, but created more of a divide across the student community as a whole than had previously been the case, and we have been keen to address this. The overall goal for the DLP has to be providing first class tutoring and support to all students, and making innovative use of pedagogy and technology appropriate to the context of the learners.

Neither e-learning nor m-learning are seen as panaceas or comprehensive solutions for achieving this goal, but they are part of a blend of approaches that are relevant if they help to solve identified problems and shortcomings of the existing approach. The context is also dynamic and, much as it might be desirable to design a programme from scratch that draws on latest technologies, the reality is that it will take significant time and resources to adapt existing course materials, and provide the students with learning resources that are designed in a consistent way that is easy to support from a distance.

Before looking further at the relevant literature and moving on to the activities piloted, we set out below some of the challenges that have influenced our thinking and encouraged us to explore the role of m-learning.

Challenge	Initial Status (at start of the pilot project)
Improving Communication	Whilst regular Internet access for many DLP students remains problematic, email is now regularly used by nearly 100 per cent of the students. Recognising this, the DLP has introduced email digests (e-digests) where tutors summarise online discussions, and encourage inputs from those not online so that they can participate.
Improving access and participation	Whilst e-learning has brought some students into closer contact with each other and with their tutors, this is not universal, and in some respects there is an uneven playing field. A goal of a global programme like the DLP is to ensure that all students irrespective of location have the opportunity to access and fully participate in the learning environment (however that is designed). Only when all students have reliable means of rapid communication with the programme, will we be able to implement educational developments such as continual assessment, and a more constructivist approach to learning that draws on the experience and context of the learning community.
Improving tutoring support to students in diverse locations	Over the last three years we have also explored the possibility of developing networks to provide in country support in countries where online access is limited. However, with students spread across many countries, this is a very expensive approach, and in practice the in-country tutorials piloted were poorly attended, as distance learning students typically work full time, and had difficulties taking time off and travelling to locations where tutors were visiting.
Improving the usability of leaning resources for students who are very mobile	DLP students are typically highly mobile, sometimes internationally, and often within their own country. Studying whilst on the move and away from the office and home presents its own problems and many students can get behind with their studies. Whilst books are portable, study guides and bound volumes are typically heavy and not that easy to have at hand whilst travelling. It is also difficult without a computer to work on assignments efficiently.

Improving access to content and programme materials	The OLE offered a convenient repository for sharing learning resources and programme related documentation. Large files did not need to be sent as email attachments and were available for download wherever a student was able to access the Internet. However, the strategy of the DLP has not been to develop an entirely web based e-learning programme, but to use the OLE and learning materials on CD-ROM to support the DL approach. Resources such as sample exam papers that were initially only made available on the OLE are now also included on a study resources CD sent to students at the start of each academic year. These approaches illustrate how the DLP seeks to recognise access issues. Digital design and distribution of materials also offers scope for replacing a lot of the investment in printing and despatching materials with digital CD based versions, but this in itself presents a difficult issue as it transfers the task and cost of printing to students.

Given the nature of these challenges, the increasing availability and power of mobile technologies confirms that a pilot to explore the potential ways in which m-learning can enhance existing approaches would be very valuable. First, however, we need to consider whether suitable m-learning approaches would be feasible in the developing country context. We will do this by exploring the profile and needs of a group of students who provided the specific southern African focus for the m-learning project.

2. THE SADC BASELINE

The DLP currently supports 108 Commonwealth Scholarship students pursuing postgraduate master's level distance learning courses, and in 2006 at the time of the survey there were 88 (see Table 1 below). These students are based in Commonwealth countries within the Southern African Development Community9 (SADC) region. In order to improve support to these students, the DLP has worked in collaboration with the University of Pretoria's Department of Agricultural Economics and Department of Educational Innovation (EI) since 2002.

9. SADC comprises Botswana, Lesotho, Malawi, Mauritius, Mozambique, Namibia, Tanzania, South Africa, Swaziland, Zambia (and formerly Zimbabwe).

TABLE 1 SADC student numbers in 2006

Country	SADC Student Nos	M.Sc. Programme	SADC Student Nos
Botswana	12	Agribusiness for Development	9
Lesotho	3	Agricultural Economics	5
Malawi	13	Applied Environmental Economics	1
Mauritius	9	Biodiversity Conservation and Management	10
Mozambique	2	Environmental Management	13
Namibia	7	Food Industry Management and Marketing	1
South Africa	7	Managing Rural Change/Development	18
Swaziland	4	Sustainable Agriculture and Rural Development	17
Tanzania	15	Sustainable Development	14
Zimbabwe	7		
Zambia	9		

In March 2006 a baseline survey was conducted with the 88 SADC based students registered on the programme at that time. There were 43 responses and the table below shows the access that the respondents have to different types of technology and application:

TABLE 2 SADC student survey – ICT access

Computer	At Home	24	At Work	40	No Access	0		
CD ROM Drive	Yes	41	No	1	N/A	1		
Cell Phone	Personal	38	Provided by Employer	11	No Access	1		
Internet	At Home	8	At Work	38	Cyber café	18	No Access	1
Email access	Regular	37	Occasional	6	No	0		

These responses are unlikely to be typical of the whole survey group, since survey responses were sent in by email. The respondents generally rated themselves highly in relation to their level of ICT literacy – "very good" (16), "good" (21) and "average" (6).

The graphs that follow illustrate the respondents' ratings for the current e-learning approaches. Graph 1 shows that the majority of students who responded found the online learning environment and the recently introduced email digests written by tutors useful.

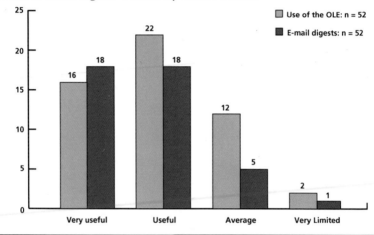

GRAPH 1 Usefulness of e-learning support

Graph 2 shows that course materials (including both printed and CD courseware) were also rated highly, but the tutoring support, whilst rated by many as of a very high standard, was not as highly regarded as the courseware.

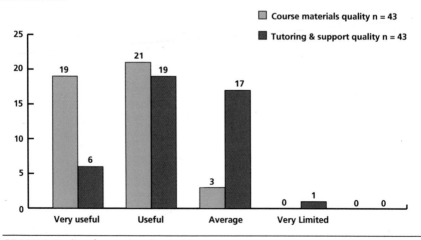

GRAPH 2 Quality of support and materials

Whilst these responses are encouraging, the constraint on OLE access (illustrated below in Graph 3) was regarded as a problem, and several in-country tutorials were organized to overcome this limitation. These workshops were rated as useful, but many students found it difficult to get time off to attend, or too expensive to travel to a workshop location. This type of event is also very expensive to organize.

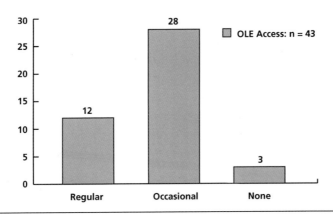

GRAPH 3 OLE access

Computer and Internet access are most likely to be via the workplace, and yet by contrast most indicated that they study mainly "at home," followed by "in the office."

Few students study when they are "away on field work," but the amount of time spent out of the office was significant. Eighteen respondents indicated that they spend one to three months per annum in the field, and thirteen indicated that they spend more than three months.

All respondents indicated that they used their phones for receiving voice calls and almost all sent and received text messages. Interestingly a lower proportion (70 per cent) made voice calls. The amount of money spent was also revealing as it varied from US$4 to US$100 per month.

The survey details summarized so far suggest that there is a potential role for use of mobile phones to improve tutoring in terms of overall access and quality. Since almost all respondents have mobile phones that they keep with them all the time, they offer the only technology that offers the potential for contact with the tutors and use of course materials "anytime, anywhere."

3. INSIGHTS FROM THE CONTEXT

The project focused initially on understanding the context and student profile, and determining which mobile technologies should be considered. The context of the distance learner is highly important, as is the need to understand how they work and study. In developing countries, for example, a student may study while travelling on a bus to the field or by candlelight when there is a power cut. Political disturbances may disrupt communications. Appropriateness of technology needs to be considered with an appreciation of such factors.

Four students were selected to be involved with the project in the first year, and this was deemed to be sufficient to enable us to obtain qualitative feedback. Students were selected based on location, mobile coverage availability, modules studied and progression within the MSc programme (in year two or beyond), and gender. One male and one female student were selected from Tanzania and two male students from Malawi. Three students are based in major towns (Dar es Salaam, Arusha, and Lilongwe) and one in a rural area, near Dwanga in Malawi. These locations are shown on the map illustrated in Figure 6. The modules that the students were studying were reviewed, and two modules were selected for the focus of the project. These modules are "Rural Development" and "ICT for Development."

FIGURE 6 Map highlighting student locations in Tanzania and Malawi

During the project, new content and activities designed specifically to make use of the features of mobile technologies are being developed and tested, and since 2007 the tutors on these two modules have also become directly involved. Visits were made to Malawi and Tanzania in February

2006 to find out more about local ICT trends and explore the realities, constraints, and possibilities of the context where the students were based. The main cell phone operators offering services in the countries selected are shown in the Table 3 below:

TABLE 3 Cell phone operations

Malawi	Tanzania
CelTel	CelTel
Malawi Telekon	Tigo (formerly Mobitel)
	Vodacom
	Buzz

Mobile coverage maps were reviewed for all SADC countries and it was noted that there was reasonable coverage in most of them, particularly in major cities and towns, and on major routes. Significant demand for coverage in villages and rural areas was also noted, driven by people wanting to "call in" as well as "call out."

Meetings were held with CelTel and Vodacom in Tanzania, and it became clear that plans to roll out 3G networks are moving ahead quickly. GPRS services are becoming widely available supporting data services, including multimedia and MMS applications. The price of GPRS services remains high: In Tanzania, for example, one kilobyte of data costs Tsh 50 (2006 rate), which was the same as the cost of sending a text message. Significant usage of GPRS services at this stage was therefore not realistic for students, and transfer of large files between students and the DLP is best done via transfer to a PC and email or Internet services. Operators did sell phones, but handsets tend to be sold separate from usage contracts, and are similar in price to SIM free handsets purchased in the UK.

The students were interviewed and videoed, and these interviews provided a rich picture of how students use their current phones, computers, and the Internet, and how they prefer to study. Personal factors such as wanting to keep on existing phone networks, or keep an existing phone number, were identified and initial suggestions about how a mobile device could support learning were explored. It became clear that in three out of four cases the students selected had reasonably good access to the Internet, and the fourth student could access e-mail on an occasional basis. It was also clear that the students travel a lot locally and sometimes internationally, and mobility is therefore an important factor to be considered during the pilot project and in scaling up mobile learning to the wider student community. The selection of quotes that follow are drawn from interviews and provide some indicative impressions of the context, and initial ideas the students had in relation to the potential for m-learning.

Student Insights from Malawi and Tanzania – THE CONTEXT

Student 1 – Malawi: "In Dwanga there are more cell phones than computers."

Student 2 – Tanzania: "Coverage is getting better and better. Three or four years back it was mainly available in the centre of town but now you can even go into the villages and there is very good coverage."

Student 1 – Malawi: "We have the cell phones when we are out in the field so that we can be reached there and given information which we can pass on to the farmers."

Student 3 – Tanzania: "With the call back services available I can call my mum in a village far away – she can just send me a message 'call me' and I can call her."

Student 1 – Malawi: "Most people know how to charge their cell phone batteries. If they don't have power they will go to their friends house or use a charger (which work on car batteries)."

Student 4 – Malawi: "I think the cell phone technology in Malawi has changed the way we live and the way we do things basically in terms of communication. Nowadays you don't see many people posting letters; also in terms of the younger generation most of their money is been spent on cell phones because they call their friends. It has become easier to communicate and almost every young person has got a cell phone."

Student 2 – Tanzania: "SMS banking is available – you can send credit through a mobile phone to somebody else."

Student 4 – Malawi: "Right now people are advertising on the cell phone and it is used for public awareness. In election times you see messages coming in terms of voting."

Student 3 – Tanzania: "I think one of the changes that can happen to the distance learning programme is that somebody could use the cell phone to connect to the Internet or use an application in order to access the online learning environment."

Student 2 – Tanzania: "I remember last year when I had to travel because we travel a lot, I had to take the printed material with me, which is heavy. Sometimes when you are doing a TMA you have to write it down on paper and you have to have your books with you so when you come back and you have access to computers you retype the thing. It makes life difficult but if you had a device where you can process some words or access some things even when you are away from your PC that would be the best option."

Student 1 – Malawi: "Sometimes as a distance learning student I have some questions which I would like to have somebody answer for me immediately. If it then could be done through my cell phone it would be wonderful; with limited access to the Internet it means that I will receive that answer in two or three weeks time; it is frustrating."

Student 2 – Tanzania: "If you are mobile and your learning is also mobile then it could make a lot of difference because if you spend two weeks without going through your materials then you may not be able to catch it up."

Student 1 – Malawi: "If you can read information from your cell phone, add information to it, and transfer it to your PC, that will be easier to read because of the screen size... But I think storing material on the phone could be quite useful."

Student 4 – Malawi: "If you hear the sound of somebody speaking something, and even see pictures or something which is audio visual, I think that will be very very interesting."

Student 2 – Tanzania: "It would make a lot of difference if I could listen to some recordings of lecturers. Sometimes it is interesting to hear and see rather than to go through the books."

Student 1 – Malawi: "It will be helpful to interact with other students using the cell phone."

4. Preliminary Activities

The four students helping with the project were given an initial task of finding out about available phones, and recommending a model that they should test for future use by a larger group of students in the next phase of the project. The activity made use of their existing phone models, and a combination of e-mail and SMS, confirming our ability to communicate with the students in these ways.

Mobile phone services fall into three main groupings:
- Basic level services; voice call and text messaging.
- GPRS services; transfer of data and multimedia on an asynchronous basis.
- 3G services; real time video calls.

Handsets typically have features that are designed to operate well at one of these levels, and students surveyed currently make use of basic level services. From the exercise carried out by the four students involved in the initial pilot phase it became clear that, within the context of this project, we were going to be looking more to the future with the selection of a mobile phone with smartphone capabilities (that support GPRS and potentially 3G services). The model chosen by the students is shown in Figure 7.

FIGURE 7 Nokia N70 phone selected by DLP students for piloting m-learning

One of the major perceived benefits of this model to the students was that it avoids device proliferation, as it incorporates the capabilities of a phone, FM radio, video and still camera, music and video player, and audio recording in a single device. It also supports storage of files on a removable storage card.

The model selected can be purchased and maintained locally (2006 price: Tsh 570,000 = approximately USD 450), but transferring money and arranging contracts locally was problematic, so it was decided to supply phones from the UK, although this may not be practical in any future scaling-up of activities. The phones (with a monthly credit allowance transferred to the student to encourage usage) were supplied to the students in exchange for a commitment to support the project research activities. Through the provision of a specific model we established better control over the variables, and rather than getting varied feedback due to diverse equipment we could concentrate our own learning on the appropriate and effective educational use of the device.

The opportunity arose to deliver the phones personally to the two students in Tanzania and show them how to use different features. By contrast the phones were sent by DHL courier to students in Malawi. This has allowed us to contrast the two groups, and determine the extent to which training makes a difference. In practice, both groups progressed well and required no additional support or help from each other.

A wide range of practical issues were identified from the survey and country visits that highlighted important concerns to be considered further in any scaling-up of the project to a larger group of students. These include costs of handset and usage, coverage of access, theft of the device, reliability, damage, power supply, insurance, and import duty. There are also issues in determining the most affordable ways to offer mobile support to the learners, and whether to supply a specific handset to students, or support a wide range of models that students have, provided they meet minimum specifications.

When they received their phones the four students were asked to carry out the following preliminary activities aimed at testing their ability to use the technology, without significant levels of support, and communicate with the DLP:

- Texting messages to the project team.
- Recording of audio, video and images, making use of two different cameras included on the phone, and sending the files to the project team via their PCs.
- Communicating with other members of the team.

These tasks were all successfully completed without the need for substantial guidance given to the students on how to carry out the task. This confirmed to us that it was feasible to design activities that involved SMS, file transfer, and communication via email. Students also proved to be very competent in making use of resources stored on their phone, and view or listen to audio resources made available on a removable storage card.

5. PILOTING M-LEARNING SUPPORT FOR TWO COURSE MODULES

Once these tests were completed work focused on designing learning activities that are being piloted with twenty students based in developing countries. These students have all been supplied with the Nokia N70 phone. Ten are based in SADC countries and studying the "Rural Development" module, and ten are based in a broader range of developing countries in Africa, Asia, the West Indies, and the Middle East, and are studying the course module in "ICT for Development."

Drawing on the pedagogic approaches identified in the literature review, three major instructional design options are now being explored:

- The design of effective learning activities (that potentially involve collaboration and sharing among students) that make use of the multimedia and communication capabilities of the mobile phone.
- The redesign of course content so that it can be readily used on the mobile phone through greater emphasis on audio visual content, and interactive features such as quizzes.
- The enhancement of remote tutoring by considering the potential role of SMS, MMS, mobile blogging, pod- and video-casting.

The module tutors for each of the two modules have become involved in exploring how these options could best enhance the module that they are responsible for. This has resulted in different approaches being explored with each module, as highlighted in Table 4 below:

TABLE 4 Mobile learning design approaches for two course modules

Rural Development	ICT for Development
Contains a lot of narrative, and is not particularly technical.	Inherently more technical, with more tables and graphs and animations.
The context where the student is based is relevant to the study. Students travel on field visits providing the opportunity to relate learning to the practical challenges students face in their work.	Audio narrative versions of the content would not be very helpful, but there are lots of practical ways students could explore this subject and undertake small research tasks.

Rural Development	ICT for Development
Materials designed and being tested include:	Materials designed and being tested include:
• Quick quizzes which students can use to test themselves on basic factual information, making use of learning moments – brief periods where they can study whilst on the move.	• Short video conversations with the course author/tutor introducing the unit, and highlighting some of the key learning points and topics for debate.
• Mp3 audio files providing a narrative of the module unit content, that the student can listen to if they have their phone with them.	• Provision of short videos supplementing the content of the study materials, or providing alternative study materials that can go further than the printed materials in illustrating a concept.
• Videos compressed to 3GP file format, that the students can watch on the phone, giving short case examples.	• Development of major new types of assignments that are based on activities and replace the traditional TMA. The approach being developed involves using the mobile device to work through a series of activities that help students reflect on the learning materials, and engage where possible in short research or practical activities. There are two deliverables: a small multimedia portfolio and an assignment in more traditional essay form. Both are submitted to the tutor for assessment and feedback.
• Polls to solicit opinion on particular topics and feedback on course materials that can be sent to the tutor by text, and responded to in the tutoring process.	
• Activities that students can do to supplement their learning by making specific use of the phones audio recording and image/video capturing capabilities.	

In both cases the students are supported by tutors based in the UK and during 2007 the pilot is also exploring the scope for:

- Preparing multimedia digests supplied to students for viewing and listening to on their mobile phone.
- Drawing on contributions submitted by students and encouraging sharing any interesting audio or video material with the wider group. Students may also be encouraged to develop and share their own audio narratives for module units.
- Use of SMS by tutors to encourage completion of work and by students when they need to ask for help – perhaps when they are studying away from their office.

Significantly, resources that the students capture on their mobile device and share with the tutor may also contribute to the development of the modules in future. They may represent useful learning resources including case studies and examples from different contexts that can form part of a repository or be integrated with the course module. In this way the students may become both beneficiaries of and contributors to the educational process, which is an important element of the evolving distance learning pedagogy of the DLP. Given the rich diversity of the DLP's student community, this also represents a wonderful opportunity to build a student community with unique global access to a pool of current knowledge.

Discussion and Practical Application

In this section, we will reflect on the pedagogic model, and also on some of the technical design decisions that the project team made.

Reflections on Pedagogy

In our background discussions, we indicated that the DLP is seeking to develop a pedagogic model to encourage contextually situated constructivist activities that involve collaborative learning. Distance learning also links strongly to processes of informal and lifelong learning. A study by Bright et al. (2004) based on a survey of all the DLP students, and meetings with students in Hong Kong and Zimbabwe, revealed that the educational and pedagogic background of many DLP students lead to expectation of the educational process being primarily shaped around a process of knowledge transfer from expert teachers. By contrast those involved within the DLP designing the OLE had assumed a more constructivists model. Alongside the access barriers, this pedagogic factor probably contributed to participation in the asynchronous online discussions being lower than hoped.

The same study indicated that many DLP students pursue further study to support career progression through gaining qualifications. Interestingly, it also highlighted that DLP students work mainly in the development sector where participatory approaches to learning and professional development are increasingly common.

Preliminary feedback from students involved in the project has welcomed the audio and video content, and suggests that this more personal contact is encouraging, and can increase student commitment. The convenience of being able to learn by using the phone in different situations and in short study sessions is also being commented on.

Set against these insights, the authors make the following observations in relation to the design of learning materials and tutoring approaches for this project:

- Provision of audio visual content, and resources that replicate familiar experiences (such as lectures and quizzes), are quickly adopted, and these approaches suited the "Rural Development" module subject matter.

- Introducing ideas that encourage learning among peers, along with sharing and contributing to the educational process, represent more progressive and innovative approaches for the students to engage in. The more collaborative activities designed around production of new types of assignment deliverables and learning-by-doing (as reflected in the "ICT for Development" module) may take more time to get student "buy in" as they have to become contributors as well as beneficiaries. Interaction with the tutor and a well designed support environment for mobile learning are likely to be more critical.

In both cases mobile technologies certainly provide suitable tools. The immediacy of instant communication and the scope for student involvement in creating and sharing learning materials and sharing experiences is more apparent and accessible than in other technology mediated models. Experiential learning can provide feedback to the learning community at large, both in the present time and for the future. This creates the opportunity for designing a more successful constructivist model for supporting distance learning.

Technical Considerations

Important technical decisions had to be made about how to develop the learning materials and make them available on the mobile phone sets. This will not be covered in depth, but Table 5 below summarizes the choices made and provides the underlying rationale.

TABLE 5 Summary of major technical decisions

Choice	Rationale
To develop content initially using XHTML, and later on consider use of Java and/or Mobile Flash for more complex interactive content and advanced quiz features.	Decision to keep the technical approach as simple as possible, and enable students to access materials through a familiar mobile equivalent of a web browser. This encourages portability, interoperability, and independence from particular phone models.
To distribute content on CD, External Storage Card (SD, CompactFlash, etc.), and exchange files via synchronisation with a PC and email attachment.	GPRS and 3G services remain expensive and coverage for these services is patchy. Web based delivery of content could be considered at a later stage. This promotes broader access, though synchronising with a PC and emailing large files is a potential problem.
To supply all students with the same phone Nokia N70 model.	Enables the project to retain a focus on the educational components, without the distraction of diverse hardware.
Not to develop any special tools that assist students in storing files in the right location when they capture audio and video or exchange files with the programme.	We are impressed by the usability of the software supplied with the phones, and are of the view that if the students know the folder structure we have developed for the mobile content (which is consistent with the CD folder structures), then with adequate documentation they can successfully do their own file management.

Designing for the small screen was a challenge, and drawing on the ideas of Jones and Marsden (2005), careful thought is being given to how best to do this. Audio and video alternatives to text are being developed where possible, and the usability features of the phone model and browser software also facilitate the design of efficient navigation. In practice, a few unexpected technical challenges have been encountered relating to audio capture time limits and slow performance if audio or video files stored on the external card are launched via the phone browser. These problems are being investigated but should not be insurmountable as the handsets rapidly become more powerful.

Future Trends and Recommendations

Since we started planning this project in 2006, the price of the Nokia N70 handset and equivalent models, together with the price of removable storage cards, has halved. Coverage and roll out of data services in Africa is also gathering pace. The assumption we started with was that whilst we were making use of expensive relatively high end equipment at the outset, the picture would look very different by 2009. We should therefore be gearing up our programme for a context where powerful handsets will be widely available in Africa along with real time data services that would remove the need for our current file transfer model.

Alongside the technological advances, we are also seeing rapid developments in the following relevant areas:

- Emergence of social software on the Internet and mobile devices, providing a global platform where individuals publish audio visual content from remote locations (for example, via mobile blogging), and collaborate on the creation and development of ideas. This trend is likely to make more people familiar with constructivist approaches.
- Emergence of standards for sharing content (learning objects), and development of new licensing approaches such as creative commons that provide incentives to innovators alongside dissemination of knowledge. Repositories of open educational resources are being developed and becoming accessible to mobile users.

MOBILE LEARNING ENVIRONMENT

These trends point to the need for further research to be carried out on how best to provide a coherent environment for mobile learners that integrates the potential of the Web 2.0 services. Figure 8 provides an overview of the bigger picture, showing different application and system components that could eventually be integrated, and need to be considered from the perspective of the mobile distance learner.

The role of tutors within this environment is not illustrated, but will be critical in facilitating student understanding of the different tools and how they support individual and group. It is also likely that formal learning environments may also be superseded or at the very least complemented by personal spaces where lifelong learning is more effectively supported.

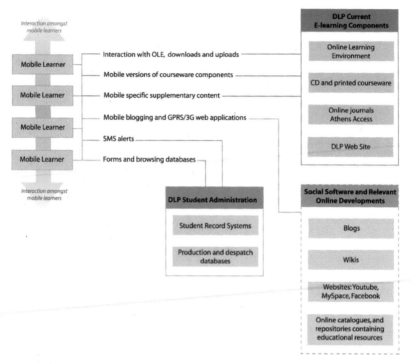

FIGURE 8 Big picture of applications and components that should be integrated for mobile learning

Conclusion

The outcomes and lessons being learned from this project should not be regarded as prescriptive, but some of the key learning points for the DLP in relation to the specific SADC context are as follows:

- The introduction of mobile learning is complex and multifaceted, and a range of pedagogic, practical, and technical issues need to be carefully understood.
- Mobile learning approaches need to be considered alongside traditional and e-learning models, and some of the emerging technical requirements for m-learning (for example, greater emphasis on audio-visual content) in turn influence the design and authoring approaches needed for the DLP's CD-based courseware and printed materials.

- Attention needs to be given to a coherent learning environment for mobile distance learners that takes account of future trends, and the emergence of social software.
- Keep it simple, personal, and avoid device proliferation.
- M-learning supports the development of new study skills:
  - learners can interact, create and share valuable learning resources such as audio versions of course materials they record themselves with appropriate regional accents, and share photos and videos providing insights into their context; and
  - make use of brief study sessions in unusual locations.

M-learning is certainly not an end in itself, so it is important to consider where it fits within a holistic learning model, and evaluation needs to identify added value in relation to clearly defined objectives. At the beginning of the DLP, we identified the needs we wanted the project to enhance:

1. Communication
2. Access and participation
3. Tutoring support to students in diverse locations
4. The usability of learning resources for students who are very mobile
5. Access to content and programme materials

In all five cases, the pilot project is providing insights into how mobile learning can help achieve these objectives, and we hope this case study has shed light that will be helpful to readers. We set out in this project to focus particularly on the needs of students based in developing countries. It is interesting to reflect that the possible solutions emerging provide the best hope for a learning environment that has global reach, and where common approaches can be developed and enjoyed equally by all students irrespective of their location. This has to be one of the major enhancements and attractions of a model incorporating m-learning.

References

ALLY, M. 2004. Using learning theories to design instruction for mobile learning devices. Paper presentation, *mLearn 2004, 3rd world conference on m-learning, June, Bracciano, Italy.* http://www.mobilearn.org/mlearn2004/

BARKER, A., G. KRULL, and B. MALLINSON. 2005. Proposed theoretical model for m-learning adoption in developing countries. Paper presentation, *mLearn 2005, 4th world conference on m-learning*, October 25-28, Cape Town, South Africa. http://www.mlearn.org.za/

BRIGHT, H., H. FRY, J. GREGSON, and R. PEARCE. 2004. The influence of educational background and culture on developing appropriate e-learning pedagogies. Unpublished research report.

JONES, M., and G. MARSDEN. 2005. *Mobile interaction design*. Hoboken, NJ: John Wiley and Sons.

KUKULSKA-HULME, A., and J. TRAXLER. 2005. *Mobile learning: A handbook for educators and trainers*. London: Routledge.

NAISMITH, L., P. LONSDALE, G. VAVOULA, and M. SHARPLES. 2004. Report 11: Literature review in mobile technologies and learning. A report for NESTA Futurelab, University of Birmingham. http://www.futurelab.org.uk/research/reviews/reviews_11_and12/11_02.htm

Project Team

The authors would like to thank the following members of our project team:

- Paul Smith who together with Jon, has designed the mobile learning resources for the ICT for Development module, and given invaluable support and advice in relation the authoring of this chapter.
- Mike Stockbridge who designed the mobile learning resources for the Rural Development module, and is tutoring that module
- Emmy Patroba and Emmanuel Kitwala based in Tanzania, and Rex Chapota and Mike Matsimbe based in Malawi, who from the outset have given us their advice and feedback from the perspective of students based in the SADC region.

Using Mobile Technologies
for Multimedia Tours
in a Traditional Museum Setting

LAURA NAISMITH
M. PAUL SMITH
UNIVERSITY OF BIRMINGHAM
UNITED KINGDOM

Abstract

Mobile technology can be used to deliver learner-centred experiences at a museum without compromising its aesthetic appeal. This chapter presents a study in which two Flash-based multimedia tours were developed for the Hypertag Magus Guide system and trialled with twenty-five visitors to the University of Birmingham's Lapworth Museum of Geology. Trial participants found the system fun and easy to use, though they requested headphones in order to hear the audio more clearly. They provided several suggestions to improve the tours including creating stronger links between the tour and the museum's objects and incorporating more interactive and competitive elements. We found that a structured multimedia tour approach was appropriate for visitors who can connect with the museum's narratives, though more flexibility was required to meet the needs of other visitor types.

Introduction

The Lapworth Museum of Geology is one of the pre-eminent geology museums in the United Kingdom. Established in 1880, its collections now number around two hundred and fifty thousand specimens, with particular strengths in vertebrate and invertebrate palaeontology and mineralogy. The collections are characterized by having a particularly large volume of supporting historical information (for example, documents, photographs and maps), that is housed in the museum's archives. As shown in Figure 1, the principal display area for the collections is the main hall of the museum, which is one of only two geology museums in the UK to retain its original Victorian/Edwardian design and fittings.

FIGURE 1 Main Hall of the Lapworth Museum

The museum is used as a resource by students at all levels of formal education, as well as by adult interest groups and the wider community. Hence, there is a broad variation in the experience and knowledge that visitors both bring to and take away from the museum. In attempting to provide flexible opportunities to support the range of their visitors, the museum is faced with several challenges. The building in which it is housed has a Grade II listed status, indicating that it is a particularly significant building. This, in addition to other historical and aesthetic considerations, means that the museum cannot be easily altered or extended, thus limiting the ability for the museum to easily introduce conventional interactive displays. These design constraints also restrict the supporting content of the exhibits to a small amount of in-case information and traditional paper-based worksheets.

Learning in Museums

The Museums, Libraries, and Archives Council (MLA) of the UK provide a highly inclusive definition of learning:

> Learning is a process of active engagement with experience. It is what people do when they want to make sense of the world. It may involve the development or deepening of skills, knowledge, understanding, awareness, values, ideas and feelings, or an increase in the capacity to reflect. Effective learning leads to change, development and the desire to learn more. (MLA 2004)

In museums, visitors are encouraged to explore and discover in order to learn the processes of inquiry and even of learning itself (Hawkey 2004). The ultimate goal of this exploration is the creation of new knowledge and personal meaning – what Falk and Dierking (2000) term "free-choice learning." Free-choice learning "tends to be nonlinear, is personally motivated, and involves considerable choice on the part of the learner as to what to learn, as well as where and when to participate in learning" (p. 13). Museums support free-choice learning by helping to reinforce existing knowledge, helping to make abstract concepts "real" and providing each visitor with a unique experience (Falk and Dierking 2000).

Previous research suggests that there are patterns in how visitors select and engage with a museum's objects in order to create meaning. A study commissioned for the West Midlands Science and Industry Collections Project (Morris, Hargreaves, and McIntyre 2004) revealed four distinct modes of this behaviour:

- **Browsers** select random objects and then require explanation. They are likely to select visually arresting objects that appeal to their sense of awe and wonder.
- **Followers** latch on to the museum's explanatory narrative themes. These visitors need points of engagement and connection as provided through thematic groupings with narrative structure.
- **Searchers** gather information on particular collections or exhibitions. They are likely to search by keyword rather than by thematic narrative.
- **Researchers** seek detailed information about specific objects, including links to authoritative, scholarly commentary and information on the location of related collections.

Browsers and Followers, who made up the largest proportion of visitors in this study, do not need to interact with many objects in order to have a meaningful experience, while Searchers and Researchers want to be able to search across entire collections. Browsers and Followers are likely to prefer information delivered in a rich sensory format, while the principal need of Searchers and Researchers is easy access to detailed information.

Using Mobile Technology to Support Museum Learning

A common problem faced by museums is that visitors often do not make good use of the range of learning opportunities that they offer. Various reasons have been cited for this, including a lack of preparation and follow-up (Oppermann and Specht 1999) and supporting materials that cannot easily adapt to the range of learner interests and needs (Not and Zancanaro 1998). Mobile technology can support visitors by providing both location-based information and guidance through this information based on the learner's interests and needs.

Museum learning has personal, physical, and sociocultural dimensions (Falk and Dierking 2000). Mobile technology may also be used to build more engaging learning experiences by directly facilitating these dimensions by their personal, portable, and networked nature. Previous work has shown that mobile technology can help to increase engagement with the visitor's physical surroundings (Naismith et al. 2005), increase the confidence, motivation, and involvement of pupils and staff visiting art museums (Burkett 2005) and promote interactivity with artworks (Proctor and Tellis 2003).

The following requirements for the design of mobile technology and content for a general audience were gathered from the literature:

- Technology should be easy to use and unobtrusive; it should enable the experience rather than detract from it (Hawkey 2004).
- Content should work with the objects, to direct the visitor's attention and require their feedback (Fisher 2005).
- Visitors should be offered choice wherever possible (Falk and Dierking 2000).
- Visually arresting objects should be incorporated in order to help Browsers transition to Followers (Morris, Hargreaves, and McIntyre 2004).
- A strong narrative should be provided to help structure the content. Multimedia should be incorporated where possible and appropriate (Mayer, 2001; Morris, Hargreaves, and McIntyre 2004).

- When using multimedia, the audio and video must be coherent (Proctor and Tellis 2003).
- The use of specialist language should be avoided where possible; unfamiliar terms need to be explained (Fisher 2005).
- Promote engagement with objects through personal challenge (i.e., quizzes) and play (Fisher 2005).

Aim of this Study

The primary aim of this study was to explore the use of mobile technology to deliver learner-centred experiences to visitors, while retaining the traditional look and feel of the museum.

Methodology

Overview

The main hall of the Lapworth Museum occupies approximately two hundred square metres. Most prominent are the four large wooden display units, each containing sixteen display cases arranged into two rows in the centre of the room. There are eight additional wooden display units containing a total of twenty-four display cases, as well as sixty display cases along the perimeter of the room. Objects may also be placed on temporary displays, or mounted directly to the wall. In total, there are 148 different display cabinets or display areas. The display cases are glass-fronted, and there is usually at least six inches between the objects and the glass. Many of the cases have no low-voltage power available within them and there are few power sockets available towards the middle of the room (Shucksmith 2005).

The current configuration of the museum suggests to the visitor an essentially linear path through the museum's displays. This corresponds to viewing the objects in chronological order. Mobile technology, however, affords the opportunity to tell different stories about the museum's objects without extending or altering the museum's infrastructure.

Study Design

STAGE 1: SELECTION OF POSITIONING TECHNOLOGY

It is important to preserve a "sense of place" when using mobile technology (Exploratorium 2005). In order to achieve this, we sought to source appropriate positioning technology in order to support context-sensitive delivery of information and activities based on physical location.

In order to cater to the needs of visitors at different educational levels, we intended to provide content in the form of tours. A tour would consist of a series of stops linked to either specific cases or individual objects. Positioning technology would then be used to identify to which stop the user was closest, in order to provide relevant information.

The small size and compact layout of this indoor museum prevented any serious consideration of absolute positioning techniques, as were used in the CAERUS project with the Winterbourne Botanic Garden (Naismith and Smith 2004; Naismith et al. 2005), as it would be necessary to determine in which direction the visitor was facing to suggest appropriate content. Instead, we considered various low or no-power tagging technologies that could be used either at the case or object level. As it would be necessary for the visitor to take some action in activating the tag, we could be fairly certain in identifying the correct location and orientation.

STAGE 2: TOUR DESIGN AND DEVELOPMENT

Two multimedia tours were developed to target different audiences. The primary motivation behind the focus on tours was to promote nonlinear exploration of the museum. By incorporating some of the museum's visually arresting objects (for example the *Tyrannosaurus rex* skull) within a narrative theme, we could also assist visitors in making the transition from Browsers to Followers.

The limited capabilities of the inbuilt Internet browser on the Pocket PC device presented challenges to the development of sophisticated multimedia content in HTML. An alternative to HTML content creation is the use of Macromedia Flash. Flash uses the concept of a movie, and allows control of content layout on a frame-by-frame basis. A simple scripting language can be used to control movement between frames. Flash also has the advantage of supporting the import of media files and producing a single output file, as opposed to the multiple files required with an HTML-only approach.

It should be noted, however, that Flash outputs a file with a SWF extension, which cannot be displayed on the Pocket PC handheld device without additional software. A free ActiveX control from Adobe (http://www.adobe.com/devnet/devices/development_kits.html) can play the SWF file if it is embedded within an HTML file. This control is licensed for development purposes only, and is not available for commercial release.

STAGE 3: VISITOR EVALUATION

The next stage of the study was to evaluate the demonstrator system for efficiency, effectiveness, and satisfaction. The objectives of this evaluation were to:

- assess the general usability of the system
- assess how the system affected user behaviour and ability to navigate around the museum
- assess desirability of the system amongst different user groups
- assess desirability of different types of content amongst different user groups

Twenty-five visitors to the Lapworth Museum participated in a trial of this system in November 2005. Table 1 describes the organization of participants in the trial.

TABLE 1 Trial Organization

Visitor Type	Tour	Number of Visitors
A. Adult Visitors	Climate Change	5
B. Undergraduate Students	Climate Change	6
C. School Visitors	Predators and Prey	14

Eight handheld devices were used during the trial, six running the Pocket PC 2002 operating system and two running the Pocket PC 2003 operating system. The Hypertag Magus Guide application and Macromedia Flash Player ActiveX control were preloaded on all devices, along with the content for the chosen tour.

Trial participants gathered in a central meeting space for a scripted overview and demonstration of the Magus Guide system. The trial participants were then free to wander around the museum and use the Magus Guide as they wished, though it was suggested that they attempt to follow the tour as set. Informal observations were made while the participants were in the museum. Participants were instructed to return the handheld devices when they had either completed the tour, or were satisfied that they had experienced the full functionality of the system. A short questionnaire was then administered, followed by a semi-structured interview on their experiences.

The trial participants covered a range of demographic groups. Table 2 shows a breakdown of the trial participants by sex, age, and experience of the museum. Trial participants spent between fifteen and thirty minutes in the museum.

TABLE 2 Trial Participant Demographics

Sex	Male	21
	Female	4
Age	under 20	14
	20-29	5
	30-39	1
	40-49	0
	50-59	1
	60-69	3
	70-79	1
Experience of Museum	First Time Visitor	11
	Returning Visitor	14

Results

STAGE 1: SELECTION OF POSITIONING TECHNOLOGY

Table provides a summary of the three main technologies evaluated: Barcodes, RFID, and Infrared.

TABLE 3 Comparison of Positioning Technologies

	Barcodes	RFID	Infrared
1. Supplier	Socket Communications	Socket Communications	Hypertag Magus Guide
2. Cost of demonstration kit	Low	Medium	Medium
3. Aesthetic appeal of tags	Low	High	Medium
4. Ease of activating tag	Medium	Low	High
5. Requires reader for each handheld device	Yes	Yes	No
6. Power required for tags	No	No	Yes (battery)
7. Requires additional software development	Yes	Yes	No

Barcodes are an established and familiar technology, and have been used extensively for many applications, including retail purchasing and general stock control. Pridden (2003) provides an extensive review of the advantages and disadvantages of using barcodes in a traditional museum setting.

As the barcodes would be placed on the individual cases or objects, the Pocket PC would need to be equipped with a barcode reader to identify the code and take appropriate action. A secure digital (SD) compatible barcode reader, and supporting software, was acquired from Socket Communications (http://www.socketcom.com). As the iPAQs used in the trial have an inbuilt SD slot, it was possible to use the barcode reader without any supporting hardware.

Barcodes were ultimately deemed unacceptable due to a number of factors. Though the process of generating the barcodes is relatively straightforward and inexpensive, it would be necessary to purchase a separate barcode reader for each Pocket PC used by the museum. Additional software development would also be necessary to use the barcode number to display the appropriate multimedia content. The barcodes would need to be affixed to the cases with some kind of adhesive, which could potentially cause damage. They are also easily damaged and, as they are quite familiar in industry, may project a "low-tech" impression to visitors.

RFID is also used extensive in the manufacturing industry. Hsi and Fait (2005) describe a custom-designed RFID application that was used to enhance visitor experiences at the Exploratorium science museum in San Francisco. An RFID demonstrator kit was acquired from Socket Communications. A selection of passive (i.e. unpowered) tags was provided, each with a read distance of approximately 2.5 inches. The tags were smaller and more visually appealing than the barcodes. The reader, however, was compact flash (CF) compatible (as opposed to SD), which required an additional expansion sleeve for the iPAQs. As with the barcode reader, it would be necessary to develop additional software to use the RFID code to display the appropriate multimedia content.

RFID was ultimately deemed unacceptable. The total cost of ownership was higher than that of barcodes, without providing any additional benefits. The iPAQ, expansion sleeve, and RFID reader together were quite bulky and difficult to manipulate. The RFID sensor was actually located on the back of the reader, meaning that the user had to hold the iPAQ flat over the tag, as opposed to the more intuitive point and click operation of the barcode reader. The short read distance of the tags meant that it would not be possible to place them in the cases, thus the same problems with affixing the barcodes to the cases would be encountered.

The Hypertag Magus Guide system was selected for this study (http://www.hypertag.com/igsolutions.html). Fisher (2005) evaluated this system in four different UK museums, so there was already some indication of its possible effectiveness. The Magus Guide system includes custom-designed battery-powered Infrared tags, as well as supporting software both to identify the tag and to display the appropriate multimedia content. Infrared capabilities are inbuilt into nearly all handheld devices, and have traditionally been used to transmit information from one device to another. This meant that it was not necessary to purchase a reader for each device, which substantially lowered the total cost of ownership.

Figure 2 shows a sample tag. Activating a tag required pointing the handheld device at it. When activated, the tag flashed a blue light, accompanied by an audible click in the software application. As the tags had a read distance of approximately one metre, it was possible to place them inside the display cases. In total, seventeen of these tags were acquired for this study.

FIGURE 2 A Sample Magus Guide Tag

STAGE 2: TOUR DESIGN AND DEVELOPMENT
Two tours were developed, a fourteen stop "Climate Change" tour directed at a general, non-specialist audience and an eight stop "Predators and Prey" tour directed at a younger, non-specialist audience. The Climate Change tour contained text, images and audio, while the Predators and Prey tour contained text, images, audio and video. Figure 3 and Figure 4 illustrate screen shots from each of these tours.

FIGURE 3 Screen shots from the Climate Change tour

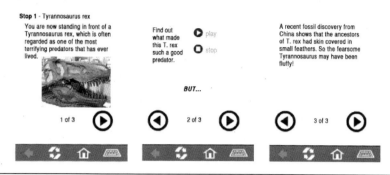

FIGURE 4 Screen shots from the Predators & Prey tour

As the Lapworth Museum did not have wireless network coverage, it was necessary to store the files on the iPAQs. This is supported by the Local Redirect feature of the Hypertag Magus Guide. It was originally intended that each tour would be developed as a single Flash file and embedded into an HTML file. Code could then be included in the HTML file to play the Flash file at a specific frame. Unfortunately this feature did not seem to be supported on the Pocket PC and it was necessary to create a separate Flash file for each stop on the tour.

Though the content was not linked to a website for the purposes of the trial, it would be possible to include these on the Lapworth Museum website without further modification.

STAGE 3: VISITOR EVALUATION

Table 4 shows the mean and standard deviation of the response to each questionnaire item, in the range from 1 (Strongly Disagree) to 5 (Strongly Agree). One sample t-test was performed on each mean, with 3 (Neither Agree nor Disagree) as the constant value. All statements showed a significant difference from Neither Agree nor Disagree ($P < 0.05$).

TABLE 2 Mean and Standard Deviation of Responses to a 5 point Likert Scale (1 = Strongly Disagree, 5 = Strongly Agree)

Statement	Mean	SD	N
a. Using the handheld device does not require much training.	4.04	1.06	25
b. It was easy at a glance to see what the options were for each screen.	4.38	0.50	24
c. It was difficult to select the option I wanted with the touch screen.	1.88	1.24	25

d. I felt that I was in control of the device.	4.17	1.27	24
e. The device responded too slowly.	1.79	1.18	24
f. I found it difficult to read the text on the screen.	1.92	1.28	24
g. The device helped me to navigate around the museum.	3.88	1.05	25
h. I felt self conscious using the device.	2.17	1.31	24
i. The way that the device presented information was clear and understandable.	4.24	0.78	25
j. It was difficult for me to determine where I was in the museum.	2.17	1.07	23
k. I would recommend the device to other visitors.	4.48	0.79	23
All items are significant at P < 0.05			

Positive Aspects of the System

Most visitors found the experience of using the Hypertag Magus Guide system to be fun and engaging. Participants were able to stay on task during the trial and did not seem to attempt to use the handheld device for other purposes. They found the action of swiping the tags easy and intuitive and felt that they could use the system independently in the future. The mix of media present in the designed content was highly desirable, particularly the audio segments.

From a management perspective, the tags themselves were small and easy to set up and move around the museum as required. Though battery powered, there was no need to replace any of the batteries during the trial.

Negative Aspects of the System

The audio was very difficult to hear clearly in the changeable environment of the museum, and many trial participants commented on the necessity of headphones. Headphones were also felt to promote a more personal experience and address the potential "embarrassment factor" of using the system alongside other museum visitors. It was also observed that the application itself is quite noisy, with many clicks and beeps, which could disturb other museum visitors.

The original decision not to offer headphones was made in an attempt to promote social interaction and prevent isolation and a heads-down experience (Hsi 2003). Proctor and Tellis (2003) identify the same issues in the decision by a museum to offer either a headset or wand for an audio-based tour. Their conclusion is that the "effectiveness of these educational experiences is based on the appropriateness of the technology used for the stated educational or interpretive goals."

Aspects of the System that Need Improvement

The introduction to the system was a bit too informal for many participants and there was some initial confusion as to where they should start and what buttons (if any) needed to be pressed. The digital map on the handheld device was both difficult to read and labour intensive to produce. Suggestions to address both of these problems included having a large poster or a handout that both outlines the use of the system and labels the stops in order.

During the trial, the white square tags were sometimes difficult to distinguish from the labels in the cases, and many participants commented that they would have appreciated more obvious visual indicators. They suggested that this could be accomplished by painting the tags in a distinctive colour, numbering the tags or both.

While the content was generally well received, some of the images selected were not well suited for the small display screen. There was also a tendency for participants to become so engaged in the experience of using the handheld device that they did not look at or interact with the actual objects in the cases. Participants commented that this could be remedied through direct instructions (for example, "Look at the [object name] in the case"), stronger linking between the object labels and the information available on the handheld device (sometimes just the common name was used in the tour, while the label contained the scientific name), and incorporating short quizzes. Increased interactivity and competition was particularly desirable amongst younger visitors. This aligns with Fisher's (2005) recommendations for designing content that works with the objects and having a screen that promotes engagement through personal challenge and play.

There was also a need to offer more flexibility within the system. In addition to the logistical problems of having many visitors start at the same place, older visitors were somewhat resistant to following a prescribed tour and wanted to be able to focus their visit on one or two areas of interest.

From a management perspective, installing the software and loading the content onto each iPAQ was quite time-consuming. It was necessary to repeat this procedure for each trial session, as the batteries on the handheld devices sometimes drained completely, losing all of the applications and content in memory.

Differences Amongst Age Groups

The adult trial group consisted of regular visitors to the museum. Whilst there were some technical problems during this first trial that were later remedied, overall the participants were generally enthusiastic, thought that this system could add to the museum experience and were willing to try it again. Unlike the younger visitors, however, they felt that they needed someone in the museum to be on call for technical support.

The adult visitors could successfully manipulate the technology but, as noted previously, there was some resistance to the idea of going on a formal tour. As specialist visitors, they were more likely to adopt Searcher and Researcher roles rather than Browser and Follower roles. There was some concern that the range of visitor needs was going to make it difficult for the museum to cater to everyone.

The group of undergraduate students responded particularly well to the structure of the tour, and quickly adopted the Follower role. They felt that this approach helped the content to "make sense," and that the content was pitched "about right" for a general audience. There was some interaction between the students during the trial, but it was primarily an individual experience. With respect to the technology, there was some initial confusion about where and how to get started, but by the end of the trial all of the students felt that they would be able to use the system again independently.

While the undergraduate students felt that this system enhanced the museum experience and made it more fun, they were pragmatic about their likely future usage of it. They would need the system to support them in a Researcher role in order that they could use the information provided for projects or essays. In their opinion, this would involve gathering specialist information on a select number of cases rather than a structured tour.

The school visitors were highly engaged by the technology. They immediately gravitated towards the handheld devices and did not wait for a formal explanation, preferring instead to figure it out as they went along.

This large group was split in two for the trial and very different behaviour was observed between the two groups, possibly due to the presence of the teacher in the second group. Not all of the students seemed to be following the tour, and several observations were made of students adopting a Browser role by trying to scan for tags on objects they deemed interesting (for example, the deer head). They were highly engaged by the device and the content, though their interaction with the actual exhibits was minimal. A common behaviour was to swipe a tag and then find some place to sit and interact with the device.

Students made several brief but supportive comments ("good," "really interesting"), and the teacher remarked that this system was "the best thing I've seen" for museum visits. The teacher felt that more structure was needed, however, in order to transform it into an effective learning experience. He and the students were very keen on the idea of introducing competitions (with awards) in order to focus attention on the objects and exhibits. The teacher also felt that competitions could be designed in the form of levels in order to cater to students with varying levels of ability. Students also suggested the incorporation of "weird facts," a finding echoed by Fisher (2005), which may help to appeal to a Browser's sense of awe and wonder.

Conclusion

In this chapter, we have seen that it is feasible and desirable to use mobile technology to deliver learner-centred experiences in the Lapworth Museum of Geology without compromising the aesthetic appeal of the museum. The structured multimedia approach taken in this study is appropriate for visitors who can adopt a Follower role, though more flexibility is required to meet the needs of Browsers, Searchers, and Researchers.

The Hypertag Magus Guide provides an easy to use mechanism for visitors of all ages to access web-based content, which can be stored locally on handheld devices in the form of HTML or Flash movie files. It is, however, necessary to provide headphones in order to hear the audio clearly. Overall, trial participants required minimal technical support and found the use of the system to be fun and engaging.

Limitations

The results of this study are based on a small trial consisting mainly of young male participants. The response of young females to this system is unknown. Additionally, all participants were geology enthusiasts to some degree. Further research is required to determine whether this system could be used to engage people with no previous relationship with either the museum or geology in general.

Vision for the Future

The results of this study have exceeded expectations in terms of the potential benefits of mobile technology for museum staff and its popularity with visitors. One of the benefits that will be developed in the future is the ability to respond quickly to global geological events, such as volcanic eruptions or earthquakes. With a modest investment in content generation by staff, it would be possible to produce thematic displays rapidly, interpreting the event using the museum collections while simultaneously publishing to the museum website and loaning resources from the museum's archives to local schools. Developing partnerships with media organizations would further increase the scope for embedding video clips. A further avenue to be explored is the generation of online worksheets and quizzes that can be taken back to the classroom to provide the basis for ongoing learning, creating an experience that is more seamless from classroom to museum, and back again.

Implications for Practice

This study has provided valuable insight into ways in which organizations such as the Lapworth Museum may develop the next generation of content and interpretation. It is important to note, however, that there are a number of remaining challenges in using mobile technology to provide meaningful learning opportunities on a large scale (Naismith and Corlett 2006).

Firstly, the technical reliability of mobile devices remains a concern. Whilst using the Hypertag system was easy and intuitive for most users in this study, the work involved to keep the Pocket PC devices charged and properly configured was significant. By keeping the device interactions simple and moving towards the use of user-owned technologies, both this workload and the cost-of-use could remain manageable. It is also important to note that it is not always necessary to seek technological solutions to the users' problems; for example, that of navigation. What is necessary, however, is to provide appropriate training and support to ensure that staff members are confident in promoting the available learning opportunities and in dealing with unexpected challenges. Designing and developing new mobile learning content requires a flexible and learner-centred approach that promotes interaction with the environment, whilst keeping the device interactions quick and simple. Finally, it is possible to future-proof project efforts by anticipating changes to various factors such as delivery options and device features, creating content that is independent of the specific delivery mechanism whenever possible and by paying attention to international standards for content creation, sharing, and reuse.

References

Burkett, E. 2005. Using handheld computers to stimulate critical studies in a-level art. Coventry: BECTA. http://www.evaluation.icttestbed.org.uk/learning/research/secondary/interest/collaboration.

Exploratorium. 2005. What are you puzzling about? In proceedings, *Electronic guidebook forum 2005: Issues and questions about wireless learning technologies and handheld computers in and beyond museums*, San Francisco.

FALK, J., and L. DIERKING. 2000. *Learning from museums: Visitor experiences and the making of meaning.* Walnut Creek, CA: AltaMira Press.

FISHER, S. 2005. *An evaluation of learning on the move and Science Navigator: Using PDAs in museum, heritage and science centre settings.* London: NESTA.

HAWKEY, R. 2004. *Learning with digital technologies in museums, science centres and galleries.* Bristol: Futurelab.

HSI, S. 2003. A study of user experiences mediated by nomadic web content in a museum. *Journal of Computer Assisted Learning* 19:308-19.

HSI, S., and H. FAIT. 2005. RFID enhances visitors' museum experiences at the Exploratorium. *Communications of the ACM* 48 (9):60-65.

MAYER, R. 2001. *Multimedia learning.* New York: Cambridge University Press.

MUSEUMS, LIBRARIES AND ARCHIVES COUNCIL (MLA). 2004. Inspiring learning for all. http://www.inspiringlearningforall.gov.uk.

MORRIS HARGREAVES MCINTYRE. 2004. *Learning journeys: Using technology to connect the four stages of meaning making.* Manchester: Morris Hargreaves McIntyre.

NAISMITH, L., and D. CORLETT. 2006. Reflections on success: A retrospective of the mLearn conference series, 2002-2005. In proceedings (ed. M. Ally), *mLearn 2006: Across generations and cultures,* Banff, Canada.

NAISMITH, L., M. SHARPLES, and J. TING. 2005. Evaluation of CAERUS: A context aware mobile guide. In proceedings (ed. H. van der Merwe and T. Brown), *mLearn 2005: Mobile technology: The future of learning in your hands,* Cape Town, South Africa.

NAISMITH, L. and P. SMITH. 2004. Context-sensitive information delivery to visitors in a botanic garden. In proceedings, *ED-MEDIA world conference on educational multimedia, hypermedia and telecommunications,* Lugano, Switzerland.

NOT, E., and M. ZANCANARO. 1998. Content adaptation for audio-based hypertexts in physical environments. In *Hypertext '98: Second workshop on adaptive hypertext and hypermedia.* Pittsburgh: ACM.

OPPERMANN, R., and M. SPECHT. 1999. A nomadic information system for adaptive exhibition guidance. *ICHIM '99,* 103-109. Washington: Archives & Museum Informatics.

PRIDDEN, I. 2003. Object tagging at the Petrie Museum. http://www.petrie.ucl.ac.uk/barcodes.pdf

PROCTOR, N., and C. TELLIS. 2003. The state of the art in museum handhelds in 2003. In *Proceedings of museums and the web 2003*. Toronto: Archives & Museums Informatics.

SHUCKSMITH, J. 2005. *Proposals for the Lapworth Museum Project: Thoughts and comments on how to create an interactive environment for the visitor within the Lapworth Museum.* Wave Solutions, University of Birmingham.

Acknowledgements

This study was funded through a grant from Microsoft UK Ltd. to the Centre for Learning, Innovation and Collaboration (CLIC, formerly CETADL) at the University of Birmingham in the United Kingdom.

Use of Mobile Technology for Teacher Training

JOCELYN WISHART
UNIVERSITY OF BRISTOL
UNITED KINGDOM

Abstract

This chapter describes a small-scale project, funded by the UK Teacher Development Agency, where all teachers and trainee teachers in one secondary school science department were given handheld Personal Digital Assistants (PDAs) for the academic year. The aims were to build m-learning and m-teaching capacity, to enable school based associate tutors to join the e-learning community linked to the local initial teacher training course, and to encourage reflective practice amongst trainee teachers. However, not all these aims succeeded. The handhelds were viewed as personal devices rather than enabling access to a community of practice. Nearly all participants praised the personal information management functions of the devices; however, the teachers did not use the handhelds to access course information and trainees did so only rarely. The ability to access Google from any location to answer students' and colleagues' questions was more popular. Most popular were the multiple methods of recording available on the handheld: video, audio, and written notes. Teachers used these to record observations on each others' lessons, students' work, student behaviour, and trainees' progress in teaching. The concept of using blogs to reflect on practice was not taken up though trainees did record personal reflections on their teaching in Pocket Word for later use in course assignments.

Introduction

In a comprehensive review of the use of mobile technologies such as handheld computers, Personal Digital Assistants (PDAs) and Smartphones in learning and teaching, Naismith et al. (2004) identified aspects of learning relevant to students' use of mobile devices in both formal and informal learning contexts. In order to help them evaluate the most relevant applications of mobile technologies in education they classified these aspects into six groups that could be used to describe the use of mobile devices with students. Four of these classifications are linked to types of learning theory:

- behaviourist
- constructivist
- situated
- collaborative

Two relate more to context and application:

- informal and lifelong learning
- learning and teaching support

It is this last area of learning and teaching support that is particularly relevant to initial teacher training where trainees move regularly between university and school placement and are expected to acquire, decipher, and understand a wealth of information, both pedagogical and practical, in the process.

Another review, this time of innovative practice with e-learning in further and higher education within the UK (JISC 2005) identified three key features of mobile technologies: portability, anytime-anyplace connectivity, and immediacy of communication that underpin their potential for learning and teaching support. These features are leading to empowerment and more effective management of learners (especially in dispersed communities): portability since PDAs are pocket sized; anytime-anyplace connectivity as PDAs with General Packet Radio Services (GPRS) or WiFi connectivity enable flexible and timely access to e-learning resources; and immediacy of communication through phone or email. Such a range of affordances for learning and teaching support bodes well for the potential use of PDAs with trainee teachers, who are expected to teach as well as learn during their training. Previous work with teachers using PDAs in schools (Perry 2003) has shown that PDAs can be supportive of teaching in that they offer considerable potential to make teachers' management and presentation of information more efficient. One science teacher described their range of potential benefits to Perry: "I would never willingly go without one now; it is my instantly accessible encyclopaedia, thesaurus, periodic table, diary, register/mark book, world map, and even star chart!"

Efficient management of information is indeed essential for trainees following the Postgraduate Certificate of Education (PGCE), a one-year science teacher training course in the UK. They need access to and a means to store information: on the National Curriculum, examination board syllabi, and school based schemes of work; to supplement their subject knowledge; for course administration; for assignments and for pastoral support. Additionally, whilst the trainees are directly supported by a mentor from the school when on placement, their university tutors need feedback on their trainees' progress to assure themselves of their well being. Access to email and the Internet has become essential to managing this process. However, whilst all community schools in England now have connected desktop computers, the socio-cultural context within the schools means that trainee teachers are reluctant to use these. They tend to be perceived as belonging to the students or other members of staff. Providing trainee teachers with PDAs is one way of resolving this issue and, indeed, previous research (Wishart, Ramsden, and McFarlane 2007) has shown that this can be effective where trainee teachers in science trialled the use of Internet enabled PDAs to support them in their teaching and learning. Another study investigating the development of e-learning communities amongst initial teacher trainees dispersed on their school placements (Hughes 2005) found that the trainees preferred PDAs to laptops as they were smaller and lighter. Wishart, Ramsden, and McFarlane (2005) reported that their PGCE trainees could and did use their PDAs to access course related information. The trainees especially appreciated just-in-time Internet access from any location for both personal and professional reasons and they stayed in email contact with their tutor though they preferred to use SMS texting or MSN to keep in touch with their peers. However, not all the trainee teachers used their PDAs regularly, and many within the group were uncomfortable about being the only ones in their class or school with a PDA.

Thus this project was set up with the main objective of building capacity within one school; enabling teachers and trainees in a science department to share their m-learning practice and allowing both trainees on placement miles away from the university and their school based teacher mentors to join the e-learning community linked to the PGCE course. Another objective was to encourage reflective practice amongst the trainee teachers. Employing reflective practice is recommended by Pollard (2005) as being of vital importance to teachers in order to develop evidence-informed professional judgement. The trainees would be able to use the PDAs anywhere and anytime to reflect on their teaching experiences by means of web-based logs known as blogs. These could enable both the recording of their reflections on teaching and allow the university tutor to have oversight of their progress as reflective practitioners. The blogs would also act as a mechanism for storing their reflections for later use in assignments.

Method

Thirteen science teachers at a local community school and six trainee teachers on the PGCE one-year teacher training course at the University of Bristol were given handheld computers to use throughout the academic year. These were PDAs chosen from the Pocket PC range then available in the UK that contained cameras and used the mobile phone GPRS network to connect to the Internet. Previous research (Wishart, McFarlane, and Ramsden 2005) had shown that initial teacher trainees preferred Pocket PC-based handheld computers to Palm OS based ones.

The models used in the study included Qtek 2020, Qtek 2020i, i-mate, XDA II and XDA IIi, almost identical hardware (shown in Figure 1) running Pocket PC 2003. The PDAs were supplied with aluminium protective cases and screen protectors. Separate collapsible Stowaway keyboards were provided where the participant requested one.

FIGURE 1 XDA II clone PDA

Mobile phone connectivity was supplied by Vodafone as it had proved reliable in the project area in the earlier study. It was arranged that staff and trainees could receive and send up to a total of 6MB data including web pages, emails, and texts a month without cost to them though they would be expected to pay for any voice calls they made.

The sample of teachers was selected through opportunity, with the head of chemistry at the school being an experienced PDA user and the head of science being willing to explore their use amongst his staff. The three trainees allocated to this school by the university during each of two teaching practices were then invited to join this study. All agreed though none of them had used a PDA before; however, they had all used Word, Excel, and Powerpoint in their studies and/or work.

On introduction to the mobile devices trainees and staff were shown how the PDAs have the potential to support them in:

- collaborating via the course Virtual Learning Environment (VLE) discussion groups and email
- accessing course documentation (via the VLE or via synchronisation with a PC)
- just in time acquisition of knowledge from the Web
- acquisition of science information from e-books and encyclopaedias
- delivering accurate figures for scientific constants and formulae
- organizing commitments, lesson plans and timetables
- recording and analysing laboratory results
- recording student attendance and grades
- photographing experiments for display and reinforcing student knowledge
- maintaining a reflective web log (blog) that could allow them to record lesson evaluations and other reflections on their teaching.

The six trainees were participant action researchers in the project acting on their teaching and learning by means of the PDA and then reflecting on and amending their practice (Wadsworth 1998); they reported in by online questionnaire twice during the academic year. There was also a dedicated discussion area on Blackboard, the course VLE, should they prefer this method of exchanging information and ideas about the PDA project. Additionally a focus group of all trainee PDA users was organized for the end of the first block of their teaching practice in order to collect impressions and share potential uses face to face.

Available teaching staff participated in a similar focus group discussion during the spring term and twelve were interviewed about their use of the PDA in the summer toward the end of the academic year. The totals given for number of teachers' responses in the results section vary as staff left during the discussions in response to student needs.

Results from teachers

Four to five months into the study, during the Spring term, teachers were asked to report whether they were still using the PDA. As shown in Table 1 below only half were using their PDA.

TABLE 1 Use of PDA

Are you still using the PDA?	n
Yes	6
No	6

On discussing reasons for not using the PDA three clear positions emerged: choosing to use an alternative technology to support teaching, lack of engagement with the study, and finding the PDA display difficult to read. Two teachers were not using the PDA as they now had alternative access to information and communication technology (ICT) which they found fitted their purposes better. Since the school had agreed to become involved with the PDA project each teaching laboratory had been equipped with a desktop computer, one teacher had purchased a digital camera and several had acquired USB memory sticks. All of these were suggested as being better for the purpose of designing presentations at home and bringing them to school for lessons. Another two teachers had failed to try out the PDA, and a third teacher found managing eye glasses (as the display was too small) and the stylus simultaneously too much trouble.

A list of the activities that were reported by more than one teacher as being used successfully to support teaching and mentoring trainee teachers is as follows:

- Making notes in meetings or for lesson observations using Word (see Figure 2)
- Calendar/Diary Scheduler (see Figure 3)
- Taking photos and videos (see Figure 4)
- Searching/Researching (Internet)

Figure 2 shows an example of the notes made by an experienced teacher during an observation of a trainee teacher's lesson, these were then beamed using infra-red to the trainee's PDA for her to include in her reflections

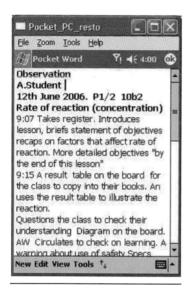

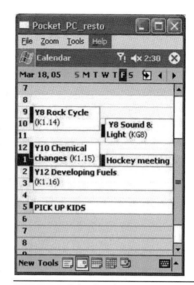

FIGURE 2 Lesson observation

FIGURE 3 Calendar showing a teacher's diary

on her teaching. The teachers noted the advantages of being able to use the PDA to quickly and easily make notes both in formal meetings and on accidentally meeting up with colleagues in the corridor between lessons.

Figure 3 is an illustration of how the Pocket PC Calendar can be used to display a teaching timetable. Whilst the diary design was not as appropriate for teaching as customized timetabling software, it was still one of the most popular applications.

Two teachers, a biologist and a chemist, were particularly enthusiastic about the potential of using images to record day to day activity in lessons, as shown in Figure 4, and displaying them to the class as a reminder of previous work or revision at a later date.

Access to the Internet was also reported particularly favourably, especially for keeping abreast of breaking news usually unavailable during the school day (such as the cricket scores). Additionally, one member of staff was very emphatic about how useful it was to set up a class administration system in Excel on a desktop computer and synchronize it to the PDA so that it could be quickly and easily updated during lessons. He used multiple windows for attendance, grades, practical skills achieved, and commendations as shown in Figure 5.

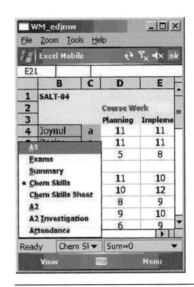

FIGURE 4 Using the camera

FIGURE 5 Using spreadsheets for class administration

However, when it came to participating in the e-learning community designed to support the trainee teachers in the school, as Table 2 shows, the teachers were less forthcoming.

TABLE 2 Participation in the e-learning community via PDA

Communication with the PGCE trainees' tutor?	n
I haven't	5
In person	1
By email from a desktop PC	1

In fact the teachers' communication using the PDA was much less than anticipated with only occasional use of SMS texts and email to contact each other or friends and family outside school. More use was made of beaming files to the trainee teachers than messaging or emailing them.

One teacher made innovative use of the PDA to support behaviour management in the classroom by recording a student's use of strong language during the lesson and playing it back to him afterwards. The student, who had previously been immensely tricky to deal with, immediately acknowledged that he had been out of order and apologized.

Results from Trainee Teachers

Results from the online questionnaires completed by the six trainee teachers (three from the autumn term teaching practice who were allowed to keep their PDAs when they moved to a different school and three from the Spring term practice) show similar trends. As Table 3 shows, just over half had given up using the PDA towards the end of the term.

TABLE 3 Use of the PDA

Are you still using the PDA?	Autumn Term	Spring Term
Yes	3	2
No	0	4

Two trainees had given up as they had allowed the PDA battery to discharge and lost their diaries and stored work, another found the PDA more hassle than a pen and paper, and another found it faster and easier to use a laptop that had become available. However, all the trainees agreed that using the PDA was easy and five of the six disagreed with the statement that the PDA was of no use to them as an individual. Though all the trainees trialled the applications used by the teachers as described earlier in this section, there was no clear agreement amongst this group as to whether having a PDA might support their learning and/or teaching. There was clear agreement though that the two most useful applications were the calendar for organizing their timetable and the task list for organizing their multiple commitments. The web browser was used (most often via Google) to answer queries and to find information to support teaching, but more often to support personal interest or need. They also used Word for making notes on lesson observations and for receiving feedback from experienced teachers on their own lessons.

The intended focus of the project for the trainees of sharing their reflections on their teaching experience with their tutors via a blog was not successful in that trainees in this study preferred not to use it. However, it was effective in proving that the software (Blogs in Hand on the PDA and Pebble on the server) worked effectively. One trainee sums it up neatly: "I saw my school based associate tutor every day, so had little need to share thoughts and ideas with him in this way. Also, I prefer to keep my personal reflections to myself." The university tutor was simply not perceived of by the trainees as being in need of this information. Another trainee teacher pointed out: "There seem to be more important things to do. Whether this is the case or not is debatable, but that is the perception when you are on the front line, teaching." The trainees did, however, use the PDAs to reflect more privately using Word to make personal notes.

Finally, several of the trainee teachers reported a feeling of confidence about their use of the PDA, especially being able to access the Internet wherever they happened to be for both personal and professional information. Also, the ability to use and then hide the PDA back in a pocket or bag led to it being perceived as educational technology that was more manageable in front of students than a desktop computer. The objective of the study to build capacity in m-learning within one school was met in that no-one reported feeling uncomfortable about using a PDA in the classroom, though sharing innovative practice was more successful amongst the chemists, amongst whom there was a keen PDA user.

Discussion

This small-scale study clearly illustrates the overwhelming nature of the social and cultural context in which new technologies are trialled. Of the three aspects cited by JISC (2005) as being key to the use for mobile and handheld technologies for learning and teaching support, portability, and anytime-anyplace connectivity were clearly important to both the teachers and trainee teachers, but immediacy of communication was not deemed relevant to their needs. The university tutor's perception that she needed to be regularly informed about trainees' development whilst on placement was not shared by the trainee teachers who reported that they felt their training needs were met by the school. In particular the concept of blogging as a way of encouraging and sharing reflections on teaching was not supported by the six trainees in this study. This result needs further research to ascertain whether it is trainee and/or school specific. For instance, other e-learning communities in initial teacher training project carried out in London (Jack and Scott 2005) investigating university tutors communicating with their trainees by means of video-conferencing found that such conferencing worked well with particularly needy trainees.

The handheld PDAs were used successfully by some of the teachers for personal support with timetabling, records of meetings, observations, students' attendance and grades, images, and just-in-time information from the Internet, thus fulfilling the enabling person-plus vision for information and communications technology (ICT) originally put forward by Perkins (1993). However, several months into the study half the participants were not using the PDA; some of these had moved on to other technology that had become available and, in the case of the teachers involved, some had not started yet. Thus the teaching staff appear to be following the bell curve model of diffusion of a successful innovation proposed by Rogers (1995) and shown in Figure 6.

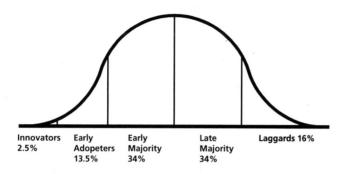

Innovators 2.5% Early Adopeters 13.5% Early Majority 34% Late Majority 34% Laggards 16%

FIGURE 6 The five categories of potential innovation adopters (Rogers 1995)

At the tail end there were the two teachers who had yet to try the technology and the four who were not convinced of its use. However, in this study, the leading edge of early adopters had not settled on the PDA as it competed with other recently acquired technological innovations. Digital cameras and USB sticks were considered better by two of the teachers for designing presentations for lessons at home and bringing them to school for lessons. Those teachers and trainee teachers who continued to use the PDA prioritized its organizational and personal management functionality which, of course, is the original design brief for a *personal* digital assistant. Though these teachers used PDAs to support their students' learning by, for example, using the camera to record layout for a class practical and audio recording to support class management, they did not use the PDA for presentations.

Both teachers and trainee teachers recognized the potential of the PDA for learning and teaching support as described by Naismith et al. (2004) and identified the same three software applications as central to this potential as in the earlier study by Wishart, McFarlane, and Ramsden (2005). These were the calendar or diary scheduler for organizing yourself, the spreadsheet of attendance or mark book for organizing your students, and the use of a word processor to make notes on information and events immediately after they are encountered.

There were clear signs that seeding a science department with PDAs led to greater confidence amongst the trainee teachers about their use than in the earlier study (Wishart, Ramsden, and McFarlane 2007). The handhelds were taken out of the participants' pockets or bags to be used only when relevant and then replaced. This was perceived as a distinct advantage by the inexperienced teachers compared to desktop or even laptop based computers in the classroom with the handhelds affording technology at a teacher's side and not in their face.

Implications for Practice

Following this study and the earlier trial reported by Wishart, Ramsden, and McFarlane (2007), the following practical applications appear to be of most benefit to teachers and teacher trainees using PDAs:

- Attendance, achievement, and behaviour monitoring – events can be captured at any location within the school. Recording may simply be via a prepared spreadsheet or tick list, but the use of video and audio to capture behaviour has the potential to provide incontestable evidence.
- Diary scheduling – a calendar application that usefully combines personal appointments with school teaching timetables and dates for student reports and parents' evenings would be welcomed.
- Making notes at point of need – teachers should explore which method of text entry they prefer, taking the time to train the character recognition if they plan to handwrite and decide where they prefer to record information. For example, some teacher trainees used Notes, yet others used Word, but the most popular place for making notes was in the Calendar.
- The application that was best received by pupils in school involved was the use of the PDA camera by the teacher to record their work and experimental set ups.

Conclusion

Despite acknowledging their potential for supporting collaboration, teachers mostly view PDAs as personal devices and used only the software that supported their personal information needs. Not all participants were sufficiently interested to trial the devices and the perceived lack of reliability where this generation of PDAs can lose their data if the battery is allowed to discharge was a significant barrier to their engagement.

However, providing a PDA for all teachers within a department enabled a culture for trainee teachers where their use could be experimented with and the experienced teachers who continued to use the PDAs found that they provided individual teaching support through:

- Internet access
- taking photos
- class administration
- diary scheduling in particular

It was clear that the just-in-time nature of the individual support – having almost instant access to personal calendar, class lists and grades, and Google was important to the trainees and supported them in their learning. Additionally, recording notes on trainees' lessons and using the infrared beam to share them was very useful to both the teachers and trainees who continued to use the PDAs. However, the objective for this study of using blogging to facilitate reflective practice was not met. The trainee teachers were not comfortable with the concept of sharing their lesson observations and their own reflections on their teaching beyond the school where they were placed.

Finally, for effective deployment of mobile devices in teaching and learning support there needs to be recognition of PDAs and other Smartphones as part of the whole ICT system within an institution. Issues such as using the WiFi to connect to the wireless network, connecting the PDAs to the data projectors and connecting the PDA cradles to the classroom desktops need a significant amount of facilitation in the school context where access to computer networks is heavily restricted.

References

HUGHES, S. 2005. JANUS Project: Looking back to the future. Training and Development Agency for Schools (UK). http://www.tda.gov.uk/upload/resources/doc/e/e-learning-case-studies.doc#_Toc92694920 (accessed November 9, 2006).

JACK, D., and R. SCOTT. 2005. Partnership with schools through WebCT and videoconferencing. Paper presentation, *TDA e-learning and teacher training conference*, November 11, London.

JISC. 2005. Innovative practice with e-learning. Bristol: Higher Education Funding Council for England (HEFCE). http://www.jisc.ac.uk/eli_practice.html (accessed March 6, 2006).

NAISMITH, L., P. LONSDALE, G. VAVOULA, and M. SHARPLES. 2004. Report 11: Literature review of mobile technologies in learning. Bristol: Futurelab. http://www.futurelab.org.uk/research/reviews/reviews_11_and12/11_01. htm (accessed March 3, 2007).

PERKINS, D. 1993. Person-plus: A distributed view of thinking and learning. In *Distributed cognitions*, ed. G. Salomon, 88-110. New York: Cambridge University Press.

PERRY, D. 2003. Handheld computer PDAs in schools. Coventry: British Educational Communications and Technology Agency. http://www.becta. org.uk/page_documents/research/handhelds.pdf (accessed March 6, 2006).

POLLARD, A. 2005. Reflective teaching: Evidence-informed professional practice. London: Continuum.

ROGERS, E. 1995. Diffusion of innovations. 4th ed. New York: The Free Press.

WADSWORTH, Y. 1998. What is participatory action research? *Action Research International*, Paper 2. http://www.scu.edu.au/schools/gcm/ar/ ari/p-ywadsworth98.html (accessed July 24, 2006).

WISHART, J., A. MCFARLANE, and A. RAMSDEN. 2005. Using Personal Digital Assistants (PDAs) with Internet access to support initial teacher training in the UK. Paper presentation, *mLearn 2005*, October 25-28, Cape Town, South Africa. http://www.mlearn.org.za/CD/papers/Wishart.pdf (accessed November 9, 2006).

WISHART, J., A. RAMSDEN, and A. MCFARLANE. 2007. PDAs and handhelds: ICT at your side and not in your face. *Technology, Pedagogy and Education* 16 (1):95-110.

Conclusion

The use of mobile technology in education is a recent initiative due to the availability and rapid advancement of mobile devices such as smart phones, PDAs, and handheld computers. Recently, there have been many research studies and applications of mobile learning in both formal and informal learning. The chapters in this book present some of these recent studies and projects on mobile learning in education and training.

The research studies presented in this book have shown benefits of using mobile technology in learning but, at the same time, suggested challenges organizations face when designing and implementing mobile learning. There are some areas that were identified in the chapters for further research. Since mobile learning is new in education, best practices and standards for mobile learning must be identified. Considerable research is needed on how to design learning materials for delivery on mobile devices and what is the right mix of technology for distance delivery. Some chapters in the book also described projects that use mobile technology to deliver formal and informal materials to students. As reported in these projects, because of the mobility of the mobile devices, they are suited for delivering instruction at anytime and to anywhere. This is important for students, workers, and citizens who are mobile and need to access information and learning materials from wherever they are located.

The following list of the lessons that were learned by the contributors to this book is presented as suggestions for the future.

1. For people who live in remote areas, connectivity is an issue. They have limited bandwidth and wireless capabilities to access learning materials on mobile devices. However, this is changing considerably as more people use mobile devices to access the Internet and to communicate with others. Governments and organizations have to work together to build the infrastructure for high bandwidth and wireless capabilities for global access.

2. At present, most mobile devices are designed for business and other industry related use rather than for use in education and training. Hence, it is important that educators and trainers work with developers

of mobile devices to build an "ideal" mobile device for education. The device must adapt to the learners' needs and preferences rather than getting the learner to adapt to the mobile device.

3. The latest mobile devices have good multimedia capabilities. Course materials for mobile devices should be in multimedia format to take advantage of the capabilities of the mobile devices and to make the learning experience more stimulating for students.

4. The use of the mobile devices in learning provides the opportunity for students to interact with each other and with the teacher using the mobile devices. Many individuals now use mobile technology for personal and workplace communication. More research is needed on how to use mobile devices as a communication tool to provide support in education.

5. The use of mobile technology is good for informal learning where learners can access information and learning materials from anywhere and at any time. As mobile technology becomes more ubiquitous, there will be more use of mobile technology for informal learning. For example, as events happen around the world, users of mobile technology will be able to get up-to-date information on these events using their mobile devices.

6. Change models should be used to help educational organizations make the transition to mobile learning. Educators need to be convinced that mobile learning is effective and will benefit them in the delivery of instruction. Results of projects that successfully use mobile technology in instruction should be communicated to educators so that they can see the benefits of using mobile technology in instruction. For example, the mobile learning projects reported in the chapters in this book shows how mobile learning can be used successfully in education. After educators see the benefits of using mobile technology, they should be provided with training on how to design learning materials for delivery on mobile devices and how to use the mobile devices for delivery and support. One approach to follow is to use a blended format where mobile learning is used for some parts of a course and other delivery methods are used for other parts of the course. This will make the transition easier for educators and trainers.

7. Because the use of mobile learning is new in education, it is important for educators, researchers, and practitioners to share what works and what does not work in mobile learning so that the field of mobile learning can be implemented in a more timely and effective manner. This is critical because mobile devices are changing constantly with

increasing capabilities and there is not enough time for everyone to conduct research and complete projects to learn about the best practices in mobile learning. This book is one attempt to give educators and trainers the opportunity to learn from the research and mobile learning projects so that they can build from where others have left off rather than start from the beginning.

8. A major challenge for educators and trainers is how to develop learning materials for delivery on mobile devices. The learning materials should be in manageable learning chunks and should make use of multimedia. One approach is to develop the learning materials in the form of learning objects and then link them to form a "learning segment." There are many advantages of using learning objects in mobile delivery including: they can be re-used and changed without affecting other learning objects, and they can be stored in an electronic repository for remote access at any time.

The research studies and projects on mobile learning presented in this book make the case that mobile learning can be successful if done properly. The chapters provide best practices for mobile learning to help educators and trainers design and deliver mobile learning. Mobile learning has already become an integral part of education in many parts of the world, and research advances in design and implementation will ensure its increasing importance. Educators and trainers will need to successfully transition to mobile learning as soon as possible to help facilitate this process.

Glossary

3G: Stands for "third generation" mobile technologies, which offer users a wider range of more advanced services than earlier mobile devices while achieving greater network capacity through improved spectral efficiency.

ActionScript: A scripting language used by Adobe Flash. It has been improved from a script syntax to one that supports object-oriented programming, and has capability comparable to JavaScript.

ADSL (Asymmetric Digital Subscriber Line): The most widely deployed form of Digital Subscriber Line (DSL) technology.

Always-online: Solutions that give the user access to the Internet at all times.

Assimilation bias: The influence of prior knowledge or skills on the acquisition of new knowledge or skills.

Audiocast: Collection of audio files that is available for access via a cell phone.

Beaming: Transmitting data between one device and another using infra-red beam. To communicate via infra-red beam, devices must be in line-of-sight with each other.

Behaviourism: An approach to psychology that emphasises observable measurable behaviour.

Blended learning: The combination of multiple approaches to learning. Blended learning can be accomplished through the use of "blended" virtual and physical resources. A typical example of this would be a combination of technology-based delivery and face-to-face sessions used together to deliver instruction/training.

Blog: A reflective journal that is hosted online.

Bluetooth: Communication standard that allows devices to communicate with each other and transfer data using short-range wireless. Bluetooth devices do not need to be in line-of-sight of each other to communicate.

Chunking: The division of information into portions of varying sizes with the purpose of reducing cognitive load on a learner. The size of the "chunk" is dependent upon the characteristics of the information or skill to be learned as well as the cognitive capabilities of the learner.

Cognitive load: The amount of information that an individual must process in one segment of time.

Cohesion: A concept from software engineering that each unit should do one thing and only one thing. For a learning object this means that it should focus on only one topic or learning objective.

Collaborative learning: The grouping and pairing of students for the purposes of achieving an academic goal.

Compact Flash (CF): A type of removable memory card for digital cameras and other portable electronic devices. See also Secure Digital (SD).

Constructivism: The focus of this learning theory is on placing the learner at the centre and designing for learning rather than planning for teaching. The underlying philosophical framework is that humans construct meaning from current knowledge structures.

Constructivist: Pertaining to the learning theory of constructivism. The central tenet is that knowledge of the world is constructed by the individual. The person, through interacting with the world, constructs, tests and refines cognitive representations to make sense of the world. Learning rather than instruction becomes the focal issue.

Data transfer rate: The rate at which one can download content from the Web.

Decoupling (minimized coupling): A term from software engineering which means that the unit (software module/learning object) should have minimal bindings to other units. Thus the content of one learning object should not refer to and use material in another learning object in such a way as to create necessary dependencies.

Demographics: This refers to selected population characteristics as used in government, marketing or opinion research, or the demographic profiles used in such research. Commonly-used demographics include race, age, income, disabilities, mobility, educational attainment, home ownership, employment status, and even location.

Digital assets: Photos, video clips, audio clips or other media items that can be used in a learning activity.

E-book: Electronic version of a book, designed to be read on a computer.

E-news: News available in electronic form, e.g. on the Web, or specifically for mobile devices.

EKKO: Norwegian acronym for "electronic combined education" the first Learning Management System (LMS) developed at NKI.

Encoding: A process in which a learner associates new, incoming information with knowledge or skills already stored in memory. Well-encoded information, in theory, should be easier to retrieve from memory when needed.

Flash: A multimedia authoring program from Adobe Systems. Flash is popular for creating animation, video and adding rich interactivity to web pages, and is available in most common web browsers.

Flashlite: A lightweight version of Flash for mobile devices.

Formative Evaluation: This is a type of evaluation that has the purpose of improving programs. It may also be referred to as developmental evaluation or implementation evaluation. It is used in instructional design to assess ongoing projects during their construction to implement improvements. Formative evaluation can use any of the techniques which are used in other types of evaluation, including surveys, interviews, data collection and experiments (where these are used to examine the outcomes of pilot projects).

GPRS (General Packet Radio Service): A wireless data service used by mobile phones to access the Internet.

GPS (Global Positioning System): Uses microwave signals broadcast by satellites orbiting the Earth to identify the geographical location of the GPS receiver. GPS devices also record altitude, speed, direction and time.

HTML (HyperText Markup Language): A programming language used to create documents for display in web browsers.

Hypertag Magus Guide: A commercial system that was designed to deliver audio, video and graphics to museum visitors with handheld devices.

ICT: Information and Communication Technology

ICT for Development (or ICT4D): A multidisciplinary area for academic study and practitioner focus that explores how technologies are used to achieve development goals.

Informal learning: Learning that is not organized and structured by an institution. It may take place in environments that already have some connections with learning, e.g. museums and art galleries, or anywhere the learner chooses, including at work.

Infrared (IR): Electromagnetic radiation of wavelengths longer than visible light. IR is typically used to transmit data through the air, for short distances, in a straight line.

Interaction: In instructional contexts, interaction can be seen as communication of any sort, e.g., two or more people talking to each other or communication among groups and organizations. Interaction in teaching and learning is typically thought of as a sustained, two-way communication among two or more persons for purposes of explaining and challenging perspectives. If done in a formal, educational environment, then, interaction is usually between a student(s) and instructor, or among students.

Interactive Voice Response (IVR): IVR is a phone technology that allows a computer to detect voice and touch tones using a normal phone call.

Interface: The components of the computer program that allow the user to interact with the information.

IP (Internet Protocol) telephony: a technology that supports voice, data and video transmission via IP-based computer network.

iPAQ: A family of Pocket PC models from HP-Compaq.

JAVA: A programming language that provides a system for developing and deploying cross-platform applications.

Language technologies or Human Language Technologies (HLT): Enables computer-based systems to understand what humans are saying, and underpins automatic machine translation.

Learning object: A self-contained learning resource that focuses on a single topic.

Learning partner: NKI has developed different kinds of social software solutions within the LMS. As such, all students are urged to present themselves in ways that invite social interaction for learning purposes. Software solutions for inviting and accepting learning partners and for establishing connections have been developed in parallel to the research on mobile learning.

LMS (Learning Management System): An online system that manages the learning process and allows students to interact with the course, other students, and the instructor.

Location-based content: Text, images, audio files and video files that relate to the place where the user is at the time, for example within a museum or heritage site. The user needs a GPS-enabled mobile device in order to access the location-based service.

Macromedia Flash: A program to create multimedia for the Web.

Mediation: The reconciliation of various processes to produce a new, harmonious entity. In terms of mobile learning and the FRAME model, the interaction of social processes, cognitive processes, and technology result in a constantly transforming method of learning.

Microsoft Reader: A program from Microsoft to read their e-book format.

M-learning: Mobile learning, using a mobile device to access and study learning materials and for communicating with the institution, tutors and fellow students.

mLMS (Mobile Learning Management System): A learning management system for mobile devices.

Mobile device: A device that can be used to access information and learning materials from anywhere and at anytime. The device consists of an input mechanism, processing capability, a storage medium, and a display mechanism.

Moblog: Blog that can be updated by posting entries directly from a PDA, phone, cameraphone or other portable device. Mobloggers are those who post to their blogs in this way.

MP3: A digital audio encoding format. Its more accurate name is MPEG-1 Audio Layer 3. MP3 uses a compression algorithm to reduce the size of audio data. It is a popular audio format on many mobile devices.

MSN (Microsoft Network): An Internet chat service that allows text communication between people who have nominated each other as 'friends'.

M-teaching: Teaching with the support of mobile, handheld devices.

Multimedia messaging service (MMS): A standard for telephony messaging systems that allows sending messages that include multimedia objects (images, audio, video, rich text).

Multimedia: A combination of two or more media to present information to users.

News feed: Also known as web feed and RSS feed. The feed is a data format that delivers frequently updated content to computer or mobile devices.

Nursing Practice Education: The planned educational credit time when nursing students have the opportunity to apply their knowledge and skills to nursing practice with real clients (individuals, families, groups, communities and populations) in a variety of settings (e.g. hospitals, community agencies or patient's homes).

Online Learning Environment (OLE): An Internet based learning environment accessible to a group of students, who can use a range of services to support their learning.

Open source: Any program whose source code is made available for use or modification as users or other developers see fit.

PBX: Telephone Private Box Exchange.

PDA (Personal Digital Assistant): A handheld device that runs cut down or "pocket" versions of most office software including word-processing, spreadsheet management. Email and web browsing are enabled through wireless or GPRS connectivity. It often includes a camera and may have a pull-out mini-keyboard as well as an onscreen keyboard.

Pedagogy: The art or science of being a teacher. The term generally refers to strategies of instruction, or a style of instruction.

Personal Development Plan (PDP): A structured and supported process undertaken by an individual to reflect on their own learning, performance and/or achievement and to plan for their personal, educational and career development.

Pervasive image capture: Spontaneous or prolific activity involving taking photographs in various locations on the move, typically with the intention of sharing them immediately with others.

Plucker: Free e-book reader for mobile devices.

PNG (Portable Network Graphic): A bitmap image format that uses data compression to make file sizes smaller.

Pocket PC: A generic term for a handheld-sized computer that runs a specific version of the Windows CE operating system.

Podcast: Video or audio podcast files designed to be syndicated through feeds via the Internet and played back on mobile devices. New content is delivered automatically when it is available.

Portable keyboard: A keyboard that is possible to put in a coat pocket, by folding it or by other means to make it smaller.

Production bias: The influence of the need for task completion on the activity level of an individual. Normally, the primary concern of an individual is to complete a specific task; other information or superfluous skills may be deliberately neglected during the learning process.

RFID (Radio-frequency Identification): Use wireless technology to identify and manage people or objects. Data stored on a small, rugged tag is transmitted to a reader via electrical or electromagnetic waves.

RLO (Reusable Learning Object): A learning object that is constructed to be reusable, i.e. it is not dependent on other objects and it is standalone. See also "Learning Object."

SADC (Southern African Development Community): A community that currently comprises fourteen member States with a vision "of a common future, a future in a regional community that will ensure economic well-being, improvement of the standards of living and quality of life, freedom and social justice and peace and security for the peoples of Southern Africa."

Scaffolding: Supporting the learner's development and providing support structures to get to the next stage or level.

Scientific Technological Park (STP): A local institution devoted to the building up and the enhancing growth of technology based companies. The goal is reached thanks to the creation of a network of contacts with universities, research centers, public bureaus and entrepreneurial associations. A STP offers a system of technology facilities and infrastructures realized to host companies whose marketing strategies include research activities, production, sale and aftermarket services.

Secure Digital (SD): A type of removable memory card for digital cameras and other portable electronic devices. See also Compact Flash (CF).

SESAM (Scalable Educational System for Administration and Management): An LMS developed at NKI distance Education.

Short Message Service (SMS): A communications protocol allowing the interchange of short text messages between mobile telephony devices.

Situated learning: Learning that draws on an understanding of the relevance of the learner's context, in the way the learning activities and resources are designed.

Skype: Skype is a widely used software program created by the Swedish and Danish entrepreneurs Niklas Zennström and Janus Friis. Skype allows users to engage in audio and video conferencing users over the Internet to other Skype users free of charge or to make telephone calls to landlines and cell phones for a fee.

Smart phone: A mobile phone with some advances features, such as a web browser.

SMS (Short Messaging Service): Allows text messages to be sent between mobile phones, also known as "texting."

Social computing: Social computing has to do with supporting any sort of social behaviour in or through the use of computers and computer software. It is based on creating or recreating social conventions and social contexts otherwise only possible in face-to-face interaction. Blogs, email, instant messaging, social network services, wikis, and social bookmarking are common examples of social software.

Social Software: The programs allow users to interact and share data with other users.

Speech synthesis: Computer-generated simulation of human speech.

Streaming: Starting the video or sound before it has downloaded to the client.

Subscriber Identity Module (SIM): Part of a removable smart card ICC (Integrated Circuit Card), also known as SIM Cards, for mobile cellular telephony devices such as mobile computers and mobile phones.

SWF (ShockWave Flash): A compiled and uneditable vector graphics format used by Flash applications. SWF files can be viewed on common web browsers (if they have the Flash Player installed) and some mobile devices.

Syncing: A method used to synchronize the data held on PDAs and mobile phones or smartphones with the data held on a computer. ActiveSync is the application used to sync Windows Mobile and Pocket PC mobile devices. Allows the user to keep things like calendar and contacts lists the same on both a desktop computer and a mobile device.

Text-to-speech (TTS): A type of speech synthesis application that is used to create a spoken sound version of text.

Transparency: The amount of time a user must focus on device usage compared with the amount of time that a user can focus on learning. A high degree of transparency suggests that a device is easy to use and that the user can concentrate on cognitive tasks rather than device manipulation.

Tutor Marked Assignments (TMAs): TMAs are assignments periodically submitted by the distance learning students, which are marked by tutors.

Ubiquitous computing: Computing technology that is invisible to the user because of wireless connectivity and transparent user interface.

Ubiquitous: Existing or being everywhere at the same time, constantly encountered or widespread.

Universal accessibility: Available to anyone independent of physical handicaps.

URL: Uniform Resource Locator, an Internet World Wide Web address.

Usability: Ease and efficiency in the use of a mobile device. In a learning situation, the device should not get in the way of the learning task. The design of the user interface is very important but contextual factors also have an impact on user experience.

User: An individual who interacts with a computer system to complete a task, learn specific knowledge or skills, or access information.

User Interface: The "bridge" through which a human interacts with a device. In mobile learning, it refers to the software and navigational features that permit a learner to complete learning tasks.

Virgin mobile: Brand used by several mobile service providers, associated with mobile entertainment such as quizzes and comedy clips.

VLE (Virtual Learning Environment): A site that hosts online resources and activities to support students' learning.

VOIP (Voice Over Internet Protocol): A new form of telephony that allows voice to be transmitted over the Internet.

Wearable Computing Devices: Devices that are attached to the human body so that the hands are free to complete other tasks.

WebCT: WebCT, or Web Course Tools, is an online or virtual learning management system (LMS) used to deliver courses over the Internet.

Weblog: An online journal or diary organized by date, with most recent posts at the top, and made publicly available via the Web.

WiFi (Wireless Fidelity): A set of standards for facilitating wireless networks in a local area, enabling WiFi devices to connect to the Internet when in range of an access point.

Wiki: Allows users to collaborate in forming the content of a web site. With a wiki, any user can edit the site content, including other users' contributions, using a standard web browser.

Wikipedia: A free, open content online encyclopedia created through the collaborative effort of a community of users.

Wireless Application Protocol (WAP): An open international standard for applications that use wireless communication. Its principal application is to enable access to the Internet from a mobile phone or PDA.

Wireless Markup Language (WML): WML, based on XML, is a content format for devices that implement the Wireless Application Protocol (WAP) specification.

XML (Extensible Markup Language): Allows users to define their own elements. Its primary purpose is to facilitate the sharing of structured data across different information systems, particularly via the Internet.

XHTML (Extensible HyperText Markup Language): A markup language that has the same depth of expression as HTML, but also conforms to XML syntax.

Index